**ORANGE CHICKEN . . .
KASHA PILAF . . .
WATERCRESS AND MUSHROOMS
IN MUSTARD DRESSING . . .
SHERBERT . . . ALL ON YOUR
DINING TABLE IN 30 MINUTES!**

KEEP IT SIMPLE

"A WORTHWHILE ADDITION TO THE KITCHEN . . .
the menus are well-designed and balanced with regard to
flavor, texture, color and especially nutrition."

—The New York Times

"AN INVALUABLE HANDBOOK FOR THE COOK
WITH LIMITED TIME WHO WANTS TO PRESENT
NOURISHING, INTERESTING AND LOW-COST
MEALS."

—Publishers Weekly

"WONDERFULLY PRACTICAL . . . Haste does not
make waste here—only good, cheap meals."

—People

"*KEEP IT SIMPLE* IS GOOD FOR BOTH THE POCKET-
BOOK AND THE GASTRONOMIC CAUSE."

—Washington Post Book World

"ALL OF THE MEALS LEAP OFF THE PAGES SAY-
ING 'TRY ME,' WHICH IS THE TEST OF A GREAT
COOKBOOK."

—Los Angeles Herald Examiner

MARIAN BURROS

PUBLISHED BY POCKET BOOKS NEW YORK

Pocket Books mass-market edition of the book published in July, 1982

 POCKET BOOKS, a division of Simon & Schuster, Inc.
1230 Avenue of the Americas, New York, N.Y. 10020

Published by arrangement with William Morrow & Co., Inc.
Library of Congress Catalog Card Number: 81-4398

ISBN: 0-671-50736-2

First Pocket Books trade paperback printing June, 1984

10 9 8 7 6 5 4 3 2 1

POCKET and colophon are registered trademarks
of Simon & Schuster, Inc.

Printed in the U.S.A.

ACKNOWLEDGMENTS

To all those who had to put up with a tornado in the kitchen, some recipes that didn't work, meals at 10 o'clock . . .

To all my editors, who dared me to create 30-minute meals, acted as guinea pigs, improved my prose, clarified my recipes, and gave me the lead to the book . . .

To my patient family . . .

To Shang Patterson, who read every single recipe and tested many; to the hardworking bureaucrats in the federal government who preferred anonymity while they kept me from making any egregious errors . . .

To all of them this book is dedicated.

MB
Bethesda, Maryland
January, 1981

CONTENTS

PART 1 | THE POLITICS OF FOOD

"NUTRITIONAL FLASH—Marian Burros, NBC's foe of junk food, has been offered five figures by a baking industry lobbyist to pose with a Hostess Twinkie. Strictly platonic, Ear's sure, but is impressed anyway."

That June, 1978, item in the *Washington Star's* gossip column "Ear" vividly demonstrates that the life of a food writer and consumer reporter in the last half of the twentieth century is never boring. In addition to the Hostess Twinkie offer, I was threatened with a lawsuit for defamation of character by a leading supermarket chain, which also cancelled its advertising for a while at the television station where I worked, and the station, NBC's WRC-TV, could have been slapped with a $10,000 fine because I suggested that viewers might want to call a chairman of a Congressional committee to register a complaint.*

I didn't pose.

They didn't sue.

---

*An FCC policy prohibits any broadcaster from telling radio or television listeners to call another person. The rule is based on a number of incidents where a talk-show host or a disc jockey has exhorted listeners to call someone, sometimes even giving out the person's private number. Since I didn't give out a number and the person is a public servant whose salary and phone bills are paid for by the taxpayers, the situation didn't seem analogous.

The fine wasn't levied.

So I'm still at it, trying to help busy people who want to play with a full deck when they read about government food policies, when they look at food ads, and when they go to the supermarket. This book is for everyone who wants to break the grip of marginally tasty, routinely salty, frequently fatty, overly sweetened, usually chemicalized, always expensive, barely nutritious, highly processed foods.

With half of the women over the age of sixteen working and more men cooking, the standard family of 2 adults, 3.2 children, and a 3-course dinner waiting for father every night no longer exists.

With all signs pointing to the diet and exercise craze of the 70s becoming a permanent way of life in the 80s for a significant part of the population, there ought to be some place where people can find out how to eat well without taking a graduate course in biochemistry or hiring a cook.

Whether people are cooking for large families or themselves, if they are interested in breaking away from bad eating habits, but are afraid new ones won't offer much that is good to eat, if they want to eat well but are sure it takes too much time and money, this *Pure & Simple* sequel (I wanted to call it "Son of Pure & Simple," but they wouldn't let me) should help.

Pure & Simple was a primer on how to do battle, on an equal footing, with the food industry: This book is a graduate course. *Pure & Simple* pointed out why additive-free foods are safest, least expensive, and best tasting; this book is meant to show why additive-free foods are all of those things plus quick to prepare.

But it's getting harder and harder to choose those foods. Even though we have become more sophisticated shoppers, manufacturers have become more sophisticated pushers. If you doubt it listen to this:

"When I use a word, it means just what I choose it to mean—neither more nor less."

That's how Humpty Dumpty put it in *Alice in Wonderland*.

Now consider these:

1. "The per capita sugar consumption in the U.S. has remained practically unchanged for the last 50 years." *From a 1977 Kellogg ad*

2. ". . . the taste of freshly squeezed orange juice." *Tang ad*

3. "Angel food cake with ice cream—a low calorie dessert." *Nutrition educational material for schools from the National Dairy Council*

4. "Sugar encourages a balanced intake of a variety of nutrients . . ." *Sugar Association literature*

5. "Uncle Ben's Chicken [or beef] Flavored Rice—made with other natural flavors." *Package label*

6. "Shasta now replaces ordinary refined sugars with simple sweeteners like fructose, a kind found in fresh fruit." *Shasta ad campaign, 1979*

7. Thomas' Whole Wheat English Muffins "made with 100 percent whole wheat." *Package label*

8. Wonder bread has "nutrition that whole wheat can't beat." *1980 ad campaign*

That's the kind of "information" we receive about food. The industry pays high-priced wordsmiths to process words, based on the assumption that the American consumer is Tweedle de Dum and Tweedle de Dumber. But here's what the Humpty Dumptys of the food industry have left out:

1. The per capita consumption of all forms of sugar (cane and beet, corn syrup, fructose) has risen from 99 pounds in 1920 to 129 pounds today.

2. In France, the Tang ad drew a 40,000-franc ($8,700) fine for misleading advertising on the grounds

that 85 percent of the product is made of sugar and chemical substances.

3. Only for a 6'7" wrestler. A slice of cake and a scoop of ice cream contain well over 400 calories.

4. Sugar is empty calories. It squeezes out consumption of essential nutrients.

5. The "other natural flavors" in Uncle Ben's flavored rice products include monosodium glutamate.

6. The fructose in Shasta soft drinks is not the pure fructose found in fruit. It is 55 percent fructose and 42 percent glucose, making it very similar in composition to ordinary sugar (sucrose).

7. Thomas' Whole Wheat English Muffins are made with *SOME* whole wheat. They are also made with white flour. The ratio is a "proprietary secret," but the muffins may contain as little as 55 percent whole-wheat flour.

8. Whole-wheat bread has about 10 percent more of the Recommended Daily Allowances for vitamin B6, pantothenic acid, folacin, potassium, phosphorus, magnesium, and zinc. It also has fiber. Wonder bread, a product of ITT Continental Baking Co. (they make Twinkies, too) withdrew the ad shortly after it first appeared.

Obviously shopping hasn't gotten any easier in the last three years. The food industry keeps finding new methods for making words mean what they want them to mean, for lowering the quality of the products they sell and then advertising them as "new and improved." What's more they are ingenious in keeping the government from regulating false advertising and removing hazardous products from the market. Not that the present government is anxious to do so.

In addition to considerably more grocery money than we've ever needed before to shop, a bachelor of science

degree in chemistry, a bachelor of arts degree in market-
ing manipulation, and an "I'm from Missouri, show me"
attitude are useful.

Despite the odds today, there is a greater public
awareness of the relationship between what we eat and
how it affects our bodies. According to a recent study, 64
percent of those surveyed said they had changed their
eating habits in the last two years for health and nutrition
reasons.

The marketplace has responded to these concerns:
some of the response is meaningful; most of it is a sham.
For those of us who shop the periphery of the supermarket where most of the produce, dairy products, meats,
and bread are displayed, there are more things from
which to choose: more whole grain (and not so whole
grain) breads, pitas, breadsticks, muffins; an expanded
selection of fresh fruits and vegetables; more dried fruits
and nuts; tofu (soybean curd); greater varieties of poultry
and fish; leaner beef ("good" grade); bulgur (cracked
wheat), brown rice, whole-wheat flour, unprocessed
bran.

For the most part, industry's response to what it
perceives as the public's concern about nutrition and
safety has produced some pretty weird foods: "nutritious" candy bars and cookies for breakfast; bread with
wood pulp; labels that rise up from every shelf and
shout, "I'm natural."

And the industry's response to previous governmental
efforts to assure the safety of food, the truth of advertising claims, and to give the public some help in sorting
out a nutritious diet, are being abandoned in the name of
de-regulation, of "getting government off people's
backs."

Anti-regulatory forces don't distinguish between necessary regulations and all the rest. But the public does.

They still want government to make sure foods are safe and that what their children are fed in school is good for them.

In 1977, the Department of Agriculture tried to remove what are called "fortified grain fruit products" from the school breakfast program. Grain fruit products are donuts and cupcakes, high in fat and sugar, often artificially colored, which have had a few vitamins and minerals glued on to them. They are used as alternatives to real breakfasts of fruit, bread or cereal, and milk. Congresswoman Shirley Chisholm explained what is wrong with these so-called breakfast foods. "Feeding our youth sugar-filled cakes teaches them poor eating habits. Part of the purpose of the breakfast program is to teach children how to eat a well-balanced meal. Breakfast bars taste like dessert. A child should not get in the habit of eating a dessert-like product for breakfast." (Television commercials for Hostess donuts and crumbcakes notwithstanding.)

The Grocery Manufacturers of America, at the request of Morton Foods, a division of ITT Continental Baking Co., and Keebler Baking Company, two of the producers of these sweets, launched an aggressive campaign in Congress to keep "superdonuts" in the breakfast program. Superdonuts are still part of that program.

The U.S. Department of Agriculture had a little better luck in court. When it tried to regulate the kind of foods that could be sold in vending machines in school, in an effort—however meager—to get some of the more obvious junk foods out of competition with school lunches, the candy manufacturers took them to court. USDA won that fight but is drawing up a proposal to undo the regulation.

Four years of watching former consumer activists try to make some changes from within the government has convinced me that the federal government is not going to be much help, even if it has the best intentions in the world. There were a couple of major breakthroughs between 1976 and 1980 but, for the most part, the pro-consumer officials were thwarted in their efforts by special interest groups which found a sympathetic ear in Congress.

Now that the thwarters are running the agencies and departments, government help for the ordinary shopper has been reduced to zero.

That means we are on our own. If you've read this far you are probably one of hundreds of thousands of people who are trying to shop, cook, and eat differently. I hope some of the ammunition you need can be found in this book. Fortunately, you are not alone.

One Department of Agriculture study conducted between November, 1979, and January, 1980, showed that from fifteen to twenty percent of the households surveyed said they were using fewer foods high in fat and cholesterol and more foods lower in fat, such as poultry, fish, and shellfish.

Twenty-five percent reported eating more fruits and vegetables.

One in seven reported substituting whole grain breads for white breads.

Seven percent shifted from sweetened to less sweetened cereals.

Twenty-two percent reported a reduction in the use of salty foods.

One in seven reported using fewer soft drinks.

Twelve percent specifically mentioned making changes to reduce nitrite intake; five percent were concerned about saccharin; ten percent said they had reduced their consumption of preservatives, colors, and other additives.

These changes had taken place before the release of the government's Dietary Guidelines in February, 1980, which are a modification of the earlier and more strongly worded publication, *Dietary Goals for the United States*. The latter was prepared in 1977 by the Senate Select Committee on Nutrition and Human Needs, chaired by Senator George McGovern. The committee went out of existence in 1978 and the senatorial career of McGovern suffered the same fate in 1980, leaving an enormous void in the Senate for those who care about nutrition.

Dietary Guidelines make seven points:
Eat a variety of foods.
Maintain ideal weight.
Avoid too much fat, saturated fat, and cholesterol.
Eat foods with adequate starch and fiber.
Avoid too much sugar.
Avoid too much sodium.
If you drink alcohol, do so in moderation.

Seems rational enough.

Judging by the furor they created, you would have thought the guidelines suggested smoking marijuana for breakfast.

Several prestigious scientific groups have come to essentially the same conclusions and several have endorsed the guidelines. Among the scores of experts who believe similar modifications are beneficial are the extremely conservative American Society for Clinical Nutrition; the Surgeon General, whose 1979 report is entitled "Healthy Americans"; the director of the National Cancer Institute; the Society for Nutrition Education; the American College of Preventive Medicine.

But the segments of the food industry that stand to lose if Americans change their eating habits have been peppering the guidelines with buckshot ever since they were released. And just when it seemed as if the furor had subsided, the Food and Nutrition Board of the National Academy of Science published "Toward Healthful Diets," which contradicted the guidelines on the issues of fat and cholesterol. The Academy's report said healthy Americans don't have to reduce their intake of fat or cholesterol. The storm that broke over the Academy's publication has left a bad taste in the mouths of many who wondered why that quasi-government advisory body was trying to make policy. There were plenty of charges about the food industry connections of a number of members of the Academy's Food and Nutrition Board and when it was all over Americans were more confused than ever.

In January, 1981, the prestigious *New England Journal of Medicine* reported on the latest study linking a high-fat, high-cholesterol diet with increased risk of heart disease. This twenty-year study, considered one of the most significant because the subjects kept a daily diary of their food intake, was just one more in a long series of studies that suggest that the prudent course for most people is a low-fat, low-cholesterol diet.

Under the Carter administration, USDA, which issued the guidelines in conjunction with the Department of Health and Human Services, attempted to use them to set policy for the school lunch program. That started another ruckus because the National Pork Producers Council and the American Meat Institute are concerned that fewer of their products will be used in school lunch programs under the new guidelines. The lobbyist for the council, C. Donald Van Houweling, directed the transition for the Reagan administration at USDA. Richard Lyng, once head of AMI, is now USDA under secretary.

The man chosen to head USDA in the Reagan administration, John Block, is a soybean and pig farmer. Asked at his Senate confirmation hearing how he felt about government giving advice to people about their diets,

Block said: "I have to say people are pretty good at figuring out what to eat and not to eat. I think people are going to balance their diets." Then Block added that even though he knows people aren't hogs, hogs know how to balance their ration. A hog won't overeat, he said. "People surely are as smart as a hog. I'm not sure government should get into telling people what they should or shouldn't eat."

Two days later, at a press conference unveiling a book of menus designed to help people follow Dietary Guidelines, the then Assistant Agriculture Secretary Carol Foreman said she was glad Block knew the difference between hogs and people. "It's fair to note," Foreman said, "the Agriculture Department has advised pork farmers how to feed hogs . . . so they will gain weight. That's the objective in raising them. I doubt [Block] intends to suggest the Department of Agriculture should do less for people than for pig producers . . . or pigs."

Despite the controversy, USDA mailed out eight million free copies of Dietary Guidelines. People are anxious for some kind of reliable information. But now, under Block and Lyng, USDA charges for the Guidelines. It's better than nothing: at one point they seriously considered scrapping them completely and there is still considerable pressure on them to do so.

PUTTING PHILOSOPHY INTO PRACTICE— WHAT DO LABELS REALLY MEAN

Let's take a look at some of the strange things you are likely to encounter in the Alice in Wonderland of food.

Natural

The interest in nutrition and safety has spawned a new buzz word . . . NATURAL. It can be found on every conceivable product, from those first natural cereals to natural ice cream, shampoo, and even cockroach poison!

At one time the Federal Trade Commission wanted to regulate use of the word natural. This is the definition the commission proposed in 1980:

"If a food wants to advertise itself as natural it may not contain synthetic or artificial ingredients and may not be more than minimally processed."

Minimal processing includes washing or peeling fruits and vegetables, canning, bottling, and freezing, baking bread, grinding nuts, homogenizing milk. For the most part, however, if you can't do it in your kitchen, it isn't minimal processing. But that would leave out anything made with bleached white flour, white sugar, brown sugar, corn syrup. So FTC has made a little exception to the minimal processing.

If a product contains brown sugar, for example, it can advertise itself as natural as long as the ad reads "natural, but contains brown sugar."

If the law took effect, what would happen to some of the products on the market?

Daisy Fresh Natural Blackberry Flavored Juice Drink—it contains 30 percent fruit juice, artificial color, citric acid, sugar, hydrogenated vegetable oil, and guar gum.

Kraft Natural Provolone Cheese—it has added smoke flavor.

Our Natural Oven Roasted Chicken Breast—it is made with chicken broth, potato starch, salt, sodium phosphates, and flavoring.

Mrs. Smith's Natural Juice Apple Pie that bakes in its own natural juices—it also contains artificial color and artificial flavor.

And what about natural and natural-style potato chips? What's natural about a potato that has been peeled, sliced, deep-fried, and salted? Is that minimal processing?

Stay tuned.

"No additives"

Products which can't claim to be natural have turned to other buzz words to imply purity and safety like "no preservatives," "no artificial colors," "no artificial flavors."

This is confusing. A product without preservatives can still have other additives.

"Sugar-free"

"Sugar-free" simply means the product has no sucrose. It may contain saccharin or it may be sweetened with high fructose corn sweetener, pure fructose, corn syrup, sorbitol, mannitol, honey, or molasses. With the exception of saccharin, which has problems enough, all of these alternatives have some calories; most of them will rot your teeth, just like sugar; sorbitol and mannitol, if used in large enough quantities, cause diarrhea.

"Non-dairy"

"Non-dairy" means only one thing: there are no milk products in the food. It doesn't mean the food is free of saturated fat. Sometimes the food is; sometimes it isn't. If you are concerned about your intake of saturated fat, watch out for those non-dairy products that contain coconut oil. Coconut oil is almost twice as saturated as lard.

"All vegetable shortening"

"All vegetable shortening" is another "gotcha." Products containing only vegetable shortening are free of animal fat, but some contain that highly saturated coconut oil.

"Reduced calories"

Lately the words "reduced calories" have been appearing on labels. FDA has made some labeling changes for foods that claim to have fewer calories than their traditional counterparts. Now, in order to label a food "low calorie," it cannot have more than 40 calories per serving. But a food qualifies for the "reduced calorie" labeling if it contains one-third fewer calories than the food with which it is comparing itself.

"Filled weight"

Take a look at some of the canned fruits and vegetables and note that in addition to the net weight something called "filled weight" is often listed. The net weight is the amount of solids and liquids. The filled weight is the amount of solids that were put into the can at the time it was packed. And there's a difference, a big difference. In a test I conducted several years ago to determine the cost of the solids in cans after the liquid was drained off, the price of the product bore little relationship to the weight of the solids. The more expensive products often had fewer solids than the cheaper items. The listing of filled weight should help.

Open dating

Very little has been done to label shelf stable products with a date that is meaningful to consumers. Almost everything is in code. But you can often find a "pull date," "use by date," "don't sell after date," or "good until date" on perishable products. And many meat counters put a "good until" date on their fresh meats. Now, if they would only stop repacking the old meat and putting on a new "good until date" . . .

Fiber

Take a look at the number of bran cereals on the shelves today, at least eleven at last count. This country is on a fiber kick. But all fiber is not the same. The fiber in bran or unpeeled apples and pears, called cellulose, is not the same as pectin, also found in apples as well as bananas, potatoes, and carrots. And all forms of natural food fiber are definitely different from the fiber found in products like Fresh Horizons bread. Discreetly labeled "powdered cellulose" in the ingredient statement, if you read the fine print on the Fresh Horizons label, you will discover that the powdered cellulose is wood pulp. Dr. Peter Van Soest, a nutrition researcher and expert in the field of fiber, has found that eating bread whose sole source of fiber is wood pulp induces constipation!

Researchers have made some startling discoveries about fiber: Browning foods by sautéing, toasting and frying increases their fiber content. Coarse grains are a more effective form of fiber than finely milled grains.

Fiber is important. Recently the extremely conservative and cautious Federation of American Scientists for Experimental Biology agreed that evidence is "strongly suggestive" that dietary fiber has some sort of protective effect against colonic cancer.

Sodium labeling

Some voluntary efforts are being made to label foods with their sodium content. Food and Drug Administration Commissioner Arthur Hull Hayes said last year that if voluntary labeling didn't work, FDA would seek mandatory labeling of some packaged foods. That would be of enormous help (and even more enormous surprise) to people who must limit their intake of salt. It's estimated that between 10 and 30 percent of the population have high blood pressure. Common table salt, which is 40 percent sodium chloride, is more ubiquitous than monosodium glutamate or sugar.

The per capita consumption of sodium in this country has been variously estimated at between 2 and 10 grams per day. Man's daily requirement for sodium is less than 1 gram (1,000 milligrams). Authorities generally agree that humans can get all the sodium they need from what occurs naturally in food.

Processed foods have far more salt in them than is needed for anything, anything that is except to disguise the fact the product isn't properly seasoned with herbs and spices.

While most people know that pickles are salty—over 1,200 milligrams (mg) of sodium per large dill pickle— they usually don't know that one Hostess Twinkie has 240 mg of sodium; one McDonald's apple pie has 400 mg; ½ cup of Jell-O Instant Chocolate Pudding contains over 400 mg; one cup of General Mills cornflakes contains over 280 mg; one cup of Del Monte canned green beans contains more than 800 mg, while one cup of fresh green beans contains less than 5 mg.

Sugar

Cereal manufacturers are putting the amount of ADDED sugar in their products on the label, but not in a meaningful way. In response to criticism about the excessive amounts of sugar in sugar-encrusted cereals, the food industry didn't lower the levels, but it now lists the number of grams of sugar per ounce of cereal on the label. An ingenious non-response to a consumer demand.

Ordinary laypersons understand when told that Sugar Smacks contain 53 percent sugar. We can easily relate that to the percent of sugar in a Hershey's Milk Chocolate Bar—51 percent. For all but the mathematicians among us, it's utterly useless to know that Apple Jacks contain 15 grams of sugar. Unless, of course, we carry around the formula in our heads to convert grams to percentages. Here's how you do it: divide the grams of sugar per ounce by .28. So Apple Jacks have 53 percent sugar.

Better still, pin the information on the refrigerator door.

And remember when you are looking for sugar on a label it can turn up in several forms and in several places. In many instances, if you put all the sweeteners together—brown sugar, white sugar, honey, dextrose, fructose, corn syrup, corn syrup solids, maltose, lactose—they could easily constitute the major portion of the product.

Fortified

Not content with fortifying cereals to a fare-thee-well, food companies have taken to fortifying candy and soda with vitamins and minerals that were never there to begin with. Well, come to think about it, what's the difference? A fortified candy bar made with peanuts and raisins is probably not much worse than a fortified cereal that is 56 percent sugar. Maybe the candy sticks to the teeth a little better and has more fat, but is there that much difference in the nutritional value? Certainly a fortified hard candy isn't any different from a fortified presweetened drink like Kool-Aid. They're both junk. And vitamin-fortified soda pop, even if it is sweetened with honey instead of sugar and colored naturally instead of artificially, is no more nutritious than a bottle of Coke. No matter how much you fortify junk it will never be anything but fortified junk. It will not become a good food.

The government is concerned about what it calls this "irrational fortification." It tried to issue regulations forbidding it several years ago but has had to content itself with guidelines. The guidelines do not have the force of law.

The FDA says "it is inappropriate to fortify snack foods such as candies and carbonated beverages. Their fortification could readily mislead consumers to believe that substitution with fortified snack foods would insure a nutritionally sound diet."

If the guidelines had been in effect thirty years ago, we might not find superdonuts in school breakfast programs or supermarket shelves filled with Kool-Aid, Tang, Betty Crocker Breakfast Bars, Carnation Instant Breakfast, or cereals with 100 percent of the Minimum Daily Requirements for certain nutrients. Cereals like Total, King Vitaman, Special K, and Product 19. Says an FDA official, "a hundred percent fortification of cereal doesn't fit the guidelines. You are just selling a vitamin pill in cereal form and that's why they're labeled a multi-vitamin supplement."

Fabricated and fortified

Fabricated and fortified foods like Tang and Carnation Instant Breakfast and the new imitation cheeses are even more of a problem than the cereals. Despite what the teacher in the Tang commercial said, the fake orange drink is not as good as orange juice. And if she thinks it is, I wouldn't want her teaching my kids. Tang has vitamins A and C added to it. It is missing nearly a dozen other nutrients found in orange juice, all of which are essential.

Imitation cheese, which has some nutrients added, is beginning to make a dent in the marketplace. For those who want to watch their cholesterol or saturated fat intake, imitation cheese may have a place, so long as the vegetable oil that replaces the milk fat is unsaturated. But what is one to make of a new imitation mozzarella cheese made with coconut oil? Coconut oil is almost twice as saturated as lard. What is one to make of the cheese, especially after they taste it? Imitation cheese is much lower in many of the essential trace nutrients found in real low-fat mozzarella. These products are often deficient or completely devoid of trace nutrients found in real food.

Neither fortified, enriched, nor fabricated—just over processed

The instant soup explosion hit the United States about four years ago. Advertised as the perfect quick lunch, the containers in which they come have about as much nutritional value as the contents. The soups are mostly noodles—about 99 percent—with 1 percent seasonings. Seasonings in this instance mean dried vegetables and meat as well as spices and herbs, mostly salt and monosodium glutamate. Often the meat is not visible to the naked eye. After picking my way through all of these instant soups, I seldom found more than scraps of those vegetables so lavishly pictured on the labels. In Oodles of Noodles dehydrated chicken meat is listed as an ingredient. None was visible to the naked eye. La Choy's Oriental Noodles with beef flavoring shows a bowl of noodles with three strips of meat. There is no beef or even natural beef flavoring in any form in the package. The only beef present in Betty Crocker's Mug-O-Lunch, artificial beef flavor, is beef fat. The "beef" pieces are hydrolyzed vegetable protein.

Such highly processed foods, what one wag calls "toy food," are not likely to be of much nutritional value. Many essential nutrients may be missing because the more processing raw ingredients undergo the greater their nutrient loss.

Consumption of so many highly processed foods is becoming an increasingly serious problem for many Americans. Says Dr. Walter Mertz, chairman of the Nutrition Institute at the Department of Agriculture,

". . . the continuation of the present trend toward consumption of more partitioned, refined and fabricated foods will eventually lead to a point where the rest of the diet cannot meet the requirements for all essential nutrients anymore."

Dr. Mertz is talking about micro-nutrients, found in natural foods in trace amounts, which the body needs in minute quantities. Few of them are added to foods because no one knows enough about most of them to determine appropriate levels. They include zinc, manganese, selenium, copper, iodine, iron, fluorine, chromium, molybdenum. Scientists have discovered tiny traces of about thirty such elements: at this time only eighteen of them have been judged essential for humans. Deficiencies in these trace elements lead to sickness and disease, so Dr. Jean Mayer's advice is worth following: "The only safe course is to continue to make sure that a large portion of our diet consists of a *VARIETY* of whole grain products, fruits and vegetables, animal products. . . ."

Careful reading of the labels on food packages will give you some clues to the nutritional value of the contents. Nutritional labeling helps. The ingredient statement will give you other important information. What you don't find on the labels is as important as what is there, especially if the food is highly processed.

Just keep in mind that ingredients must be listed in order of predominance; that the presence of artificial colors must be listed in the ingredients with the exception of ice cream, natural cheese, and butter; that products which contain saccharin or nitrites must list their presence on the label.

It took an awful lot of work to get the manufacturers to print the ingredients on the labels and they print them as small as they can. Nobody's ever gone over budget printing the ingredients big on the labels.

Buy a magnifying glass; you'll live longer.

And when you read the ads, remember, Humpty Dumpty wrote them!

Of course, you can avoid having to think about these label problems if you stick to fresh foods!

Downsizing

One of the most blatant ripoffs is reducing the size of the package without lowering the price. It's known as packaging to price, downsizing, or in some circles as watering the booze.

There has been a shortage of fresh cranberries for the last several years, so Ocean Spray, the cooperative which produces 85 percent of the cranberries in this country, came out with a new package in 1980. It was labeled "New Convenient Size." The standard 16-ounce package of cranberries was downsized to 12 ounces. The hard fact, concealed by the new package, was that the cost of a pound of cranberries doubled in one year. In 1981 it went up again. Even the price of gasoline didn't double in 1980.

For a food processor to call the new smaller package "New Convenient Size" and then write the following letter to one of the many disgruntled customers takes guts:

"In order to cope with this situation [greater demand, fewer cranberries], we have implemented the use of a smaller container which will result in a broader distribution of fresh cranberries, and we hope, satisfy more customers.

"This action was taken after researching recipes using fresh cranberries and identifying that over 90 percent of them use three cups or less fruit. We recognize that the traditional relishes frequently call for a full pound of cranberries and, in these cases, we have found that 12 ounces of fruit will suffice if all other ingredients are reduced by one-fourth. We do not recommend this approach for cakes and breads, however, where a cut in cranberries will affect the moisture and texture of the final product."

At least cranberries are a special occasion purchase. What about Cut-Rite wax paper? Remember when there were 125 feet in a roll? Remember when the 125-foot roll shrank to 100 feet in the same size box with no change in price?

Surely you haven't forgotten when all solid vegetable shortening came either in 1- or 3-pound cans. Have you noticed the 3-pound cans which now contain only 2 pounds 10 ounces of shortening? You might think they would be less than full. But no. The manufacturer has pre-creamed the shortening, which is just another way of saying air has been beaten into it. Since a can of pre-creamed shortening contains 6 ounces less than a standard can, at current prices it should be 60 cents less, but it's only 25 cents cheaper.

You do remember the raisin shortage a couple of winters ago. At that time raisins were packed two ways: single serving boxes and 15-ounce boxes. Last year I picked up what looked like a 15-ounce box of raisins that cost a lot less than the best-known brand. The box was the same size. It turned out to contain only 12 ounces of raisins and ounce for ounce the raisins in the smaller box cost 21 cents more than the raisins in the larger box.

Remember the standard 16-ounce can of coffee? It may go the way of the 16-ounce package of cranberries. Some coffee comes in 12- or 13-ounce cans now. Manufacturers claim the coffee in these smaller cans is much stronger than the coffee in 16-ounce cans so you don't need as much though you may pay as much.

Uh huh.

PARBOILED BROWN RICE

The best-known producer of processed white rice has recognized increased interest in brown rice because it has more fiber and more nutrients. So Uncle Ben's is producing a converted brown rice. Converted means it has been parboiled. Parboiling, according to a spokesperson for Uncle Ben's, changes the characteristics of the rice, making it "more uniform and fluffy." It also is supposed to improve its shelf life.

The shelf life of ordinary brown rice is six months, according to one company that packages it. The nutrient content of parboiled and ordinary brown rice is fairly similar: the price is not.

When parboiled brown rice cost 73 cents a pound, ordinary brown rice was selling for 57 cents a pound, even less if bought in bulk. I noted this price difference on television and in a newspaper article, suggesting that parboiled brown rice wasn't worth the price.

Uncle Ben's wrote to say that in addition to its product's increased shelf life, bulk brown rice was often "dirty, containing straw, stones and other foreign matter," and could be rancid.

I've been buying ordinary brown rice for six years now, usually in bulk, and I haven't found any stones, straw, or other unseemly items and the rice hasn't been rancid.

Just lucky, I guess.

ROASTING CHICKENS

Are roasting chickens making a comeback in your neighborhood? They are here . . . for a price.

At one time it might have been worthwhile to buy a roaster, but not anymore. According to a poultry expert at the Department of Agriculture, "the difference between a fryer and a roaster is essentially a labeling deal." But the biggest difference for the shopper is the price.

The miracle of modern poultry breeding (which makes all chickens too fat) has created the broiler-fryer. It roasts, it fries, it broils, it stews, it fricassees, it poaches, it steams, it barbecues. In other words, the all-around bird, which weighs between 2½ and 5 pounds. Roasters weigh between 4 and 7 pounds.

Is there any reason to buy a roaster instead of a fryer? Not for taste. Taste tests show there is no difference.

But the bigger the bird the more meat there is in relation to the bone. A 6- or 7-pound roaster provides more meat than two 3- or 3½-pound fryers. According to USDA, a fryer is 68 percent meat; a roaster is 77 percent. That 9 percent difference makes a roaster a better buy than a fryer if the price difference is less than 20 cents a pound. In Washington, roasters are from 20 to 44 cents a pound more than fryers.

BEEF

Just a step away from the poultry case is the beef counter, which has been undergoing some frightful changes, mostly in price. In two Washington markets we can now buy both "lean" beef, a cut from the "good" grade, and choice beef, one grade above good. The lean has been tenderized by machine. It costs a few pennies less per pound than choice beef and is worth buying, not only for the pennies saved but because it has less fat.

Buying the cheapest ground beef is also worth it. The Department of Agriculture has tests to prove it.

". . . There is practically no difference in cooked hamburgers whether made from extra-lean or regular ground beef, except that hamburgers made from regular beef are juicier and a bit tastier," says Dr. Russell Cross, a technologist with USDA.

For the nutrition conscious, USDA reports that the difference in fat levels of cooked hamburgers made either from extra-lean or regular ground beef is minimal. Cross explained that regular ground beef loses more fat during cooking and extra-lean loses more water. In a cooked 3.5-ounce hamburger "extra-lean patties had one gram less fat and one gram more water than regular ground beef patties." The protein content was the same and the more expensive patties were "drier and tougher. . . ."

Is the extra gram of fat, equivalent to 9 calories, worth the difference in price?

One of the more interesting meat ripoffs doesn't take place in the supermarket. It is brought to you courtesy of Montgomery Ward. Several times a year they take out full-page newspaper ads to sell frozen boxed beef that they advertise as "100 percent U.S. Government inspected." All meat sold across state lines must be government inspected. Unfortunately, many people think the inspection seal means the meat is a high grade and quality. All it means is that the meat is safe to eat.

The grades of meat sold by Montgomery Ward are "utility" or "commercial," near the bottom of the grading scale. The ads don't tell you the grade. The amount of fat (marbling) in the meat and the tenderness determine the grade. Such meat ordinarily ends up ground into hamburgers or in canned stews because it isn't tender enough to eat any other way. It can also be tenderized with chemicals; so Montgomery Ward's "steaks" contain water, dextrose, and papain.

The "steaks" are cheaper than supermarket steaks and they ought to be, considering the quality. They are no bargain.

BOTTLED WATERS

Interest in health and nutrition has sparked an interest in bottled waters. The imported waters are getting some competition not only from domestic bottled waters but from something called SELTZER. It's ordinary tap water that has been purified to remove the chlorine, off tastes, and odors, then charged with carbon dioxide, CO2. No salts are added.

CLUB SODA is purified, carbonated tap water with added salts.

SPARKLING WATER—sometimes spring water, sometimes tap water—is usually carbonated with CO2. Occasionally the carbonation in spring water comes from the same source as the water. Then it is called naturally carbonated. Sparkling waters have no added salts.

Even the president of the company that imports Perrier could not distinguish his own product from Canada Dry in a test. Bruce Nevins appeared on Michael Jackson's radio show in Los Angeles and was confronted with seven glasses of sparkling water. Jackson says Nevins "picked out Perrier on his fifth guess."

If you are buying sparkling waters to reduce your sodium intake, I highly recommend the cheaper seltzers.

FRUCTOSE

Noticed the ads for the "new" sweetener, fructose? Sweeter than sugar so you use less of it. Good for diabetics even though they shouldn't use sugar.

Bad enough that very little of the above is true. Worse still that some companies are using a product that is only 55 percent fructose—the rest is glucose—and passing it off as pure fructose, like the natural sugar found in fruits. When a product containing 55 percent fructose is called by its proper name, it is High Fructose Corn Sweetener (HFCS). It is also very little different from sucrose (sugar). A 12-ounce can of soda sweetened with HFCS instead of sugar has only about 16 fewer calories than a sugar-sweetened soft drink.

The reason soft drink manufacturers use HFCS in place of sugar has nothing to do with your diet. It has everything to do with the manufacturer's pocketbook. High fructose corn sweetener is much cheaper than sugar.

GENERICS

Generics, the no-name products in the plain wrapper, bring shoppers the best value among packaged goods. The quality is usually not as high as that of national or house brands, but in food items the nutritional value is exactly the same. And when you are putting canned tomatoes in a stew it hardly matters what they look like. The food industry said generics wouldn't last, but people need some relief from higher prices. This is one place where they can get it.

COUPONS

Coupons are supposed to be another. Some people have made careers out of coupon clipping, but the fact remains most of those coupons are for the kinds of food people who have bought this book want to get away from. Besides, you will still come out ahead buying house brands instead of name brands with coupons. Esther Peterson, consumer advisor to Presidents Johnson and Carter, tried it once. Her bill for store brand items was $2.22 less than the bill for national brands using coupons.

INDIVIDUAL PRICE MARKING

As if shopping weren't enough of a hassle, some super-markets are looking to make it even worse. Those that have electronic, computer-assisted check-outs can remove prices from individual items, leaving them just on the shelves, because the scanners "read" the Universal Product Code (UPC), the lines and numbers on the products. The UPC tells the scanner the price. It's difficult enough to follow the electronic cash register because the prices fly by in a flash. Think what it will be like (and already is in some stores) if you are supposed to "remember" the price from the shelf. Of course, if you have nothing better to do, you can always carry around a grease pencil, which the store so generously provides, and mark the prices yourself on each item you buy. I tried that once. It took exactly twice as long to shop.

On the other hand, you can simply place your faith in the accuracy of the computer. Well, maybe YOU can, but I won't. I hear from too many people about the errors these fancy new cash registers make and it's happened to me, too. Seldom more than a few cents, but, as one checker said: "I've never seen an error in the customer's favor."

This conversation with one man who'd had it with the system is typical of the complaints: "I'm not opposed to modernization," he said and then catalogued his experiences with a computer check-out. "Cans of cat food marked 6 for $1.85 were rung up at $1.89. Cookies on sale for 53 cents were recorded at the non-sale price of 63 cents. Loaves of bread marked 2/79 at the shelf cost 49 cents each according to the machine. Fortunately," continued the shopper, "they [supermarkets] have not been able to take prices off. If they had, I wouldn't have known. The potential for unscrupulous practices is large. This is the real justification for keeping prices on each product."

Removal of prices from individual items also makes price comparisons within the store difficult. How will you know if it's cheaper to buy fresh, frozen, or canned peas if you have to keep all the price information in your head?

Loss of individual price marking reduces price awareness, but to make the removal of prices more palatable to customers stores hint that they will be able to lower prices. When Giant Food, a Washington-based supermarket chain, removed individual prices in all its stores, it reduced prices on many items, but the reductions were short-lived. After four months, prices were back up at the levels of all the other stores and individual price marking had gone the way of free chocolate jimmies on your ice cream cone.

ELSEWHERE ON THE FOOD FRONT

As if worrying about what the food industry is trying to put over on you as a shopper weren't enough, those of you who have children ought to be worrying about what the industry is doing to them. Trying to win their hearts and minds in school. That's what.

Companies and trade associations offer schools reams of free material that parade as nutrition information. Most teachers are delighted to receive these slick, highly professional films, bright workbooks, and recipe guides with four-color illustrations and photos not available from other sources.

Here is a sampling of what industry's "nutrition" information contains:

A Sugar Association brochure, used in home economics classes, says: "The Association has not found concentrated opposition to sugar in responsible medical circles, but it has detected concern among many individual doctors and dentists unfamiliar with the facts. This, unfortunately, seems to influence the thinking and actions of national and local politicians."

Material from Kraft's consumer relations department tells students that additives put into food are "beneficial" and "essential" and specifically that "safe human tolerances can be established for some substances that have induced cancer in experimental animals which have been submitted to questionable tests."

There are a lot of scientists eagerly waiting to see those experiments!

Betty Crocker offers a filmstrip extolling the virtues of convenience foods—Betty Crocker's convenience foods, that is. Each recipe suggestion calls for a General Mills product.

"Cooking with Dr. Pepper" features the history of soft drinks, nutrition information about the product (that part is quite short), plus about forty recipes. And you wondered why your child wants to make corn bread with a package of corn bread mix and a bottle of Dr. Pepper!

FOOD SAFETY

Besides these concerns about nutrition and economic deception, the last five years have not eased anyone's mind about the safety of what we eat. The same concerns that existed in 1977, when I wrote *Pure & Simple*, exist today. They've been joined by a few new ones, particularly environmental pollutants. But as individuals we have little control over them. What we have control over are questionable ingredients which are deliberately added to food.

You'll recognize them immediately: nitrites, saccharin, DES (which has been banned), artificial colors. To this list, an even more familiar ingredient—caffeine—must be added.

In December, 1980, a review of the Generally Recognized As Safe list (GRAS) was completed. There are 415 food additives on the GRAS list. The reviewers said 19 of the substances needed additional studies because there are unresolved questions about their safety. These include caffeine, BHA, and BHT.

The committee recommended that FDA establish safer conditions of use or prohibit the addition to food of five additives, salt, and four starches.

Because of a technicality in the law, nitrite is not part of the GRAS list. DES is not on it either because it is a drug. FDA, as you know, has already attempted to deal with saccharin.

Caffeine

Unlike saccharin, nitrites, or DES, caffeine has not been implicated as a carcinogen (cancer-causing agent). But a body of evidence has been building to show that caffeine, found not only in coffee and tea, but in chocolate, certain soft drinks, and drugs, may cause birth defects. The caffeine crosses the placental barrier. Enough evidence exists relating caffeine to birth defects in test animals that in 1980 FDA undertook the following steps:

It proposed removing caffeine from the GRAS list and placing it on what is called an interim list while additional studies are undertaken to determine safety.

It proposed a change in regulations so that "cola" and "pepper" soft drinks, which now are required to contain caffeine, will be permitted on the market in decaffeinated form.

The agency also planned to advise pregnant women about the hazards of caffeine consumption, but in 1981 those plans simply faded away.

In addition to posing a risk for the fetus, caffeine and its relatives, theobromine and theophylline, appear to be related to fibrocystic disease, a benign breast disease that produces lumps. These lumps are not cancerous, but there is some evidence that women with fibrocystic disease are more likely to develop breast cancer.

Dr. John Minton, a surgeon at Ohio State University College of Medicine, has published studies linking caffeine and the breast disease. Dr. Minton discovered that the levels of certain chemicals in cells that act as messengers between hormones and organs were highest in cancerous tissue, second highest in tissue from women with fibrocystic breast disease, and lowest in normal tissue.

Then Dr. Minton discovered that the substance which normally breaks down those chemicals after they have delivered their message is blocked by another group of chemicals—caffeine, theobromine, and theophylline. They are known collectively as methylxanthines.

In a study, forty-seven women with fibrocystic breast disease were told to stop drinking or eating anything containing methylxanthines. Twenty of them followed the doctor's instructions and in thirteen of those twenty women the disease disappeared in six months.

Minton has been criticized by other researchers because his study wasn't very large. Since that study was completed, Minton has replicated his findings in additional research. And he has found that most women whose diet does not respond to a methylxanthine-free diet will respond when they stop smoking, too. Whether or not his findings are statistically significant, a methylxanthine-free regime worked for me.

Caffeine is a drug. It affects the central nervous system and should be used in moderation, if at all.

Saccharin

Another threat to the fetus is posed by saccharin. Five years after the FDA attempted to ban saccharin as a cancer-causing agent, it is still with us. Even though no reputable scientist argues that saccharin is safe, Congress, bowing to intense pressure from the saccharin lobby, has placed three moratoriums on the saccharin ban, the third one set to expire in June, 1983. In the meantime, millions of children, those whose risk is second only to the unborn fetus, continue to drink the major share of diet sodas in this country. Not diabetics, for whom some might make an argument that saccharin is necessary, not old people who probably can't ingest enough of it in the time they have left to cause cancer, but adolescents and young people. Former FDA Commissioner Jere Goyan said in his first press conference in 1979: "My biggest concern is that a tremendous amount of younger people are drinking huge amounts, literally, of these . . . drinks. I hope we are not sitting on some future time bomb."

In an editorial the *New England Journal of Medicine* said: *ANY* use of saccharin by non-diabetic children or pregnant women, heavy use by young women of child-bearing age and excessive use by anyone is ill-advised.

None of these warnings has diverted the Calorie Control Council from its mission. The Council, which lobbies for suppliers and manufacturers of diet foods and drinks, has developed a unique public relations campaign ever since it broke into the news with its full-page ads opposing the original saccharin ban.

The Council has been quite successful in getting favorable stories on TV and radio, in newspapers and magazines, by distorting the results of sound scientific studies. I was sent some of the organization's confidential materials that provide an eye-opening picture of how they go about doing this.

In one letter to potential contributors they ask for money to keep saccharin on the market. Attached to the letter is a summary of the Council's work with the press. It includes: launching a counter blitz every time a new scientific report on saccharin is issued; meeting with editorial boards of newspapers; sending out public relations material to all meetings of interested journalists; sending thank-you notes to those who write articles the Council considers favorable.

What kind of success are individual consumers going

to have against a well-funded, professional organization like that?

Artificial Colors

All risks, no benefits. Today we consume sixteen times the amount of artificial colors we were consuming in 1940. The only thing new about artificial colors is that FDA plans to give industry additional time to test twenty-three artificial colors before deciding whether or not they should be removed from the market. The industry has known since 1960 it would have to prove the safety of all artificial colors. What with a little litigation here and there it wasn't until 1977 that FDA really put its foot down and said you have four more years in which to prove the safety of the remaining untested colors, or else. Or else turns out to be . . . more time.

FDA has made a special exception of Yellow #5, which is one of the untested colors. As long as Yellow #5, tartrazine, remains in the food supply it must be listed by name on products in which it is used because so many people are allergic to it.

DES

The food industry's attitude toward public health and food colors is positively cooperative compared to some cattlemen and their use of DES, diethylstilbestrol. DES causes a rare form of vaginal cancer and testicular abnormalities in some offspring of women who took the drug during pregnancy. DES was also used as a growth stimulant in cattle until FDA Commissioner Dr. Donald Kennedy banned its use after November 1, 1979.

In outright defiance of the ban, a number of feedlot operators continued to use DES after the cutoff date.

About 14 percent of the annual beef supply was affected when it was discovered in April, 1980.

A spokesman for the cattlemen said the violators were probably driven by sheer frustration. They had been losing a lot of money, he said, and thought they could get away with it. And they probably would still be doing it if a disgruntled feedlot employee hadn't squealed.

Nitrites

At the beginning of this chapter I mentioned most of the fascinating things that had happened to me as a food writer since I wrote *Pure & Simple*. I neglected one event: FDA's claim that it was forced to release the Newberne study on nitrites prematurely because I had written a story of the study's results in advance of the official release. FDA was preparing to say that the Newberne study showed nitrites caused cancer in test animals.

Between the time the results were available and my story was written, FDA had ample time to validate the study, but it didn't. If it had, there is the possibility the agency would have discovered that the study was faulty and did not prove that nitrites cause cancer. So it announced that the study showed nitrites caused cancer in laboratory animals and then had to backtrack.

Well, the press gets blamed for everything, why not this, too.

What is unfortunate about the entire episode is that the processed meat industry has seized on FDA's reversal as proof that nitrites are safe. We still don't have that answer, but it is totally irrelevant. Whether or not nitrites cause cancer by themselves, they definitely cause cancer in combination with amines. Nitrosamines are a potent carcinogen that can form in the stomach. They cause cancer in every species of animal tested, in every organ. If you didn't eat food cured with sodium nitrite before, there is no reason to start eating it now.

In an effort to help people who want to eat meats cured without nitrites and to make it easier for producers of nitrite-free products to market them, in 1978 USDA proposed a regulation to allow nitrite-free products to be called by the same names as those cured with nitrites. So "beef pups" could be called "uncured hot dogs," "pork strips" could be named "uncured bacon," and so on. Such uncured meats would have carried a warning on the label: "NO NITRITE OR NITRATE ADDED—NOT PRESERVED, KEEP REFRIGERATED BELOW 40 DEGREES AT ALL TIMES."

The regulation was scheduled to go into effect in the fall of 1979. The pork producers would have none of it. (You remember C. Donald Van Houweling on page 11.) They went to their congressmen, who in turn wrote to the Secretary of Agriculture. The congressmen said the regulation was "a dangerous proposal" and that if children take nitrite-free meats to school, keep them in a "warm school locker for hours on end," the children are subject to "potential disaster."

The congressmen wanted the nitrite-free meat to have different names: for example, "cold dogs" instead of hot dogs. They wanted the shape of the cold dogs changed, too, from round to square.

The Agriculture Secretary turned them down, so the pork producers took USDA to court . . . in Iowa, where they produce a lot of pork. A sympathetic judge stayed the regulation, but in the fall of 1980 the appeals court overturned the judge's decision. USDA should have been free to implement the regulation. It was not to be. The pork producers took the case to the Supreme Court! The Court refused to hear the case.

What will happen now that a pig farmer is Secretary of Agriculture!

Delaney clause

Food safety issues aren't going away, but the food industry wants to make it harder to ban carcinogens in food. For the last four years there has been increasing talk of modifying the Delaney Clause.

The Delaney Clause says that any substance ingested by man or animal must be banned if it causes cancer. The Congressional moratorium on the saccharin ban was the first successful attempt to weaken the Delaney Clause. In 1981 a bill was introduced in Congress by Sen. Orrin Hatch which seeks to loosen the food safety laws so that benefits can be weighed against risks. If it were enacted, it would virtually destroy the Delaney Clause.

But who's going to do the weighing?

Scientists?

Whose scientists?

Politicians?

We already know they think the benefits of saccharin outweigh the risks. Even Elizabeth Whelan, a self-styled consumer advocate, who strongly opposes a ban on saccharin, was forced to admit to a group of food writers that saccharin has "very little medical benefits . . . but it does provide enjoyment."

Whelan opposed a saccharin ban because "it would throw the soft drink and diet industry into chaos and the cost would be passed on to consumers."

Are people like Whelan, executive director of the American Council on Science and Health, going to make the benefit-risks decision?

Whelan, co-author of a book on food safety with another scientist closely allied with the food industry, Dr. Frederick Stare, believes that "food additives now in use are safe and contribute to good health." Her organization takes no money directly from industry but many members of its board of directors and advisors are consultants for the food industry on a regular basis.

Organizations like Whelan's sound scientific and impartial. They produce prodigious quantities of material proving that one or another food additive is safe and that people who think otherwise are guilty of "cancerphobia."

So it may be useful to keep in mind that studies from similar groups are likely to have industry bias.

The Nutrition Foundation is one of them. Its trustees are officials of Coca-Cola, Nestlé, Campbell's, Borden, Kraft, General Mills, and so on. Over half of its financial support comes from food, drug, and chemical industries.

Council on Agricultural Science and Technology, known as CAST, gets much of its financial support from agribusiness.

The membership of The Institute of Food Technologists is made up of the scientists who bring us food colors, food flavors, fabricated foods, additives in general. They may be connected with a company producing such food or the ingredients for it, or they may be connected with a university where experimental work in food technology is carried out.

And then there is an organization called Consumer Alert, founded and directed by Barbara Keating-Edh. Its seed money came from a company called Precision Valve whose chairman is Robert Abplanalp, the close friend of former President Nixon who perfected the aerosol spray valve. The company strongly opposed the ban on fluorocarbons in aerosol cans. Keating-Edh was director of Reagan's transition team for the Consumer Product Safety Commission. Consumer Alert also gets money from chemical companies and the soft drink trade association.

Its board of advisors includes Elizabeth Whelan.

Fortunately, there are still people who will continue to fight the food industry.

There are people who continue to believe that the sun will rise in the West, that those who sell us food will voluntarily change their ways, that we will enter a new era where packages will be labeled properly and fair prices will be marked clearly, where nothing harmful will be added to our foods, where advertisers will tell the truth, the whole truth, and nothing but the truth.

And pigs will fly.

ABOUT THE BOOK

In addition to the preceding chapter on the politics of food, the book has four additional chapters; all of them contain "from scratch" recipes. You don't have to read the political chapter to cook from the remaining chapters, but it would be enormously helpful if you read the introductory material to each of the recipe chapters before plunging ahead.

The next chapter, sixty-one 30-minute meals from scratch, which is referred to in the book's subtitle, is the main reason for the book's existence.

It is the result of a challenge issued to me by one of my editors, Chuck Conconi, who loves to eat well but lives in a two-person household where both people work. He wanted to know if you could put together a presentable meal in 30 minutes and dared me to try. After I had succeeded with several I asked another editor friend, who doesn't cook often, to try one or two menus. He beat the clock and commented: "If I can do it, anybody can."

The two chapters following 30-minute meals are for quick hors d'oeuvres and desserts. You can pick out any of the recipes to use with any meals, but they also can act as bookends to a 30-minute meal and quickly turn it into a meal for company.

The final chapter, homemade convenience foods, is for those who like to have ready-made dishes on hand so that they can spend even less than 30 minutes preparing dinner. With a few exceptions, these convenience foods are the kind you make when you have the time and store as you would a similar commercially prepared product.

Most of the recipes have been constructed to reduce calories, excess fat, salt, and sugar. Occasional indulgences are permitted. After all, if you treat your body well all week, you are entitled to treat yourself on occasion.

In short, *Keep It Simple* is a book for people who care about food and themselves, but who are in a hurry.

PART **2** | # 30-MINUTE MEALS MENUS AND RECIPES

30-MINUTE MEALS

CHICKEN

Summer, fall
FRENCH MENU FOR THREE   79
Chicken breasts in tarragon
Sautéed cherry tomatoes
Boiled tiny new potatoes
Berries and cookies

Spring, fall, winter
MENU FROM NORTH AND SOUTH OF
      THE BORDER FOR TWO OR
      THREE   83
Chicken in lime
Sautéed sunchokes
Baked acorn squash slices
Pears or grapes

Summer, fall
MENU FOR TWO OR THREE FOR A
      "MORE SPECIAL" DINNER   87
Chicken with marsala and grapes
"Creamed" spinach
Rice with mushrooms and onions
Purple plums and crystallized ginger

Avocado, mushroom and sprout salad
Sliced pineapple, papaya, or berries

Spring
SPRING DINNER FOR TWO   108
Chicken with yogurt
Whole-wheat pasta with caraway seeds
Steamed asparagus
Strawberries and orange liqueur

Summer
AN AMERICAN VERSION OF AN
    INDIAN MENU FOR TWO   111
Curried chicken
Saffron rice
Fresh fruit, chopped peanuts and chutney
Frozen yogurt

Any season
SPECIAL BUT INEXPENSIVE DINNER
    FOR THREE   115
Orange chicken
Kasha pilaf
Watercress and mushrooms in mustard
    dressing
Sherbet

Spring, fall, winter
CHINESE DINNER FOR THREE   119
Chicken and sweet peppers with hoisin
Spinach with sesame seeds
Vermicelli
Orange or mango

FISH

Fall, winter
MODERATELY FRENCH MENU FOR
    THREE   135
Fish bonne femme
Glazed brussels sprouts
Rice cooked in broth
Sliced pineapple with yogurt and brown
    sugar

Summer, fall
A LIGHT MIDSUMMER MENU FOR
    TWO   138
Seafood and nectarines
Sautéed cucumbers
Corn on the cob with cumin butter
Sorbet or ice

Any season
FISH DINNER FOR THREE   142
Fillets with lemon butter
Green beans in peanut sauce
Lisa's noodles
Grapes

Spring, summer, fall
FISH DINNER FOR TWO   145
Salmon fillet poached in vermouth
Cucumbers with mint in yogurt
Boiled new potatoes
Raspberries

MEATLESS

Summer, fall
MEATLESS ITALIAN MENU FOR FOUR   162
Zucchini and rotini
Tomato and mozzarella salad
Italian bread or dark peasant bread
Lemon ice

Any season
**MENU MINUS MEAT FOR THREE OR
       FOUR**   165
Bulgur with everything
*Sherley's creamy dressing for red lettuce (or
       green)*
Whole grain bread or whole grain pitas
Navel oranges, apples or papayas

Any season
MEATLESS MENU FOR FOUR   169
Green and yellow pasta
Oriental cucumbers
Garlic bread
Peaches, pears or strawberries

Spring, fall, winter
VEGGIE MENU FOR TWO   173
Tofu pasta sauce
Spaghetti squash
Sandy's salad
*Apple wedges, or strawberries with yogurt
       and brown sugar*

*Blueberries and strawberries or grapefruit
and banana*

Any season
SAN DIEGO VEGETARIAN MENU FOR
TWO   194
Deborah's huevos rancheros
*Boston or bibb lettuce with buttermilk
dressing*
Crusty dark bread and butter
Fruit and ice cream

Spring, winter
MEATLESS MENU FOR THREE OR
FOUR   198
Macaroni and cheese "nouvelle"
Cucumbers in orange sauce
Stewed tomatoes
Apples or strawberries with honey

Spring, fall, winter
MENU WITHOUT MEAT FOR THREE   202
Low-calorie cheese soufflés
Mexican zucchini
Warm pitas
Broiled grapefruit halves with honey

BEEF

Any season
CALIFORNIA MENU FOR FOUR   206
California picadillo

Avocado salad
Tortillas
*Cream cheese and guava paste with crackers
     or fruit*

Summer, fall
A "LITTLE" STEAK DINNER FOR TWO   210
Beef teriyaki
Green beans, tomato and savory
Boiled new potatoes
Peaches or nectarines

Spring, fall, winter
HUNGARIAN MENU FOR FOUR   213
Beef paprika "stew"
Broad egg noodles
Hungarian cucumber salad
Grapes with camembert

Spring, fall, winter
TEX-MEX DINNER FOR THREE   217
Chili
Beans with onion
Chicory with vinaigrette
Apples with camembert

Summer, fall
ITALIAN MENU FOR FOUR   221
Spaghetti squash with meat sauce
Chunky tomatoes and cucumbers
Breadsticks
Berries or pears

Any season
CHINESE MENU FOR TWO   225
Chinese beef and noodles
Leaf lettuce with garlic-caraway dressing
Tangerines, nectarines or grapes

Spring, fall, winter
TUESDAY NIGHT SPECIAL FOR THREE   229
Individual meat loaves
Steamed cauliflower
Cheese bread
Broiled grapefruit sprinkled with brown sugar

Any season
STIR-FRY MENU FOR TWO   233
Stir-fried beef and tomatoes
Vermicelli
Oriental broccoli
Honeydew or frozen fruit

Any season
MOCK CHILI MENU FOR TWO OR
THREE   237
Chili and sausage
Romaine salad with garlic dressing
Spaghetti squash
Frozen yogurt

Fall, winter
TWO DISH MENU FOR FOUR   241
Beef and bulgur
Braised fennel
Bananas with yogurt and brown sugar

Strawberries, peaches, or oranges with
    brown sugar and sour cream or yogurt

Spring, fall, winter
MELTING-POT MENU FOR TWO   261
Pork chops with apple, cabbage, and cumin
Yellow squash with provolone sauce
Bulgur with garlic and parsley
Papaya or frozen fruit

Any season
CHINESE MENU FOR TWO   265
Pork chops with mushrooms
Noodles
Pat's bean sprouts and scallions
Murcotts, strawberries or blueberries

Any season
FAR EAST MENU FOR THREE   269
Pork saté
Mushrooms and sprouts with
    mustard-vinegar
Asian rice
Pineapple spears or blueberries

Fall
ITALIAN MENU FOR TWO   273
Italian sausages in pepper-basil sauce
Spaghetti
Spinach, apple, walnut salad
Melon and lemon wedges

Summer, fall
GERMAN MENU FOR TWO   276
Bratwurst
Cabbage, apples, and onions
Hot potato salad
Pumpernickel rolls or bread
Boysenberry sherbet

Spring, fall, winter
A HYBRID MENU FOR TWO   280
Polish pork chops
Macaroni
Curly endive with chili-cumin dressing
Grapefruit with or without honey

TURKEY, "VEAL" AND LAMB

Any season
ITALIAN MENU FOR TWO   283
"Veal" parmesan
Pasta pizzaiola
Mushrooms and scallion salad
Frozen or fresh strawberries or peaches

Any season
CELEBRATION MENU FOR FOUR   287
Veal piccata "sting"
Whole-wheat pasta with yellow squash and
    tomato sauce
Whole-wheat breadsticks
Raspberry sorbet

Summer, fall, winter
POOR MAN'S VEAL DINNER FOR
    FOUR 290
"Veal" with rosemary
Thin egg noodles
Zucchini with apples
Plums or tangelos

Fall, winter
THANKSGIVING MENU FOR SIX 293
Turkey-sesame cutlets
Mushroom rice
Tomatoes provençale
Cranberry-orange sherbet

Spring, fall, winter
LAMB CHOP DINNER FOR THREE 297
Lamb chops oregano
Sweet potatoes and apples
Baked mushrooms
Fruit sherbet

30-MINUTE MEALS FROM SCRATCH

Lorelei Kilbourne was held up at the paper, on deadline with a story about a man who was trying to scale the tallest building in town. There's nothing in her refrigerator at home and two people waiting to eat it. So she opts for carry-out—cold cuts, potato salad, coleslaw, and ice cream. To heck with the diet. Fortunately, it had been payday the day before and she had enough money for the $20 dinner.

Elizabeth Furnace is on her way to the third protest meeting of the week. This one has been called in an effort to abolish plastic peas, cardboard tomatoes, and bread made with wood pulp.

But the manufacturers of these products aren't the least bit worried. As a matter of fact, they love the protest meetings. The Elizabeth Furnaces of the world are in such a hurry to get to their meetings that their families end up eating . . . plastic peas, cardboard tomatoes, and bread made with wood pulp.

Both Kilbourne and Furnace are busy.

But being busy doesn't mean you have to settle for second best. The alternative to a limited amount of time to prepare dinner doesn't always have to be a restaurant, carry-out food, or convenience packages. Since no one is going to lower those restaurant prices, improve the quality of the carry-out, or make the non-nutritious, oversalted, additive-ridden convenience food all natural, the ball is in your court . . . as usual. The alternative to a limited amount of time, limited funds, and limited patience with the second rate is the subject of this section.

Using the menus in this chapter it will take you only 30 minutes from the time you put on your apron (if you wear one) until the dinner is ready to go on the table to prepare a two- or three-dish meal from scratch for two to four people, dessert not included. That's how long it takes McDonald's to sell 230,000 hamburgers.

If one of the speakers at the annual newspaper food editors' conference in 1980 was reading the surveys correctly, speed in food preparation is what people care about. "The 'perfect housewife' ethic is quickly being supplanted by that significant consideration, 'saving time,'" he said. "For the household of the 1980s faster meal preparation and clean up will be critical."

Today, half of the women in this country are in Betty Furnace's category—not working outside the home but busy. And the other half are like Lorelei Kilbourne. If you include only women under thirty-five, the Kilbournes account for 75 percent of the female population. And let's not forget working men.

Working people, in general, suffer from a lack of time to plan and shop economically. The problem afflicts anyone who likes to eat dinner at home, whether alone or with family.

The food industry has taken full advantage of the situation, creating and advertising prepared foods that are supposed to save time. That they may not be as palatable, that they probably are less nutritious, that·they definitely cost more, none of that is part of the advertising campaign.

Surveys have found that working women feed their families on a par with full-time homemakers, but often spend 50 percent more to do so. Some of the extra money goes into ready-to-serve foods.

It doesn't have to.

There are simple alternatives to TV dinners, cold-cut platters, cans of chili, boxes of macaroni and cheese, and boil-in-the-bag-mixed-vegetables-in-cream-sauce-with-toasted-almonds. The alternatives are not simply the equal of the factory-prepared foods, they are infinitely better. They offer a lot more for a lot less and can be ready to eat in half the time it takes a lot of TV dinners to heat. (I know this is off the subject, but one of my favorite examples is TV breakfast—sausage, eggs, and French toast. You have to get up at least an hour before breakfast in order for it to be ready on time!)

But weaning yourself from anonymous food that is prepared by anonymous machines involves a certain amount of reorganization and rethinking.

First you must decide whether or not you believe the commercials that imply that cooking from scratch is a tedious, time-consuming job for an expert. If you can't abandon that ridiculous notion, return this book to the store.

Then you have to get organized, organized enough to keep the cupboard stocked with staples, to know where they are, to keep your cooking equipment in good repair, your knives well sharpened.

Next you have to pick out a menu, check the staples list to be sure you have them, and make a quick trip to the grocery store on your way home to buy what's on the shopping list. (If you don't want to decide the night before, or in the morning before you go to work, you can always take the book to the office.) The shopping list is almost always less than ten items, which means you can go to the quick check-out in most supermarkets. (Sometimes that means quick; sometimes it doesn't.)

The meals in this chapter assume that all the hungry people waiting at home are incapable or unwilling to do anything in the kitchen except set the table. The menus can be prepared in 30 minutes by one person, working alone, just as long as the dog doesn't get underfoot, the utensils aren't dirty, and no one else wants to cook something entirely different at the same time. The 30 minutes do not include a dessert or washing the dishes, though some preparation of the meals takes less than 30 minutes so you will have time to straighten up before dinner is ready. And all those helpless people in the house who can't cook certainly know how to wash dishes. If they don't, they should take a self-improvement course.

Cooking a meal in 30 minutes is not for the rank beginner. There are no complicated techniques to perform, but there isn't any time to look up the meaning of "mince" or figure out how "hot" hot is. But the novice can certainly cook this meal . . . it will just take longer.

For some experienced or relatively experienced cooks, preparing a 30-minute meal will require rethinking. If you feel compelled to finish one dish before starting another, you will have to discard that idiosyncrasy. You will have to discard your leisurely pace and your military precision. Here neatness doesn't count. If a piece of parsley falls on the floor, it can be left there until after dinner when it can be swept up along with the peppercorns that rolled off the counter.

You will also have to stop worrying about exact measurements. It's OK if it isn't exactly one tablespoon of parsley or one-half cup of cheese on the button. Such exactitude is necessary only for baking. Accurate measurements are given in the recipes so you will know where to start. You may like less cumin in a recipe anyway; you may also like more.

If you've been around a kitchen long enough you probably don't have to measure out one tablespoon of chopped parsley; you know what it looks like. And you know not to worry if the pork chops aren't browned evenly all over. No one will notice the difference in the finished product. And you won't worry if a recipe calls for a 28-ounce can of tomatoes and all you can find is a 29-ounce can. It will do just as well.

I had to learn a lot of these things by doing, or finally giving up. When I started I thought I never could include green beans in a meal like this because it would take too long to trim them. Not true if you are cooking for two or three. True, I'm sure, if you have to cook for more.

I was also determined to find a way to cook potatoes in 30 minutes without peeling and cutting them because that removes many of their nutrients. Well, I didn't succeed completely. Even half a potato with a skewer through it will not bake in 30 minutes no matter how high you set the oven. But the season for new potatoes, the ones that are no larger than golf balls, finally solved the problem, and you will notice that in the spring and summer menus there are numerous recipes calling for those wonderful little potatoes. You don't have to peel them, as a matter of fact you shouldn't, and they cook, whole, in less than 30 minutes.

I also discovered that I didn't need any fancy equipment to make all but a couple of these meals, although a food processor, blender and/or electric mixer might speed up some of the operations. (In the chapters on hors d'oeuvres and desserts some of the recipes call for such equipment.)

There are some basic decisions you have to make when you are trying to pare down to the basics and don't want to sacrifice quality. Certain niceties of preparation must go by the boards.

Forget about mincing onions and green peppers, or much of anything else. As long as onions are being cooked a while they can be coarsely chopped; the same is true of most vegetables. Garlic can be put through a garlic press for speed, though mincing a clove with a sharp knife is pretty speedy work. (I found I couldn't use shallots too often because it took too much time to peel and chop them.)

Forget about peeling and seeding tomatoes. If you have a very juicy one, you can give it a quick squeeze to get rid of some seeds and juice, but for the kinds of dishes included here, whether or not the tomato is peeled is a refinement of little consequence.

Forget about marinating food to tenderize it. If the

marinade is used to impart flavor, most mixtures are powerful enough to add flavor to the food in 15 minutes. In addition the marinades in these recipes are also used in the final dish.

Most of the cooking is on top of the stove: if a dish should be run under the broiler to brown, it ought to be cooked, if possible, in a pot or skillet that can be put under the broiler. It takes time to transfer pots and it just means something else to clean.

If you have a toaster oven it's more economical as well as quicker than the oven for browning and for heating breads or toasting nuts.

The size of the food you are cooking is of great importance. You will have to give up whole roast chickens, whole roasts, period. Chicken pieces—legs, thighs, breast quarters—take much less time to cook than a quartered chicken. Pork cubes rather than chops, though thin chops cook quickly; thinly sliced beef and ground beef, of course, will cook in a short time. Some vegetables—broccoli or cauliflower—must be cut up or broken into small pieces instead of left in whole stalks or heads; slices of acorn squash, quarters of spaghetti squash, in place of a whole squash. The aforementioned tiny new potatoes, of course. On the other hand, you can't select vegetables that require time-consuming peeling and cutting.

The cooking techniques are broil, boil, sauté, or simmer. Stewing and roasting are out.

If all the staples are in the cupboard, the just-bought groceries in the bag, the knives sharp, the pots and pans clean, everything in its place, you are ready to start.

One of the most important instructions given to cooks is to read a recipe through before cooking it. It's pretty hard to put a 30-minute meal together in the allotted time if the cook is totally unfamiliar with the recipes. Give them a once-over.

As you will see by reading the Game Plan, you start with the food that takes longest to cook. The plan directs you to move back and forth among the recipes so that everything will cook on time. You may, for example, start by frying pork chops and then while they are frying, you will put on the water to boil the noodles. Note that you are told to put hot water on to boil in a covered pot. Hot water from the tap reduces the amount of time it takes the water to boil; so does covering the pot. Next you may return to the chops to prepare the onion and garlic for them and add them to the pan. Then you may wash the vegetables for the salad, and so on.

Again, the Game Plan is just a guide. You may need to do some switching around for the style in which you work or because something isn't quite ready for the next step.

A number of recipes do not specify cooking times. If you follow the directions and the Game Plan, they will be finished in the 30 minutes. But use your discretion.

You will also find that some of the dishes can't be started until just a few minutes before the 30 minutes are up; otherwise they will be overdone. It's better, though, to have the boiling water waiting for the pasta or vegetables than the other way around.

You will see that these recipes form a fairly standard American dinner for the 80s. There are numerous dishes with foreign flavor; that's how Americans are cooking. If you examine the components carefully, you will find some subtle and not-so-subtle changes from ten or fifteen years ago: the portions of meat are often smaller; the portions of vegetables and grains larger. Most of the meals are lower in calories, specifically fat calories. This has been accomplished by frequent substitution of yogurt for sour cream and cream; by reduction of the ratio of oil to vinegar in salad dressings; by reduction of the amount of fat needed for sautéing; by draining off excess fat when browning or cutting it away before cooking.

An entire section is devoted to meatless menus. There are more recipes for chicken and fish than for beef and pork and when you include meatless menus with chicken and fish the recipes for pork and beef are greatly outnumbered. Few of the suggested family desserts contain sugar.

Even in the separate dessert chapter the majority are fruit-based.

Salt fanciers will have to do their own thing. "Salt and freshly ground black pepper to taste" can be found eternally linked together in almost every recipe. But how much you use is up to you. We don't use any salt in our house at all and because of the extensive use of herbs and spices in most recipes we don't miss it.

While greens are specified for salads, you can choose whichever you like and whatever you can easily buy.

If you have a big eater in your family, you can do several things: increase the size of the recipes; add some good-tasting warm bread; convince him or her to eat less if overweight.

While about ten of the sixty-one menus are not budget-minded (scallops, shrimp, salmon, sirloin, chicken breasts), they still beat the prices for what you can buy already prepared. Cooking from scratch means keeping close to the budget, eating better for less. It means not only controlling the fat, salt, sugar, and calories, it means controlling the chemical additives. There's no mono-sodium glutamate, sodium nitrite, BHA, BHT, saccharin, powdered cellulose (wood pulp), artificial color, and artificial flavor. We can't control a lot of the pollutants in our environment, but we do have control over most food additives, a control it's easy to exercise.

There may be some criticism because there seem to be several recipes for cooking Chinese or Italian pasta, several recipes for rice, and several for boiled new potatoes. I plead guilty. But plain dishes are the appropriate ones for many of the menus and including fancy ones just for the sake of change doesn't do justice to the menu.

The menus are keyed for the appropriate seasons. Often it's a matter of changing just one item to make a menu work for another season, so if you want a spring menu with asparagus, just substitute broccoli or zucchini when there is no asparagus.

At the end of this introduction is a list of the staples you should have for a 30-minute kitchen and a list of the bare essentials in equipment.

This chapter is followed by a chapter on hors d'oeuvres and another on desserts. They are included to help turn these family dinners into something more festive. If you add one of the speedy hors d'oeuvres to the "cocktail" hour (while you are doing your 30-minute stint) and a dessert, you should be proud to serve any of these meals to company and that includes your mother-in-law and your spouse's boss.

While the 30-minute menus suggest a fruit dessert* (they are not included in preparation time), usually just a piece of fruit in keeping with health concerns, many of the recipes from the dessert chapter can be tagged on to the end of the meal for the family. Some of them won't add more than a few minutes preparation time.

The meals are for two, three, or four people. Many of them can be made for six without going over the 30-minute limit. It depends on how much cutting, chopping, and peeling is involved. Several of the meals have been prepared for six people and have added only five or seven minutes onto the preparation time.

SHORTER CUTS

There are additional ways to cut down on preparation time without sacrificing quality and taste, but they are not available to everyone and/or they cost a lot. For those who are interested, here are some of them, with suggestions on how to prepare your own Shorter Cuts at home.

Freshly grated Parmesan cheese is available in supermarkets in many big cities and in Italian markets. You can do that yourself by grating a large wedge of Parmesan in a

---

* Dessert ingredients are enclosed in parentheses under "Staples" and "Shopping List."

food processor and keeping the grated cheese in the refrigerator or freezer. The cheese doesn't freeze solid so it can be spooned out easily.

Chopped garlic, preserved in oil, is becoming more readily available. Restaurants have been using it for years. It keeps indefinitely in the refrigerator. You can do the same. Chop several heads and store it, covered with oil in a jar.

Chopped onions and chopped green peppers are often sold frozen in plastic bags. They aren't bad at all for cooking, but they do throw off moisture when they are cooked. You can do the same thing, chop a large quantity at a time—in the food processor if you have one—and store it in the freezer. If you use the frozen kind, you will have to compensate for the moisture and if you want crisply cooked green pepper, such as you find in a Chinese recipe, the frozen won't do.

Since I have yet to find whole-wheat bread crumbs, I make them in the food processor and keep them in the freezer to use when bread crumbs are needed.

After you have tried the 30-minute menus you like, you will have the hang of the concept and be able to adapt many of your favorite recipes to this style of cooking. I'd love to hear from you if you have any shortcuts cooking from scratch at the last minute.

This chapter is proof, if you needed it, that the old saw was wrong: Haste doesn't make waste; it makes a 30-minute meal.

THE BARE ESSENTIALS FOR A 30-MINUTE KITCHEN

EQUIPMENT

Pot sizes recommended are for two to four people. If you are cooking for a larger number, you will need some larger pots and skillets.

KNIVES, FORKS, AND SPOONS

chef's knife

paring knife

bread knife

2 stirring spoons, 1 slotted, preferably

1 large fork

POTS AND PANS

12-inch skillet with lid

sauté pan with lid

6-quart pot with lid

2- or 3-quart pot with lid

holder for steaming that fits into pot, or steamer

muffin tins or Pyrex cups

2-quart casserole

jelly-roll pan or baking sheet

OTHER UTENSILS

spatula

garlic press

4-sided grater

set measuring spoons

bottle opener

vegetable peeler

whisk

juice squeezer

quart measuring cup	can opener
set measuring cups (¼, ⅓, ½, 1)	electric or hand beater (for soufflé)
large colander or strainer	pot holders

STAPLES

Clearly, if you can't stand some of the ingredients that follow you aren't going to stock them. And just as clearly, some of the ingredients listed below are not considered staples in the American kitchen. But if you have these items on hand you will not have to go out of your way to buy them at the local ethnic market when you are in a rush to cook dinner. That way you can keep the amount of time spent in the supermarket to a minimum and take advantage of the quick check-out line.

If you have access to fresh herbs, you are in luck. If you have access to them for at least part of the year, either in the supermarket or in your own garden, freeze them and use frozen herbs instead of dried wherever possible.

I have designated herbs as staples, whether fresh, frozen, or dried, because it is seldom that the supermarket stocks any but parsley and dill.

HERBS AND SPICES

Aniseed or star anise	Ginger—fresh, frozen, powdered
Basil—fresh, frozen, dried	
Bay leaves	Marjoram—fresh, frozen, dried
Caraway seeds	
Chili powder	Mustard, dried
Cinnamon, ground	Nutmeg, ground
Cloves, ground	Oregano—fresh, frozen, dried
Coriander seed, crushed	
Cumin, ground	Paprika, preferably sweet Hungarian
Curry powder	Pepper—freshly ground black, ground white, ground red (cayenne)
Dillseed	
Dillweed—fresh, frozen	Poppy seeds

Rosemary—fresh, frozen, dried

Salt

Savory—fresh, frozen, dried

Sesame seeds

Tarragon—fresh, frozen, dried

Thyme—fresh, frozen, dried

CONDIMENTS

Capers

Chili sauce

Hoisin sauce

Honey

Mayonnaise

Mustard, Dijon

Oil—Olive, vegetable, sesame

Oyster sauce—watch out for the kind with monosodium glutamate

Sesame paste (preferred), tahini or creamy peanut butter

Soy sauce—either Japanese or imported Chinese

Vinegar—red and white wine, distilled white, rice

Worcestershire sauce

SPIRITS

Brandy

Marsala

Orange-flavored liqueur

Dry sherry

Dry vermouth

BASICS

Beef stock, bouillon, or broth*

Dry bread crumbs

Butter, unsalted

Chicken stock, bouillon, or broth*

Eggs

Flour, unbleached

Garlic

Lemons

Milk

Onions

Rice—enriched long grain white and/or brown

Sugar—granulated and brown

---

* If you do not make your own stocks and choose to buy them, watch out for those that contain monosodium glutamate. Some are available unsalted, too.

NICE BUT NOT ESSENTIAL EXCEPT THAT IF YOU HAVE THEM IT SAVES TIME

Bulgur (cracked wheat)

Chinese vermicelli

Egg noodles, thin and wide

Italian pastas, especially thin spaghetti and linguine

Muenster, Monterey Jack and/or Cheddar cheese

Kasha (buckwheat groats)

Tomato purée

Vegetable stock or broth*

Plain yogurt, with active cultures

NON-STAPLES—WHAT TO LOOK FOR

Cheese: buy white uncolored.

Cottage cheese: check ingredient statement.

Cream: buy pasteurized, not ultra-pasteurized. The latter does not whip well. It has an off taste and it doesn't make crème fraîche.

Sour cream: check the ingredient statement.

Wine: buy the kind you drink, not the kind which has been adulterated with salt and is called "cooking wine."

BROWN RICE IN A 30-MINUTE MEAL

To use brown rice in a 30-minute meal, you will have to think about it 4 hours or more in advance. You can soak the rice when you get ready to go to work in the morning, the night before, and so on. Soaking the kernels softens them but does not destroy any appreciable amount of nutrients.

To cook, drain off soaking liquid and proceed with recipe directions for white rice. The rice will be cooked in 20 minutes or less.

---

* If you do not make your own stocks and choose to buy them, watch out for those that contain monosodium glutamate. Some are available unsalted, too.

SUBSTITUTIONS

Allspice: 1 teaspoon equals ½ teaspoon cinnamon and ⅛ teaspoon ground cloves.

Baking powder: 1 teaspoon equals ¼ teaspoon baking soda plus ½ teaspoon cream of tartar.

Bread crumbs: ¼ cup dry bread crumbs equals 1 slice bread; ½ cup soft bread crumbs equals 1 slice bread.

Butter: 1 cup equals ⅞ cup oil or 14 tablespoons solid shortening plus ½ teaspoon salt.

Buttermilk: 1 cup equals 1 cup yogurt, or 1 cup whole milk plus 1 tablespoon vinegar or lemon juice: let stand 5 minutes, or 1 cup milk plus 1¾ teaspoons cream of tartar.

Catsup: ½ cup equals ½ cup tomato sauce plus 2 tablespoons sugar, 1 tablespoon vinegar, ⅛ teaspoon ground cloves.

Chocolate: 1 ounce unsweetened equals 3 tablespoons carob powder plus 2 tablespoons water.

Chocolate: 1 ounce unsweetened equals 3 tablespoons cocoa plus 1 tablespoon butter or other kind of fat.

Chocolate: 1 ounce unsweetened plus 4 teaspoons sugar equals 1⅔ ounces semisweet.

Chocolate: 6 ounces semisweet (chips or squares) equal 6 tablespoons cocoa plus 7 tablespoons sugar and ¼ cup shortening.

Chocolate: premelted unsweetened, 1-ounce envelope equals 3 tablespoons cocoa plus 1 tablespoon oil or melted shortening.

Coffee: ½ cup strong-brewed coffee equals 1 teaspoon instant coffee powder in ½ cup water.

Cracker crumbs: ¾ cup equals 1 cup bread crumbs.

Cream: 1 cup half-and-half equals ⅞ cup milk plus 3 tablespoons butter.

Cream: 1 cup whipping cream equals ¾ cup milk plus ⅓ cup butter. (It won't whip.)

Cream: 1 cup whipping cream equals ⅔ cup well-chilled evaporated milk, whipped, or 1 cup nonfat dry milk powder whipped with 1 cup ice water.

Egg yolks: for thickening, 2 yolks equal 1 whole egg.

Flour: for thickening, 1 tablespoon equals 2 teaspoons quick-cooking tapioca or 1½ teaspoons cornstarch, potato starch, or arrowroot.

Cake flour: 1 cup equals 1 cup minus 2 tablespoons sifted all-purpose flour.

All-purpose flour: 1 cup equals 1 cup plus 2 tablespoons cake flour.

Self-rising flour: 1 cup equals 1 cup all-purpose flour plus 1¼ teaspoons baking powder plus ⅛ teaspoon salt.

Whole-wheat flour: ¾ cup whole-wheat flour equals 1 cup white flour. Reduce shortening by using 2 tablespoons for every 3 tablespoons called for. Add 1 or 2 tablespoons liquid for cakes, slightly more for bread.

Garlic: 1 clove equals ¼ teaspoon garlic powder or 1 teaspoon garlic salt (reduce added salt by ½ teaspoon in recipe).

Gelatin: ¼-ounce envelope equals a little less than 1 tablespoon.

Ginger: 1 tablespoon fresh equals 1 teaspoon powdered or 1 tablespoon crystallized with sugar washed off.

Herbs: 1 tablespoon fresh equals about 1 teaspoon crushed dried or ⅔ teaspoon powdered.

Hot pepper sauce: few drops equal pinch cayenne or red pepper.

Lemon juice: 1 teaspoon equals ½ teaspoon vinegar.

Milk: 1 cup skim equals ⅓ cup instant nonfat dry milk plus approximately ¾ cup water.

Milk: 1 cup whole milk equals ½ cup evaporated milk plus ½ cup water.

Milk: 1 cup whole milk equals 1 cup reconstituted nonfat dry milk plus 2½ teaspoons butter (or margarine).

Milk: in baking 1 cup whole milk equals 1 cup fruit juice.

Mushrooms: 6 ounces canned, drained mushrooms equal ½ pound fresh.

Mustard: 1 tablespoon prepared equals 1 teaspoon dried.

Onion: 1 small fresh onion, chopped, equals 1 tablespoon instant minced onion or ¼ cup frozen chopped onion.

Raisins: ½ cup equals ½ cup cut, plumped, pitted prunes or dates.

Sour cream: ½ cup equals 3 tablespoons butter plus ⅞ cup buttermilk or yogurt.

Sour cream: for dips, 1 cup equals 1 cup cottage cheese puréed with ¼ cup yogurt or buttermilk, or 6 ounces cream cheese plus enough milk to make 1 cup.

Sour milk: Place 1 tablespoon lemon juice in distilled white vinegar in the bottom of a measuring cup. Add enough milk to make 1 cup. Stir and let mixture clabber, about 5 minutes.

Soy sauce: ¼ cup equals 3 tablespoons Worcestershire sauce plus 1 tablespoon water. Soy sauce can be found in Oriental shops in light, and dark (or black) in imported Chinese. Except where specified, light soy sauce is used.

Japanese soy sauce, manufactured in this country, can be substituted for light Chinese soy sauce. It also comes in a reduced sodium version. But even that still has a lot of sodium.

SWEETENERS

Sugar: 1 cup granulated equals 1¾ cups powdered, but do NOT substitute in baking.

Brown sugar: 1 cup firmly packed brown sugar equals 1 cup granulated sugar.

Turbinado sugar: 1 cup equals 1 cup granulated, with a heavier molasses flavor.

Corn syrup: 2 cups corn syrup equal 1 cup granulated sugar, but never use corn syrup to replace more than half the amount of sugar called for in a recipe. In baking, you are taking a chance in making the substitution, but if you must, "for each 2 cups of sugar, reduce the liquid called for—other than syrup—by ¼ cup."

Honey: 1 cup equals 1¼ cups sugar. For baking, also decrease liquid in recipe by ¼ cup. If there is no liquid in recipe, add ¼ cup flour. Unless sour cream or sour milk is used in recipe, add a pinch of baking soda.

Molasses: 1 cup unsulphured molasses equals ¾ cup sugar. In baking, decrease liquid by ¼ cup for each cup of molasses; omit any baking powder and add ½ teaspoon baking soda.

Tomatoes: 1 cup canned equals 1⅓ cups chopped fresh tomatoes, simmered.

Tomato juice: 3 cups equal 1½ cups tomato sauce plus 1½ cups water or 1 6-ounce can tomato paste plus 3 cans water, dash salt, sugar.

Tomato paste: 1 tablespoon equals 1 tablespoon catsup.

Tomato purée: 1 cup equals ½ cup tomato paste plus ½ cup water.

Tomato sauce: 1 cup equals 1 6-ounce can tomato paste plus 1½ cans water and seasoning.

Wine: For marinade, ½ cup dry equals ¼ cup vinegar plus 1 tablespoon sugar and ¼ cup water.

Worcestershire sauce: 1 teaspoon equals 1 tablespoon light Chinese soy sauce plus dash hot pepper sauce.

Yeast: 1 cake compressed equals 1 package dried.

Yogurt, plain: 1 cup equals 1 cup buttermilk.

MENUS AND RECIPES

FRENCH MENU FOR THREE

Chicken breasts in tarragon

Sautéed cherry tomatoes

Boiled tiny new potatoes

Berries and cookies

CHICKEN in tarragon is a classic French recipe. Its directions have been shortened a bit to accommodate the 30-minute meal, but the results are still delicious. The recipe has also been decalorized a bit by the omission of flour to coat the breasts and by the use of half-and-half instead of heavy cream.

Sautéed cherry tomatoes have been hanging around my cookbooks for a long time. Everyone loves them, no matter the seasonings.

I hope you won't look at tiny new potatoes during their season and say, "Oh no, not those again!" I must admit, I'm addicted to them.

GAME PLAN

Cook potatoes.

Sauté chicken breasts.

Prepare tomatoes, garlic, and parsley.

Keep breasts warm; deglaze pan with wine.

Add mustard, tarragon, salt, half-and-half.

Sauté tomatoes, parsley, garlic, bread crumbs, and seasonings.

Return breasts to pan; heat through.

STAPLES

butter

white wine or dry vermouth

Dijon mustard

tarragon

salt

garlic

bread crumbs

pepper

olive oil

SHOPPING LIST

6 halves boneless chicken breasts

¾ cup half-and-half

pint cherry tomatoes

3 tablespoons parsley

10 to 12 (1 pound) tiny new potatoes

(berries, cookies)

Chicken breasts in tarragon

3 SERVINGS

3 tablespoons butter
6 boneless chicken breast halves
¾ cup dry white wine or dry vermouth
1½ teaspoons Dijon mustard

¾ teaspoon dried tarragon or 2 teaspoons fresh
Salt to taste
¾ cup half-and-half

Heat butter in large skillet. Sauté chicken breasts, skin sides down, until golden; turn and sauté on second side until golden, about 3 minutes on each side. Remove and keep warm. Deglaze pan with wine, stirring over medium heat. Chop fresh tarragon. Add mustard, tarragon, and salt; mix. Whisk in half-and-half and cook at high simmer until mixture reduces and thickens a little. Add the breasts; spoon sauce over them and heat until mixture is heated through. Serve.

Sautéed cherry tomatoes

3 SERVINGS

1 pint cherry tomatoes
1 large clove garlic
3 tablespoons chopped fresh parsley
2 tablespoons olive oil

½ cup white or whole-wheat bread crumbs
Salt and freshly ground black pepper to taste

Wash and stem tomatoes. Put garlic through press. Chop parsley. Heat oil. Add tomatoes, garlic, parsley, bread crumbs, and salt and pepper. Sauté over low heat stirring occasionally, about 15 or 20 minutes, until tomatoes begin to soften but before they burst. Be sure crumbs don't burn.

Boiled tiny new potatoes   3 SERVINGS

10 to 12 (1 pound) tiny new   **Salt to taste**
    potatoes

Scrub potatoes, but do not peel them. Place in pot with water to cover. Bring to boil, covered, and boil 15 to 20 minutes, depending on the size of the potatoes, until tender. Drain and serve either with sauce from the chicken or with a little butter. Season with salt.

MENU FROM NORTH AND SOUTH OF THE BORDER FOR TWO OR THREE

Chicken in lime

Sautéed sunchokes

Baked acorn squash slices

Pears or grapes

THE seasonings for the chicken are strictly Mexican, the rest of the meal is strictly north of the Rio Grande. That makes it typically American.

Chicken in lime was originally made with large pieces of chicken. Of course it works just as well with smaller pieces, and they cook much more quickly.

It took a bit of experimenting to figure out how to cook acorn squash in less than 30 minutes. Now that I know, it seems ridiculously easy.

Sunchokes—if you go back far enough you remember them as Jerusalem artichokes, which hardly anyone ever ate, and you seldom saw in supermarkets. That is beginning to change. Now Jerusalem artichokes—under a new and more appropriate name and not related to artichokes at all, but to sunflowers—are more readily available at the stores. They are easy to prepare and can be scrubbed and eaten raw, too. Nice and crunchy.

GAME PLAN

Turn oven to 400.

Prepare squash and bake.

Brown chicken.

Cut up garlic and onion and add to chicken.

Prepare sunchokes and sauté.

Add seasonings to chicken and simmer.

Add lime juice to chicken.

STAPLES

oil

onion

garlic

hot red pepper

ground cumin

crushed coriander seeds

turmeric

soy sauce

butter

salt

pepper

SHOPPING LIST

6 chicken thighs or 3 large chicken breast halves

2 limes

½ pound sunchokes (Jerusalem artichokes)

1 small acorn squash (pears or grapes)

Chicken in lime   2 or 3 SERVINGS

6 chicken thighs or 3
  large chicken breast
  halves
2 tablespoons oil
1 medium onion
1 clove garlic
⅛ teaspoon hot red
  pepper

½ teaspoon ground cumin
½ teaspoon crushed
  coriander seeds
¼ teaspoon turmeric
2 tablespoons soy sauce
2 limes

Heat oil in large skillet. Add the chicken pieces and cook over medium heat until both sides are brown. While chicken is browning, cut onion coarsely and put garlic through press; add to chicken. When chicken has browned on both sides, add red pepper, cumin, coriander seeds, turmeric, and soy sauce. Reduce heat; cover and cook until chicken is tender, 15 to 20 minutes, depending on cut of chicken. Cut 1 lime into quarters. Just before serving, sprinkle chicken with the juice of 1 lime, about 2 tablespoons. Serve with lime quarters.

Sautéed sunchokes   2 or 3 SERVINGS

½ pound sunchokes
  (Jerusalem artichokes)
2 tablespoons butter or
  oil

Salt and freshly ground
black pepper to taste

Wash the sunchokes thoroughly, using hand to rub away any dirt. (It is not necessary to scrape off skin or scrub chokes with brush.) Trim off any soft or pink parts. Slice thinly, less than ⅛ inch thick. Heat butter until hot in large skillet and sauté slices until they soften and begin to brown. How soft the sunchokes should be depends on personal taste. Season with salt and pepper.

Baked acorn squash slices

2 or 3 SERVINGS

---

1 small acorn squash
Oil

Salt and freshly ground
black pepper to taste

Turn oven to 400 degrees.

Wash the exterior of the squash and slice into ¼-inch-thick slices. Remove seeds from center. Rub both sides of slices with a little oil. Season with salt and pepper. Place in shallow baking dish and bake about 25 minutes, until tender.

Spring, Fall, Winter / 69

MENU FOR TWO OR THREE FOR A "MORE SPECIAL" DINNER

Chicken with marsala and grapes

"Creamed" spinach

Rice with mushrooms and onions

Purple plums and crystallized ginger

ONE night I made this dinner for four people, doubling everything. I found that I had to add 5 minutes to preparation time, making it a 35-minute meal. But for two or three people (depending on their appetites), it is easy to put this together in less than 30. Be sure, however, to allow the full cooking time for the chicken. Whatever chicken isn't served immediately will pick up even more flavor as it sits.

A new entry from California is a seedless red grape. Delicious. Even sweeter than the green grapes. You can use either kind.

The idea for the "creamed" spinach was lifted from the Golden Door, the health spa in Escondido, California. Everything is supposed to be low calorie, and is, so obviously there is no cream used. But the melted Muenster cheese gives the same effect.

STAPLES

oil	onion
salt	butter
pepper	nutmeg
Marsala	chicken broth or bouil-
rice	lon

SHOPPING LIST

4 or 5 small chicken breast halves

2 shallots

1 cup seedless grapes

¼ pound mushrooms

10 ounces frozen chopped spinach or 10-ounce package fresh spinach or 1 pound loose fresh spinach

½ cup (about 2 ounces) Muenster cheese

(purple plums, crystallized ginger)

GAME PLAN

Brown chicken.

Chop shallots and add to skillet when chicken is turned.

Cook rice.

Prepare spinach and cook.

Chop onion; rinse and slice mushrooms for rice.

Add Marsala to chicken; cover and cook over low heat.

Cook onion and mushrooms in small skillet.

Grate cheese.

Add grapes to chicken.

Combine cooked rice with onion and mushrooms.

Process spinach with cheese and season.

Chicken with marsala and grapes
2 or 3 SERVINGS

2 tablespoons oil
4 or 5 small chicken breast halves
1½ tablespoons finely chopped shallots

Salt and freshly ground black pepper to taste
½ cup Marsala
1 cup seedless grapes

Heat oil in large skillet. Add breasts, skin sides down, and brown over medium-high heat. Chop shallots finely. Turn chicken and add shallots. Brown chicken on second side. Season with salt and pepper. Add Marsala; reduce heat; cover and simmer 10 minutes. Add grapes; continue cooking until grapes are heated through and serve.

"Creamed" spinach
2 or 3 SERVINGS

10-ounce package frozen chopped spinach
or
10-ounce package fresh spinach or 1 pound fresh loose spinach
Few shakes nutmeg

½ cup coarsely grated Muenster cheese
Salt and freshly ground black pepper to taste

Cook frozen spinach in covered pot without additional water until it is completely defrosted. Drain. Season with nutmeg. Coarsely grate cheese and pack tightly in measuring cup. Just before serving, stir cheese into spinach; melt completely and season with salt and pepper.

If using fresh spinach, wash spinach and remove tough stems. You don't have to remove them all because the spinach will be puréed. Steam spinach in covered pot in its own liquid until wilted. Drain. Combine the spinach with cheese in food processor with steel blade. Process until puréed. Season with nutmeg and salt and pepper. (This produces a bright green dish.)

Rice with mushrooms and onion

2 or 3 SERVINGS

½ cup enriched white or brown rice*

1 cup chicken broth or bouillon

¼ pound mushrooms

1 medium onion

2 tablespoons butter

Salt and freshly ground black pepper to taste

Combine rice with broth or bouillon. Bring to boil. Reduce heat to simmer and cook, covered, until liquid evaporates, about 17 to 20 minutes. Rinse mushrooms and trim off ends of stems. Slice mushrooms. Chop onion coarsely. Melt butter in small skillet. Add mushrooms and onion and sauté until onion is soft. Add mixture to cooked rice. Season with salt and pepper.

---

* See page 74 for directions on how to use brown rice in a 30-minute meal.

GREEK MENU FOR THREE

Chicken oreganato

Tangy Brussels sprouts with tomato sauce

Greek salad

Oranges with rum and sugar

WHILE there is a definite Greek flavor to this meal, I've never seen a recipe for Brussels sprouts in tomato sauce in a Greek cookbook.

But that simple recipe for chicken oreganato is authentic, except for the fact that pieces of chicken are used. The original recipe, collected at one of Washington's many Greek church bazaars, where the best Greek food is found, is made with split chicken halves.

Greek salads, especially the kind you find in delis, always seem to have tomatoes in them, but this menu is designed for the time of year when tomatoes taste about as good as the cardboard in which they are shipped.

Perhaps you will not be able to find Calamata olives easily. You can substitute the salty Greek olives, but go easy because the feta cheese is salty, too.

At one time the Brussels sprouts were served with plain yogurt as a sauce to be spooned on, but it seemed to be a bit too much with the feta, so it was eliminated. If you like, try it, though.

GAME PLAN

Turn on oven.

Prepare chicken and bake.

Prepare Brussels sprouts; bring hot water to boil in steamer.

Chop onion and sauté.

Cook Brussels sprouts.

Add purée to onions.

Turn chicken after 15 minutes.

Prepare salad.

Combine Brussels sprouts with sauce.

STAPLES

oregano

salt

pepper

olive oil

vegetable oil

red wine vinegar

ground cinnamon

dry mustard

lemon

onion

(rum, sugar)

SHOPPING LIST

6 chicken thighs

10 ounces Brussels sprouts

16-ounce can tomato purée

½ pound greens, such as red lettuce or romaine

1 medium cucumber

3 ounces feta cheese

2 scallions

9 Calamata olives (Greek olives in olive oil and brine)

(oranges)

Chicken oreganato   3 SERVINGS

---

6 chicken thighs
2 tablespoons crushed
  dried oregano
  Salt and freshly ground
  black pepper to taste

¼ cup olive oil
Juice of ½ lemon

Turn oven to 500 degrees.

Rinse and drain chicken thighs. Mix oregano with salt and pepper. Rub seasonings into chicken pieces on both sides. Place chicken pieces in shallow baking pan. Whisk oil with lemon juice and drizzle half of it over chicken. Bake chicken 15 minutes; turn; drizzle on remaining oil-lemon mixture, and continue baking until 30 minutes are up, or for another 10 minutes.

Tangy Brussels sprouts with tomato sauce   3 SERVINGS

---

10 ounces Brussels
   sprouts
1 large onion
1 tablespoon vegetable oil

1 cup tomato purée
  Salt and freshly ground
  black pepper to taste

Bring hot water to boil in steamer. Wash and trim Brussels sprouts. Chop onion coarsely. Heat oil in skillet. Sauté onion until tender. Steam sprouts about 10 minutes. When onion is tender, stir in purée. Add cooked sprouts. Season with salt and pepper.

Greek salad 3 SERVINGS

½ pound greens (red leaf lettuce, romaine)
2 scallions
1 medium cucumber
3 ounces feta cheese
9 Calamata olives
1½ tablespoons olive oil

1 tablespoon red wine vinegar
Few shakes cinnamon
Few shakes dry mustard
Freshly ground black pepper to taste

Wash and dry greens. Tear into bite-sized pieces. Chop scallions. Peel cucumber, if waxed. Cut in quarters lengthwise, then into slices. Crumble cheese. Mix together in salad bowl with olives. In small bowl beat oil with vinegar. Beat in cinnamon, mustard, and pepper, pour over salad, and toss.

A CHINESE-AMERICAN MENU FOR THREE

Deviled chicken thighs

Marinated tomatoes and onion rings

Rice

Nectarines, plums or apples

IF you have access to fresh herbs, they add such wonderful flavor to the salad. They really make a difference. That doesn't mean the salad won't be good with dried herbs; it will. But what makes an even more significant difference is the quality of the tomatoes. Hothouse tomatoes cannot compete with garden fresh tomatoes whether you are lucky enough to grow them yourself or have a convenient source such as a farmer's market, a roadside stand, or a truck that drives into the city in the summer and sets up shop until the day's produce is gone. Out of season the only substitute for standard-sized tomatoes are cherry tomatoes. They haven't figured out how to pick them green yet.

GAME PLAN

Combine garlic, ginger, soy, sherry, hot pepper, and water in large pot; add chicken and cook.

Cook rice.

Prepare salad dressing.

Turn chicken.

Prepare tomatoes and onion for salad and dress salad.

STAPLES

soy sauce	olive oil
dry sherry	basil
garlic	tarragon
ginger	oregano
hot pepper	salt
rice	pepper
red or white wine vinegar	

SHOPPING LIST

9 chicken thighs
3 tomatoes
1 red onion

(nectarines, plums, or apples)

Deviled chicken thighs   3 SERVINGS

1 large clove garlic
1 large slice ginger or ½ teaspoon powdered ginger
3 tablespoons soy sauce

¼ cup dry sherry
⅛ teaspoon hot pepper, such as cayenne
½ cup water
9 chicken thighs

Put garlic through press. Mince fresh ginger. Combine garlic and ginger with soy sauce, sherry, hot pepper, and water and bring to boil in heavy pot, large enough to hold chicken. Add chicken; reduce heat and simmer in covered pot 10 minutes. Remove cover; turn chicken pieces over and raise heat so liquid boils briskly. Boil chicken 10 to 12 minutes, until liquid evaporates and chicken takes on golden coloring.

Marinated tomatoes and onion rings

3 SERVINGS

1½ teaspoons dried basil or 1½ tablespoons minced fresh basil

¾ teaspoon dried tarragon or 2¼ teaspoons minced fresh tarragon

⅛ teaspoon dried oregano or ½ teaspoon minced fresh oregano

¼ cup red or white wine vinegar

6 tablespoons good quality olive oil

3 tomatoes

1 red onion

Salt and freshly ground black pepper to taste

Mince fresh herbs if using them. Combine fresh or dried herbs with vinegar and olive oil and whisk or shake in tightly covered bottle. Slice tomatoes and onion. Separate onion slices into rings. Alternate slices of tomato and onion on salad plates and pour on dressing. Season with salt and pepper. If time allows, refrigerate.

Rice

3 SERVINGS

1 cup enriched white or brown rice*

2 cups water

Salt

Combine rice with water. Season with salt. Bring to boil. Stir once. Reduce heat and cook, covered, below simmer until water is absorbed, about 17 to 20 minutes.

---

* See page 74 for directions on how to use brown rice in a 30-minute meal.

HUNGARIAN MENU FOR THREE

Chicken paprikash

Buckwheat groats

Steamed broccoli

Tangelos or strawberries

HUNGARIANS will doubtless look askance at this speedy version of chicken paprikash, especially after I suggest that if you can't find Hungarian paprika you can use regular paprika. It will not, it is true, taste the same or as good, but it can be used. Hungarians don't use yogurt in their paprikash either, but it does very nicely and certainly cuts the calorie load down considerably.

Buckwheat groats, a.k.a. kasha, are a wonderful nutty grain that we don't use enough of in this country. They are available in many, many supermarkets in fine, coarse, medium cuts as well as whole. Whole has the best flavor and texture to my taste. Most Americans come in contact with buckwheat in the form of pancakes. It's the same plant.

GAME PLAN

Brown chicken on one side.

Prepare onions, green pepper, and tomato; turn chicken and add vegetables with paprika.

Stir groats with egg over heat.

Bring hot water to boil in steamer for broccoli.

Add water and salt to groats; cover and cook.

Prepare broccoli.

Add water, salt, and pepper to chicken; cover and cook.

Cook broccoli.

Add sour cream-yogurt mixture to chicken.

Drain broccoli.

STAPLES

oil	salt
onions	pepper
sweet Hungarian paprika	egg

SHOPPING LIST

4 or 5 chicken breast halves

1 green bell pepper

1 tomato

1 cup sour cream or ½ cup sour cream and ½ cup plain yogurt

1 cup buckwheat groats (kasha)

1½ pounds broccoli (tangelos or strawberries)

Chicken paprikash　　　3 SERVINGS

3 tablespoons oil

4 or 5 chicken breast halves

2 medium onions

1 green bell pepper

1 tomato, well ripened*

2 tablespoons sweet Hungarian paprika

1 cup water

Salt and freshly ground black pepper to taste

1 cup sour cream or ½ cup sour cream and ½ cup plain yogurt

Heat oil in skillet. Add chicken, skin sides down, and brown on one side over medium heat. Cut onions coarsely; add to chicken. Seed and cut pepper coarsely. Cut tomato coarsely. Add to skillet; turn chicken. Add paprika and cook about 10 minutes. Add water and salt and pepper;

---

* If the tomato is not well ripened, you may want to add 1 tablespoon of tomato paste to sauce to add more flavor.

reduce heat; cover and cook until chicken is tender and vegetables are soft, about 20 to 25 minutes total cooking time.

Just before serving, stir in sour cream or mixture of sour cream and yogurt. Do not boil. Just warm and serve.

Buckwheat groats (kasha)
3 SERVINGS

1 cup buckwheat groats	2 cups water
1 egg	Salt to taste

Lightly beat egg in saucepan. Mix groats with egg and stir frequently over medium heat until all the grains are separated. Add water, as hot as it comes from the tap. Season with salt. Cover and bring to boil; reduce heat and simmer until all water is absorbed, about 20 minutes.

Steamed broccoli
3 SERVINGS

1½ pounds broccoli	Salt to taste

Bring hot water to boil in steamer. Trim broccoli of thick stems with knife. Rinse flowerettes under water and divide into small portions. Start steaming broccoli about 7 minutes before you are ready to serve the meal. Steam until crisp-tender. Season with salt.

COLD NOODLE SALAD MENU FOR THREE

Chinese noodle salad with chicken

Piquant cucumbers

Honeydew with mint leaves

IF you happen to live or work near a Chinese grocery store, you may want to purchase some of the authentic ingredients called for in these recipes. Otherwise you can make the substitutions, as suggested.

When I put this menu together, I wondered how yogurt, so foreign to Chinese cooking, would taste with Chinese flavors, but the dishes marry well.

This is also the kind of menu that can wait as long as you like after it is prepared. Just refrigerate the cucumbers.

GAME PLAN

Bring hot water to boil in pot for noodles.

Poach chicken breasts in covered pot.

Mix together sauce ingredients for noodles.

Cook noodles.

Chop scallions.

Peel cucumbers, if waxed, or wash and slice thinly.

Mix yogurt with mustard; mix in cucumbers.

Drain noodles; rinse under cold water.

Remove chicken; skin and shred meat.

Mix chicken with sauce.

Mix noodles with sauce.

Place chicken on top of noodles.

Sprinkle with scallions.

STAPLES

sesame oil	sugar
soy sauce	garlic
sesame paste or tahini or peanut butter	pepper
	Dijon mustard
ginger	white wine or dry ver-
dry sherry	mouth (optional)
red wine vinegar	(mint leaves)

SHOPPING LIST

12 ounces very thin spaghetti or 12 ounces fresh or frozen or dried Chinese noodles

2 scallions

4 chicken breast halves

½ cup plain yogurt

1 pound cucumbers (honeydew)

Chinese noodle salad with chicken

3 SERVINGS

4 chicken breast halves
Water, or white wine, or dry vermouth
3 tablespoons water
2 tablespoons soy sauce
2 tablespoons sesame paste*
1½ tablespoons dry sherry
2 teaspoons red wine vinegar
1½ teaspoons sugar

3 medium cloves garlic
1-inch piece ginger
12 ounces very thin spaghetti or fresh, frozen, or dried Chinese noodles
2 teaspoons sesame oil
2 scallions
Freshly ground black pepper to taste

---

*Sesame paste from China is different from sesame paste from the Middle East. But the Middle Eastern kind—tahini—can be substituted if that is what is readily available. If neither is on hand, use natural peanut butter.

Bring 3 or 4 quarts hot water to boil in covered pot. Salt, if desired. Place chicken in skillet. Pour enough water, wine, or vermouth into skillet to cover chicken halfway. Season with salt, if desired. Cover and simmer chicken until tender, about 20 minutes.

Combine water, soy sauce, sesame paste, sherry, vinegar, sugar. Put garlic through press. Mince ginger. Add garlic and ginger to soy mixture.

Cook dried noodles about 7 minutes or, if using fresh, add to pot, return water to boil, and cook about 30 seconds, until tender. Watch carefully. Drain and rinse under cold water. Sprinkle with sesame oil. Chop scallions finely. Remove chicken from skillet and skin, using fork and knife because chicken will be too hot to handle. Shred chicken. Mix chicken with a little of the sauce; set aside. Mix noodles with remaining sauce; top with chicken and sprinkle on scallions.

Piquant cucumbers   3 SERVINGS

1 pound cucumbers
½ cup plain yogurt

1 tablespoon Dijon mustard

Peel cucumbers if waxed. Otherwise just scrub them and slice thinly. Mix yogurt with mustard. Stir in cucumbers. If not serving immediately, refrigerate.

MEXICAN MENU FOR THREE

Cinnamon chicken

Chili cheese rice

Avocado, mushroom and sprout salad

Sliced pineapple, papaya or berries

A colorful meal with a Mexican flavor, but several American touches. In other words, a real American meal, taking the best from another culture and making it our own.

I just hope you have a better source of ripe avocados than I do. Otherwise you will have to think about having this meal several days before you are ready to eat it!

GAME PLAN

Brown chicken.

Cook rice.

Chop onion.

Put garlic through press.

Slice mushrooms.

Add garlic and onion to chicken.

Cut up Monterey Jack cheese.

Cut up Cheddar.

Make salad dressing.

Add remaining ingredients but almonds to chicken.

Add remaining ingredients to rice.

Finish salad: cube avocado.

Dress salad.

Add almonds to chicken.

STAPLES

salt	garlic
pepper	onion
ground cinnamon	rice
ground cloves	wine vinegar
olive and vegetable oils	ground cumin

SHOPPING LIST

6 or 7 chicken drumsticks or thighs	4-ounce can chopped green chiles
¾ cup of orange juice	2 tablespoons Cheddar cheese
2 tablespoons raisins	
1 tablespoon capers	1 medium avocado
2 or 3 ounces slivered almonds	12 medium mushrooms
2 ounces Monterey Jack cheese	2½ to 3 ounces alfalfa sprouts
½ pint yogurt (and sour cream)	(pineapple, papaya, or berries)

Cinnamon chicken   3 SERVINGS

6 or 7 chicken drumsticks or thighs	1 medium onion
	1 large clove garlic
Salt and freshly ground black pepper to taste	¾ cup orange juice
	2 tablespoons raisins
Ground cinnamon and cloves, about ¼ teaspoon each	1 tablespoon capers
	⅓ cup slivered almonds
1½ tablespoons oil	

Sprinkle chicken with salt and pepper, cinnamon, and cloves. Brown chicken over medium-high heat in hot oil on one side. Chop onion coarsely and put garlic through press. When ready to turn chicken, add onion and garlic. Cook until chicken is brown all over. Add orange juice, raisins, and capers and cook, covered, until chicken is tender, about 15 minutes. Add almonds; stir a minute and serve.

Chili cheese rice   3 SERVINGS

½ cup brown or enriched white rice*

1 cup water

2 ounces (about 6 sticks) Monterey Jack cheese

¾ cup plain yogurt or mixture of yogurt and sour cream

¾ of a 4-ounce can chopped green chiles

Salt and freshly ground black pepper to taste

2 tablespoons Cheddar cheese, cut into small cubes

Combine rice with water. Salt, if desired. Bring to boil. Reduce heat to simmer and cook, covered, until all liquid is absorbed and rice is tender. Cut Jack cheese into strips. Cube Cheddar. Mix yogurt with chiles. When rice is cooked, stir in Jack cheese, yogurt mixture, Cheddar cheese and season with salt and pepper. Cover and allow cheeses to melt.

*See page 74 for directions on how to use brown rice in a 30-minute meal.

Avocado, mushroom, and sprout salad

3 SERVINGS

2 tablespoons wine vinegar

2 tablespoons olive oil

1 tablespoon vegetable oil

¼ teaspoon ground cumin
Salt and freshly ground black pepper to taste

1 medium, ripe avocado

12 medium mushrooms

2½ to 3 ounces alfalfa sprouts

Beat vinegar with oils, cumin, salt, and pepper. Cube or slice avocado. Rinse and trim off ends of mushroom stems. Slice mushrooms. Divide mushrooms and avocado among 3 plates and top each with a handful of sprouts. Whisk dressing and pour over salads.

SPRING DINNER FOR TWO

Chicken with yogurt

Whole-wheat pasta with caraway seeds

Steamed asparagus

Strawberries and orange liqueur

CHICKEN with yogurt is sort of a shorthand version of an Indian dish. It can be made with other parts of the chicken, of course.

You don't have to use whole-wheat pasta to make a satisfactory dish, but it is nice for a change and has a different texture and bite to it.

Prepare asparagus as often as possible when in season. When it isn't, it's better to wait until next year, rather than eat the canned or frozen variety.

GAME PLAN

Brown chicken.

Chop onion.

Bring hot water to boil in pot for pasta.

Bring hot water to boil for asparagus.

Mix yogurt and tomato paste.

Stir yogurt into chicken with cumin, coriander, and salt and pepper; cover.

Cook pasta.

Steam asparagus.

Grate cheese.

Drain pasta.

Stir caraway and salt and pepper into pasta.

Sprinkle pasta with cheese.

STAPLES

vegetable oil	salt
onion	pepper
ground cumin	caraway seeds
ground coriander	

SHOPPING LIST

6 chicken thighs	½ cup (2 to 2½ ounces) sharp cheese, such as Parmesan or Cheddar (strawberries, orange liqueur)
½ pint plain yogurt	
6-ounce can tomato paste	
1 pound fresh asparagus	
4 ounces whole-wheat pasta	

Chicken with yogurt   2 SERVINGS

2 tablespoons vegetable oil	½ teaspoon ground cumin
6 chicken thighs	½ teaspoon ground coriander
1 small onion	Salt and freshly ground black pepper to taste
1 cup plain yogurt	
½ cup tomato paste	

Heat oil in skillet. Brown chicken thighs in hot oil over medium-high heat. While they are browning, coarsely chop onion. Add to chicken and continue cooking over medium high until onion is soft. Mix yogurt with tomato paste. Reduce heat under chicken. Add yogurt mixture with cumin, coriander, and salt and pepper. Cover and cook below simmer about 15 or 20 minutes longer, until chicken is tender.

Whole-wheat pasta with caraway seeds

2 SERVINGS

4 ounces (2 cups) whole-wheat pasta

1½ teaspoons caraway seeds

½ cup coarsely grated sharp cheese, such as Parmesan or Cheddar

Salt and freshly ground black pepper to taste

Bring about 3 quarts of hot salted water to boil in covered pot. Add pasta; stir and cook 10 minutes, or until pasta is tender. Grate cheese. Drain pasta; stir in caraway seeds. Season with salt and pepper. Sprinkle with cheese and serve.

Steamed asparagus

2 SERVINGS

1 pound asparagus

Salt to taste

Bring hot water to boil in steamer. Break tough stems off asparagus at point where they break easily. Soak while preparing rest of meal. Steam asparagus about 10 minutes, until tender but still crisp. Season to taste.

AN AMERICAN VERSION OF AN INDIAN MENU FOR TWO

Curried chicken

Saffron rice

Fresh fruit, chopped peanuts and chutney

Frozen yogurt

COOKS who know Indian food will tell you there is no such thing as curry in Indian cooking. And in India there is no such thing. But there are certain dishes that use combinations of spices much like what you find in a decent curry powder.

To be authentic, such a dish would be made with the individual spices. But even if the recipe that follows is not truly authentic, it is certainly typical of what Americans do with other peoples' foods: we take what we like of it, adjust it to the ingredients we have available, and often come up with something quite good, just different.

As you will note in the recipe for fruit platter, if you want to serve it any other time of year, buy according to what is in season.

GAME PLAN

Heat oil and stir in curry.

Add chicken.

Prepare onion and garlic; add both to skillet.

Bring rice, water, and optional saffron to boil and cook.

Turn chicken and brown on second side.

Cut up tomato.

Cut up banana.

Wash and cut up peach or nectarine and sprinkle with lemon juice; arrange on plate with grapes.

Add tomato, banana, broth, yogurt, and salt and pepper to chicken; reduce heat, cover and cook at high simmer.

Spoon chutney and peanuts into individual small dishes.

STAPLES

vegetable oil

curry powder

onion

garlic

salt

pepper

chicken broth

rice

saffron or turmeric

lemon

SHOPPING LIST

4 small chicken breast halves

1 large tomato

1 small banana

½ cup plain yogurt

1 large peach or nectarine

1 cup seedless grapes

small jar chutney

¼ to ⅓ cup chopped or halved unsalted roasted peanuts

(frozen yogurt)

Curried chicken   2 SERVINGS

2 tablespoons vegetable
  oil
1 teaspoon good quality
  curry powder
4 small chicken breast
  halves
1 medium onion
1 small clove garlic

1 large tomato
1 small ripe banana
½ cup chicken broth or
  water
½ cup plain yogurt
  Salt and freshly ground
  black pepper to taste

Heat oil in large skillet. Add curry powder and stir. Add
chicken, skin sides down. Chop onion and add. Put garlic
through press into skillet. Cook over medium-high heat
until chicken is golden brown on one side. Turn and brown
chicken on second side. Cut up tomato. Cut banana into
small cubes. Add tomato, banana, chicken broth, yogurt,
and salt and pepper. Stir; reduce heat and simmer,
covered, about 20 minutes, until chicken is tender.
Toward the end, if the sauce is too thin, remove cover and
cook until thicker.

Saffron rice   2 SERVINGS

½ cup enriched white long
  grain rice or brown
  rice*
1 cup water

Salt to taste
⅛ teaspoon saffron or
  turmeric

Combine rice with water, salt, and saffron or turmeric.
Bring to boil. Reduce heat to simmer and cook, covered,
until water is absorbed and rice is tender, about 17 to 20
minutes.

*See page 74 for directions on how to use brown rice in a 30-minute
meal.

Fresh fruit, chopped peanuts, and chutney

2 SERVINGS

1 large peach or nectarine, cut up and sprinkled with fresh lemon juice

1 cup seedless grapes

¼ to ⅓ cup chopped unsalted roasted peanuts

Few tablespoons chutney

Arrange fruit on platter and put chutney and nuts in small dishes. Serve with curry.

When peaches, nectarines, and seedless grapes are not available, use 1 large tart apple, like a Granny Smith or Jonathan and 1 large orange, tangerine or tangelo. Sprinkle the cut apple with lemon juice.

SPECIAL BUT INEXPENSIVE DINNER FOR THREE

Orange chicken

Kasha pilaf

Watercress and mushrooms in mustard dressing

Sherbet

You want to make this dinner for six people quickly? If so, don't do what I did. I thought I was completely organized when I began. As the guests had cocktails, I spent several minutes looking for the kasha. The closest I came was white rice, so that's what I substituted, but I had wasted precious minutes hunting through my cupboard.

Preparing the meal for six, not counting the fruitless kasha search, took 35 minutes. For three people, 30 minutes is a snap. One less orange to peel, one less garlic clove, less ginger to mince, and so on.

To make it a company meal I served Frozen Peach Purée (see page 321).

For hors d'oeuvres, Angels on Horseback (see page 306) and Spinach Spread (see page 315).

Postscript. Among the guests for dinner that night were Senator and Mrs. Mark Hatfield. He was chairman of the Congressional Inaugural activities for the Reagan swearing-in. Part of those festivities include a lunch for the new First Family and their guests. Antoinette Hatfield liked the rice pilaf so much she included it in the menu for the lunch.

STAPLES

oil	pepper
garlic	egg
ginger	chicken stock or broth
basil	Dijon mustard
white vinegar	capers
salt	onion

SHOPPING LIST

9 chicken thighs
2 navel oranges
1 cup orange juice
½ cup kasha (buckwheat groats)
1 stalk celery
½ cup (2 ounces) slivered almonds

12 medium mushrooms
1 bunch watercress
1 scallion
½ cup plain yogurt (sherbet)

GAME PLAN

Brown chicken.

Prepare garlic, oranges, and ginger.

Add garlic to chicken.

Cook kasha with egg.

Add oranges, ginger, basil, vinegar, orange juice, and salt, pepper to chicken.

Prepare celery and onion for kasha.

Cook celery and onion.

Prepare mushrooms and watercress.

Add chicken stock and seasonings to kasha.

Toast almonds.

Prepare salad dressing.

Stir almonds into kasha.

Dress salad.

Orange chicken   3 SERVINGS

2 tablespoons oil
9 chicken thighs
2 medium cloves garlic
2 navel oranges
2 tablespoons minced ginger

1 teaspoon dried basil
4 teaspoons white vinegar
1 cup orange juice
Salt and freshly ground black pepper to taste

Heat oil in large skillet. Brown thighs. Put garlic through press and add to skillet when chicken is turned. Peel oranges, cut in half; cut each half in half. Separate into segments and add to chicken when second side is browned. Add ginger to chicken with basil, vinegar, orange juice, and salt and pepper. Cover and cook over medium-high heat, until chicken is tender, about 15 minutes more.

Kasha pilaf   3 SERVINGS

1 egg
½ cup kasha (buckwheat groats)
1 stalk celery
1 small onion
1 tablespoon oil

1 cup chicken stock or broth
Salt and freshly ground black pepper to taste
½ cup toasted slivered almonds

In saucepan beat egg slightly and then spoon off about one teaspoon of it; discard. Mix kasha with remaining egg. Stir frequently over medium heat until each grain is separate and dry. Slice celery thinly. Chop onion coarsely. Push kasha to one side of pan. Add oil. When oil is hot, add celery and onion and sauté over medium heat a few minutes, until onion has just begun to soften. Add chicken stock; mix ingredients together and season. Reduce heat; cover pan and simmer about 15 minutes, until kasha is tender. While kasha cooks, toast almonds in toaster oven or regular oven until golden brown at 400 degrees for 3 to 4 minutes. Stir into cooked kasha. Serve.

Watercress and mushrooms in mustard dressing

3 SERVINGS

12 medium mushrooms
 1 bunch watercress
 1 scallion
 ½ cup plain yogurt
1½ teaspoons Dijon mustard

1½ teaspoons capers
    Salt and freshly ground black pepper to taste

Rinse mushrooms and trim off most of stems. Rinse watercress, drain, remove tough stems. Chop green and white part of scallion. Combine scallion with yogurt, mustard, capers, and salt and pepper. Spoon over watercress and mushrooms.

A CHINESE DINNER FOR THREE

Chicken and sweet peppers with hoisin

Spinach with sesame seeds

Vermicelli

Orange or mango

DON'T worry if you can't find Chinese vermicelli for this dish—Italian vermicelli is a delicious substitute. Also, at least in Washington, hoisin sauce is beginning to make its appearance in regular supermarkets. In fact, you could easily think of it as a staple. A jar keeps in the refrigerator almost indefinitely.

STAPLES

soy sauce	garlic
dry sherry or	ginger
apple juice	onion
vegetable oil	sesame seeds
sesame oil	salt

SHOPPING LIST

12 ounces boneless skinless chicken breasts or turkey breasts

4 red or green bell peppers
hoisin sauce

1½ 10-ounce packages fresh spinach or 1½ pounds loose

4 or 5 ounces Chinese vermicelli or 6 ounces Italian vermicelli

(orange or mango)

GAME PLAN

Slice chicken; combine soy and sherry and marinate chicken in it.

Chop onion; mince garlic and ginger; sauté. Cut up peppers.

Prepare spinach.

Bring hot water to boil in pot. If using Chinese vermicelli, pour water over.

Sauté ginger, garlic, onion in hot oil.

Add peppers and cook.

If using Italian vermicelli, cook.

Steam spinach.

Add chicken to peppers; cook, uncovered.

Add water, marinade, hoisin; continue cooking.

Toast sesame seeds.

Drain spinach; mix with sesame oil; sprinkle with sesame seeds.

Drain vermicelli.

Chicken and sweet peppers with hoisin

3 SERVINGS

12 ounces boneless, skinless chicken breasts or turkey breasts

3 tablespoons soy sauce

3 tablespoons dry sherry or apple juice

1 large onion

1 large clove garlic

2 tablespoons minced fresh ginger

1 tablespoon vegetable oil

4 red or green bell peppers

¼ cup water

1 tablespoon hoisin sauce

Slice chicken on diagonal into thin slices, less than ¼ inch wide. Mix the soy and sherry and marinate the chicken in that mixture. Chop onion coarsely; mince ginger and put garlic through press. Heat the oil in a heavy skillet or wok. Add onion, garlic, and ginger and cook over medium heat about 2 minutes, until onion begins to soften. Seed peppers and cut into strips less than ¼ inch wide. Add to skillet and cook about 3 minutes, stirring occasionally. Push peppers and onions to the side; add chicken, without marinade and cook quickly until chicken loses pink color, about 3 minutes. Add water, remaining marinade, and hoisin. Reduce heat and cook a minute or two, until peppers are crisp-tender.

Spinach with sesame seeds
3 SERVINGS

1½ 10-ounce packages fresh spinach or 1½ pounds loose spinach

2 teaspoons sesame seeds

Few drops sesame oil
Salt to taste

Wash spinach and remove tough stems. Steam spinach in covered pot in its own liquid until just limp. Toast sesame seeds. Drain thoroughly, pressing out excess moisture. Toss with sesame oil. Season with salt, if desired. Sprinkle with sesame seeds.

Chinese vermicelli
3 SERVINGS

4 or 5 ounces Chinese vermicelli

Bring 3 quarts hot water to boil. In a heatproof bowl pour water over vermicelli and allow to sit 15 minutes, until noodles are tender. Drain and serve.

OR

Italian vermicelli
3 SERVINGS

6 ounces Italian vermicelli

Salt

Bring 3 quarts hot water to boil in covered pot. Salt, if desired. Add vermicelli and cook, uncovered, until al dente, about 3 minutes. Drain and serve.

AN ITALIAN FISH DINNER FOR TWO

Fish fillets marinara

Zucchini and vermouth

Green noodles

Blueberries or frozen fruit

THERE is very little fat in this entire menu. As a matter of fact, the oil in the fish marinara recipe has been cut way back, from 6 tablespoons to 2. So if you are a dieter, or at least a calorie watcher, this menu should be to your liking—Dr. Stillman's, Dr. Atkins's, Drinking Man's, or any other such diets notwithstanding. What those diets do is cut way down on carbohydrate intake, but the only sensible way to lose weight (and keep it off) is to cut down on fat and portion size. (That's the kind of information no one really wants to hear, and I know what happened to the king's messenger who brought bad tidings!)

By changing the suggested dessert, this menu is equally appropriate any time of year.

STAPLES

olive oil	pepper
garlic	capers
salt	dry vermouth

SHOPPING LIST

¼ cup parsley

1 can anchovy fillets

2 (4- to 6-ounce) fish fillets

16-ounce can tomatoes

4 ounces green noodles

2 or 3 medium zucchini

(blueberries or frozen fruit)

GAME PLAN

Prepare parsley and garlic for sauce.

Heat oil for sauce.

Sauté parsley and garlic.

Bring hot water to boil in pot for pasta.

Add tomatoes to sauce.

Grate zucchini.

Cook zucchini in hot oil.

Prepare garlic and parsley for fish and sauté in hot oil with anchovy and capers.

Cook noodles.

Add fish to skillet.

Add vermouth to zucchini.

Turn fish.

Drain noodles.

Pour sauce over fish.

Fish fillets marinara   2 SERVINGS

*Marinara
Sauce:*

1 tablespoon olive oil

2 tablespoons chopped fresh parsley

1 large clove garlic

1 16-ounce can tomatoes
Freshly ground black pepper to taste

Fish:

1 tablespoon olive oil	3 small capers
1 small clove garlic	2 4- to-6-ounce fish fillets,
2 tablespoons chopped	such as perch, snapper
fresh parsley	or flounder
1 anchovy fillet	

Heat 1 tablespoon oil in small skillet. Chop 2 tablespoons parsley and put garlic through press. Sauté until garlic begins to turn golden. Add tomatoes and liquid, squeezing tomatoes in fingers to break them up before adding them to skillet with pepper to taste. Cook over medium-high heat while fish cooks.

To cook fish, heat 1 tablespoon oil in large skillet. Chop parsley; put garlic through press. Sauté parsley, garlic, anchovy, and capers over medium heat for a minute. Add fish fillets, flesh sides down, and cook 2 minutes. Turn fillets. Cook over low heat 5 to 8 minutes, depending on thickness of fillets, until fish flakes easily with fork.

Pour sauce over fish and serve.

NOTE: Cooking fish: Allow 10 minutes per inch, measuring fish at thickest part, whatever the cooking method. If frozen, double cooking time.

Zucchini and vermouth   2 SERVINGS

2 or 3 medium zucchini	Salt and freshly ground
1 tablespoon olive oil	black pepper to taste
1 or 2 splashes dry	
vermouth	

Scrub zucchini and trim. Grate zucchini coarsely. Heat oil in skillet. Add zucchini and cook over medium-high heat until it begins to soften and liquid evaporates, about 6 minutes. Add vermouth and continue cooking until liquid has evaporated, about 3 minutes. Season and serve.

Green noodles   2 SERVINGS

4 ounces (2 cups) green   Salt to taste
   noodles, thin or
   medium

Bring 2 or 3 quarts hot water to boil in covered pot. Salt, if
desired. Add noodles and cook, uncovered, until noodles
are al dente, about 5 minutes, depending on their width.
Drain and serve with sauce from fish.

A VERY SIMPLE MENU FOR TWO

Shrimp with apple and brandy

Cucumbers in yogurt-dill dressing

Herbed pitas

Orange sherbet

IF you don't have any brandy in the house and don't want to stop at the liquor store, substitute apple juice.

If you keep chopped fresh dill in your freezer, you won't have to bother with the dried, which doesn't taste the same, or with stopping at the store to buy some. In certain seasons the supermarket carries fresh dill where I live. It's almost always more than I can use, so the remainder gets chopped up and put in the freezer in a plastic bag, ready to be hacked off as needed.

GAME PLAN

Remove butter from refrigerator.

Chop dill and scallion; combine with yogurt.

Prepare cucumbers and mix with dressing.

Spread split pitas with butter and sprinkle with herbs and paprika.

Prepare shrimp.

Prepare apple and cook with shrimp.

Toast pitas.

Season shrimp.

Add brandy to shrimp.

STAPLES

butter
brandy or apple juice
salt
pepper

dill
basil
oregano
paprika

SHOPPING LIST

½ pound fresh or
frozen peeled
shrimp
1 medium apple
½ cup yogurt
1 scallion
1 large or 2 small
cucumbers or 3 or
4 pickling
cucumbers

2 large whole-wheat
pitas
(orange sherbet)

Shrimp with apple and brandy

2 SERVINGS

2 tablespoons butter
½ pound fresh or frozen
peeled, deveined
shrimp
1 medium apple

3 tablespoons brandy or
apple juice
Salt and freshly ground
black pepper to taste

Heat the butter in the skillet. If the shrimp are frozen, add
them first and cook until they have defrosted. Pour off
most of the liquid.

Quarter, core, and slice apple. Add apple to skillet and
sauté until it begins to soften. If shrimp are not frozen, add

apple and shrimp together and cook until shrimp are done and apple is softened, 5 to 7 minutes.

Add brandy and cook about 1 minute over low heat. Season with salt and pepper.

Cucumbers in yogurt-dill dressing

2 SERVINGS

½ scallion, white and green part
½ cup plain yogurt
½ teaspoon dried dill or 1½ teaspoons chopped fresh dill

1 large or 2 small cucumbers or 3 or 4 pickling cucumbers*

Chop scallion. Combine yogurt, dill, and scallion. Peel cucumbers and slice thinly. Mix with dressing.

Herbed pitas

2 SERVINGS

Softened butter
2 large whole-wheat pitas
Dried basil

Dried oregano
Paprika

Take butter out of refrigerator to soften.

Split pitas into 2 rounds each. Spread with butter. Sprinkle about ¼ teaspoon each basil and oregano on each half pita. Sprinkle paprika on top a little more sparingly. Toast in toaster oven or under broiler about 3 minutes, until butter is bubbly and top begins to brown.

---

*If you can find pickling cucumbers, they usually are unwaxed and do not have to be peeled, merely well washed.

FISH DINNER FOR TWO

Snapper in orange sauce
Stir-fried broccoli with lemon
Green and white potatoes
Strawberries

COMBINING citrus fruit with fish is Spanish in origin. Even people who say they don't like fish like it this way because of its sweetness and tang.

The elements that go into making up this meal could only have come together in the late 20th century and then probably only in this country.

STAPLES

butter   olive oil
salt   garlic
white pepper   lemon
milk

SHOPPING LIST

¾ pound red snapper   ¼ cup plain yogurt
   fillets or other   1 small cucumber
   firm-fleshed moist   1 scallion
   fish, such as   3 stalks broccoli
   flounder,   (strawberries)
   pompano, croaker
1 large orange
7 or 8 (¾ pound)
   small new potatoes

GAME PLAN

Turn oven to broil.

Cook potatoes.

Chop cucumber; chop scallion.

Grate orange rind; squeeze orange. Melt butter with rind and juice.

Chop garlic.

Prepare broccoli.

Sauté garlic in skillet or wok; remove and stir in broccoli.

Spoon orange mixture over fish in pan and broil.

Add water to broccoli; reduce heat, cover, and cook.

Drain potatoes; add remaining ingredients.

Baste fish.

Squeeze lemon juice over broccoli.

Baste fish again.

Snapper in orange sauce 2 SERVINGS

¾ pound snapper fillets or other firm-fleshed moist fish, such as flounder, pompano, croaker

Salt and white pepper to taste

1½ tablespoons orange juice

1½ teaspoons grated orange rind

2 tablespoons butter

Turn oven to broil. Place fillets in foil-lined shallow baking dish. Season fish with salt and pepper. Grate orange rind. Squeeze juice. Heat orange juice and rind and butter in small pan until butter is melted. Spoon some of sauce over fillets. Broil fillets 2 inches from heat, turning once if they have been skinned. Baste once or twice with orange mixture and broil 8 to 10 minutes, until fish flakes easily with fork.

Stir-fried broccoli with lemon
2 SERVINGS

3 stalks broccoli
1 clove garlic
2 tablespoons olive oil
2 or 3 tablespoons water

Salt and freshly ground pepper to taste
2 teaspoons fresh lemon juice

Trim tough stems from broccoli and separate heads into small flowerettes. Rinse and drain.

Chop garlic. Heat oil in skillet or wok and sauté garlic over medium-high heat until golden, but not browned. Remove garlic. Add broccoli and stir-fry over high heat 2 minutes. Add water, salt and pepper, and garlic. Reduce heat to medium, cover, and cook until broccoli is crisp-tender, about 4 minutes. Sprinkle with lemon juice.

Green and white potatoes
2 SERVINGS

7 or 8 (about ¾ pound) small new potatoes
3 tablespoons chopped cucumber
1 scallion

¼ cup plain yogurt
1½ teaspoons milk
Salt and freshly ground black pepper to taste

Scrub potatoes, but do not peel. Cook in water to cover in covered pot, 15 to 20 minutes, depending on size of potatoes. Drain. Do not peel. Peel cucumber, if waxed; chop cucumber. Chop scallion. Add cucumber, scallion, yogurt, milk, and salt and pepper to potatoes; cover and keep warm.

SIMPLE FISH MENU FOR FOUR

Orange-salmon patties

Egg noodles

Piquant spinach

Pears or watermelon

THE salmon patties once upon a time were salmon loaf, but that took too long to bake. The orange sauce was once made with sour cream instead of yogurt. I like this version better because it's tangier and has fewer calories. The orange sauce does double duty—over the salmon patties and the noodles.

STAPLES

onion	pepper
bread crumbs	vegetable oil
Worcestershire sauce	soy sauce
salt	

SHOPPING LIST

2 navel oranges	8-ounce package wide egg noodles
1-pound can salmon	¾ cup plain yogurt
1 6-ounce can frozen orange juice	(pears or watermelon)
1½ 10-ounce packages fresh spinach or 1¼ to 1½ pounds fresh loose spinach	

GAME PLAN

Prepare oranges and onion; drain salmon; combine these ingredients with bread crumbs, Worcestershire, salt, and pepper. Shape patties.

Bring hot water to boil in pot for noodles.

Prepare spinach.

Sauté salmon patties.

Make orange sauce.

Cook noodles.

Turn patties.

Heat oil for spinach and cook with soy.

Drain noodles.

Orange-salmon patties   4 SERVINGS

---

2 navel oranges

1 medium onion

   1-pound can salmon

½ cup bread crumbs

2 teaspoons Worcestershire sauce

   Salt and freshly ground black pepper to taste

2 tablespoons vegetable oil

Peel and seed oranges and cut into small pieces. Chop onion medium-fine. Drain salmon. Combine all the ingredients except for the oil and mix well. (It's quickest with your hands.) Shape into 8 patties. Heat oil in large skillet. Saute patties in hot oil over medium heat until golden brown on one side. Turn and brown on second side.

  Serve with Orange Sauce.

Orange sauce

¾ cup plain yogurt

6 tablespoons frozen reconstituted orange juice

Combine ingredients and mix until smooth. Serve at room temperature or warmed slightly.

Egg noodles   4 SERVINGS

Water   **Salt to taste**
8 **ounces (½ pound) wide**
egg noodles

Bring 2 quarts hot water to boil in covered pot. Salt, if desired. Add noodles and cook about 5 to 7 minutes, until noodles are just al dente. Drain. Serve with Orange Sauce.

Piquant spinach   4 SERVINGS

1½ **10-ounce packages fresh**   2 **tablespoons vegetable**
spinach or 1¼ to 1½   **oil**
pounds fresh loose   1 **tablespoon soy sauce**
spinach

Wash spinach and remove tough stems. Heat oil in large skillet. Add soy sauce and spinach. Cover and cook about a minute, until spinach begins to wilt. Uncover and cook spinach, stirring, until it is barely cooked.

MODERATELY FRENCH MENU FOR THREE

Fish bonne femme

Glazed Brussels sprouts

Rice cooked in broth

Sliced pineapple with yogurt and brown sugar

FISH Bonne Femme—French and, therefore, difficult. French, yes; difficult, no, and certainly not time-consuming. I think we haven't yet shaken off the myth that all French food takes a long time to prepare. Many dishes are as simple to make as a meat loaf.

The Brussels sprouts don't need to be glazed in the butter and touch of sugar. They are tasty just steamed. The rice, by the way, is especially good with a little of the fish poaching liquid spooned over it.

GAME PLAN

Cook rice.

Bring hot water to boil in steamer for Brussels sprouts.

Prepare sprouts.

Prepare mushrooms, shallot, and parsley;

place in skillet with wine and butter; top with fish; season with salt and pepper. Cook.

Cook sprouts.

Drain sprouts; sauté in butter with sugar.

STAPLES

shallot
salt
white and black pepper
leftover white wine
or dry vermouth
butter

white sugar
brown or enriched white
rice
chicken broth or stock
(brown sugar)

SHOPPING LIST

1 pound fish fillets,
such as flounder,
sole, blue
3 ounces mushrooms
1 teaspoon parsley

1 pint Brussels
sprouts
(pineapple, ½ pint
plain yogurt)

Fish bonne femme   3 SERVINGS

3 ounces mushrooms
1 teaspoon minced shallot
1 teaspoon minced fresh
parsley
⅓ cup white wine or dry
vermouth

1½ tablespoons butter
1 pound fish fillets, such
as flounder, sole, blue,
rock
Salt and white pepper
to taste

Rinse mushrooms and slice. Mince shallot and parsley. In
heavy skillet with cover place mushrooms, shallot, parsley,
wine, and butter. Cut fillets in half if pieces are large. Add
fish to skillet, flesh sides up. Sprinkle with salt and
pepper. Bring to simmer. Cover and simmer 10 to 12
minutes, depending on thickness of fillets, until fish flakes
easily with fork. During cooking, spoon some of liquid over
the fish once. Serve immediately.

Glazed Brussels sprouts   3 SERVINGS

1 pint (about 10 ounces)
Brussels sprouts
1 tablespoon butter

½ teaspoon sugar
Salt and freshly ground
black pepper to taste

Bring hot water to boil in covered steamer. Wash and trim sprouts and slice off bottom of stem ends. Steam 7 to 10 minutes, depending on size of sprouts. Drain. Sauté cooked sprouts in melted butter and sugar for 1 or 2 minutes. Season with salt and pepper.

NOTE: You don't have to glaze the sprouts in butter and sugar; they taste fine just steamed. You can eliminate the sugar, too, and just coat the sprouts in butter. As it is the amount of sugar in the recipe has been halved, the amount of butter cut by 50 percent.

Rice cooked in broth   3 SERVINGS

¾ cup enriched white or
brown rice*
1½ cups chicken broth or
stock

Salt and freshly ground
black pepper to taste

Combine rice with broth. Bring to boil. Reduce heat to simmer, and cook, covered, until all liquid is absorbed and rice is tender, about 17 minutes. Season with salt and pepper, if desired.

*See page 74 for directions on how to use brown rice in a 30-minute meal.

A LIGHT MIDSUMMER MENU FOR TWO

Seafood and nectarines

Sautéed cucumbers

Corn on the cob with cumin butter

Sorbet or ice

THE idea of fish with fruit is a bit out of the ordinary, but the sweet tartness combines perfectly with either shrimp or scallops.

The idea of cooked cucumbers may be a bit unusual, too. The flavor of the cucumber doesn't change, but the texture does, making the vegetable silky and crunchy at the same time.

Finally, spreading cumin-flavored butter over corn on the cob may be the most unusual of all. It is absolutely delicious, intensifying the sweet flavor of the corn.

In sum, an unusual dinner.

STAPLES

butter	ground cumin
salt	garlic
pepper	lemon
onion	

SHOPPING LIST

¾ pound fresh or
frozen peeled
shrimp or ¾
pound scallops

2 medium nectarines

3 tablespoons
parsley

2 large cucumbers or
5 small pickling
cucumbers

2 to 4 ears fresh corn

2 tablespoons plain
yogurt (optional)

(sorbet or ice)

GAME PLAN

Prepare cucumbers.

Chop onion. Chop parsley for shrimp and cucumbers.

Melt butter with cumin.

Boil water for corn.

Sauté onion for cucumber.

Prepare garlic; heat butter for shrimp; add garlic; add seafood and season.

Add cucumbers to onion; season.

Cook corn.

Slice nectarines; add to shrimp; squeeze in lemon juice.

Add yogurt, if used, to cucumbers with parsley.

Garnish shrimp with parsley.

Seafood and nectarines 2 SERVINGS

¾ pound fresh or frozen peeled uncooked shrimp or ¾ pound scallops
2 cloves garlic
2 tablespoons butter
Salt and freshly ground black pepper to taste

2 medium nectarines
2 tablespoons fresh lemon juice
1 tablespoon chopped fresh parsley

If frozen shrimp are used, do not defrost.

If scallops are used, wash and dry. Cut sea scallops in half. Leave bay scallops whole. Put garlic through press. In large skillet heat butter; add garlic, shrimp or scallops, and salt and pepper. Cook quickly over high heat, stirring occasionally, until shrimp turns pink, 5 to 7 minutes, or scallops begin to brown, 5 minutes. (Pour off most of accumulated liquid from frozen shrimp.)

Slice nectarines. Add for last 2 or 3 minutes of cooking time. Squeeze lemon. Chop parsley. Add lemon juice and stir. Sprinkle parsley over dish just before serving.

Sautéed cucumbers 2 SERVINGS

2 large cucumbers*
1 medium onion
2 tablespoons butter
Salt to taste

2 tablespoons plain yogurt (optional)
2 tablespoons chopped fresh parsley

*If you are fortunate enough to pick up the little pickling cucumbers, they are crisper, have less water, and are preferable. You can use 5 small ones in place of the 2 large ones called for.

The pickling cukes as well as other cukes purchased at roadside stands or farmer's markets are not likely to have wax on them. They don't need to be peeled, therefore, just scrubbed.

Peel and coarsely grate cucumbers into a colander. Let stand until cooking time. Coarsely chop onion. Chop parsley. Squeeze water with hands out of cucumbers. Heat butter in skillet and sauté onion until softened. Add cucumbers and cook, stirring occasionally, until mixture is soft, about 5 minutes. Salt, if desired. To serve, either blend in yogurt, if desired; or sprinkle with parsley.

Without the yogurt, this mixture has a more oniony flavor and is sweeter. The yogurt has been substituted for sour cream in the original recipe.

Corn on the cob with cumin butter

2 SERVINGS

2 to 4 ears fresh young corn	½ to 1 teaspoon ground cumin
2 to 3 tablespoons butter	

Husk the corn. Bring enough hot water to boil in large covered pot to cover the corn. Salt, if desired. When water boils, add corn and cook, covered, 5 minutes. (If corn is older, cook longer.) Drain. Serve with cumin butter.

To make cumin butter: melt butter and stir in cumin; allow to stand about 5 minutes. To serve, roll corn in cumin butter or, using a pastry brush, paint corn with the butter.

FISH DINNER FOR THREE

Fillets with lemon butter

Green beans in peanut sauce

Lisa's noodles

Grapes

A combination of very simple broiled fish with a spicy, flavorful Chinese version of green beans and a recipe from a friend who has always contributed at least one recipe to my cookbooks. Lisa's noodles, at least the original version, came from Sherley Koteen. It was a favorite of her daughter, Lisa. But it took a lot longer to prepare, so I updated and simplified it to fit in with the 30-minute format.

GAME PLAN:

Bring hot water to boil in steamer for beans.

Bring hot water to boil in pot for noodles.

Wash and trim green beans.

Make sauce for green beans.

Steam green beans.

Make lemon butter for fish and arrange fish fillets on broiling pan; brush with lemon butter.

Cook noodles.

Grate cheese and chop scallions for noodles.

Drain green beans and mix with sauce.

Put fish on to broil.

Make sauce for noodles; drain noodles; mix with sauce.

When fish is done, brush again with lemon butter.

STAPLES

butter	garlic
white pepper	Worcestershire sauce
salt	caraway seeds
oyster sauce	lemon
rice vinegar	

SHOPPING LIST

1 to 1½ pounds fish fillets, such as scrod, flounder, trout, sole, turbot

2 teaspoons parsley

¾ pound green beans

4 tablespoons unsalted roasted peanuts

3 cups (6 ounces) very thin egg noodles

½ pint yogurt

3 scallions

¾ cup firm cheese, such as Edam, Cheddar

(grapes)

Fillets with lemon butter   3 SERVINGS

1 to 1½ pounds fish fillets—scrod, flounder, trout, turbot, sole

2 teaspoons minced fresh parsley

2 tablespoons butter

1½ teaspoons fresh lemon juice

Salt and white pepper to taste

Lemon half

Wash fillets. Mince parsley and place in small saucepan with butter, lemon juice, and salt and pepper. Heat until butter is melted. Cover a broiling pan with aluminum foil. Brush foil with some of melted-butter mixture. Place fillets on foil, skin sides down. Brush with melted-butter mixture. Broil 3½ to 4 inches from heat 8 to 10 minutes. Cut lemon half into 3 wedges. Remove fish and brush with remaining butter. Serve with lemon wedges.

Green beans in peanut sauce

3 SERVINGS

¾ pound green beans
4 tablespoons crushed unsalted roasted peanuts

2 tablespoons oyster sauce
6 tablespoons rice vinegar
1 medium clove garlic

Bring hot water to boil in covered steamer. Wash and trim beans. Steam until beans are crisp-tender, 7 to 9 minutes. Drain. Crush peanuts with rolling pin between two sheets of wax paper or in small hand chopper. Combine nuts in serving bowl with oyster sauce and vinegar. Put garlic through press into bowl and mix. Add beans and toss to coat. Stir occasionally. Serve at room temperature.

Lisa's noodles

3 SERVINGS

3 cups (6 ounces) very thin egg noodles
3 thin scallions
¾ cup coarsely grated firm cheese, such as Edam, Cheddar
1 cup plain yogurt

2 teaspoons Worcestershire sauce
1½ teaspoons caraway seeds (optional)
Salt and freshly ground black pepper to taste

Bring 3 quarts salted hot water to boil in covered medium-sized pot. Add noodles and boil about 4 minutes, until tender. (They cook much more quickly than spaghetti.) Drain. Return to pot. Chop scallions. Grate cheese. Add the yogurt, Worcestershire sauce, caraway seeds, if used, scallions, cheese, and salt and pepper and serve.

FISH DINNER FOR TWO

Salmon fillet poached in vermouth

Cucumbers with mint in yogurt

Boiled new potatoes

Raspberries

It's easier to turn some menus for two into dinners for four or more without going over the 30-minute limit. This is definitely one of them and that's because there is very little chopping or cutting.

If the price of salmon is out of your league, you can use another moist or oily fish like fresh sole, porgy, or flounder. Adjust cooking time to thickness of fillet.

This is a lovely low-calorie meal—without tasting like one.

STAPLES

dry vermouth	salt
lemon	pepper
garlic	olive oil
thyme	fresh mint*

SHOPPING LIST

½ to ¾ pound salmon fillets	6 (about 10 ounces) new potatoes
2 small cucumbers	(raspberries)
¾ cup plain yogurt	

---

*If you aren't growing mint where you live, you may be hard-pressed to find it in the grocery store. Dried mint isn't the same, but you can make this dish without any mint at all.

GAME PLAN:

Boil potatoes.

Prepare dressing for cucumbers.

Prepare poaching medium for salmon.

Cut salmon into individual fillets.

Prepare and slice cucumbers and add to

dressing; refrigerate until serving.

Poach salmon.

Drain potatoes and cut into quarters.

Remove salmon to individual dishes with slotted spoon.

Salmon fillet poached in vermouth   2 SERVINGS

½ to ¾ pound salmon fillet
1 medium clove garlic
½ cup dry vermouth
1 tablespoon fresh lemon juice

¾ teaspoon chopped fresh thyme or ¼ teaspoon dried
Salt and freshly ground black pepper to taste

Wash salmon fillets and cut into 2 portions. Put garlic through press into saucepan to be used for poaching. Add vermouth and lemon juice. Chop thyme. Add with salt and a grind or two of pepper. Place salmon, skin side down, in enamel or glass pan. Turn heat to medium. Cover. Poach, just at simmer, until salmon flakes easily with fork, 8 to 10 minutes, depending on thickness. Remove from poaching liquid with slotted spoon and serve.

Cucumbers with mint in yogurt

2 SERVINGS

1 large clove garlic
¾ cup plain yogurt
2 teaspoons good quality olive oil
2 tablespoons chopped fresh mint

Juice of ½ of a large lemon
2 small cucumbers or 1 medium

Put garlic through press into bowl large enough to hold all ingredients. Chop mint. Add yogurt, oil, and mint and squeeze in lemon juice. Mix. Peel cucumbers if waxed; otherwise just wash well. Slice thinly into yogurt mixture. Stir and refrigerate until serving.

Boiled new potatoes

2 SERVINGS

6 golf-ball-sized new potatoes (about 10 ounces)

Scrub potatoes, but do not peel them. Cook in water to cover in covered pot until tender, but not soft, about 20 minutes. Drain and cut into quarters. Do not peel.

Serve plain, with freshly ground black pepper, with butter, if desired, or with some of the sauce from the cucumbers.

COLD PASTA SALAD MENU FOR TWO OR THREE

Broccoli, tuna, and shells salad

Cheese, garlic, and parsley bread

Honeydew or cantaloupe with lime

COLD pasta salads are cool in every sense of the word. Some of them are perfect for quick meals, proof that quick, chic, and good are synonymous.

This meal is extremely simple, light but filling. Cooking is kept to a minimum so that the kitchen won't heat up and, if you have a toaster oven to finish the bread, you won't even have to turn on the oven at all.

If you want to take the time to go to a store that sells fresh or frozen pasta or happen to live near one, you can try fresh fettuccine in place of the shells.

GAME PLAN:

Bring hot water to boil in pot for shells.

Bring hot water to boil in steamer for broccoli.

Cook shells.

Steam broccoli.

Cut up tomatoes.

Drain and rinse tuna.

Mix together oil, vinegar, basil, and oregano; chop onion.

Combine shells, broccoli, tomatoes, onion, and tuna; mix in dressing.

Mix cheese, garlic, and parsley; spread on rolls and broil.

STAPLES

salt

pepper

red wine vinegar

olive oil

basil

oregano

garlic

SHOPPING LIST

2 cups (4 ounces) macaroni shells

2 or 3 large stalks broccoli

2 medium to large tomatoes

6½- to 7-ounce can water-packed tuna

small red onion

3 French or sourdough rolls

1 cup (4 ounces) Monterey Jack cheese

¼ cup parsley (honeydew or cantaloupe, lime)

Broccoli, tuna, and shells   2 LARGE OR 3 SMALL SERVINGS

2 cups (4 ounces) macaroni shells

2 or 3 large stalks broccoli, about 1¼ pounds

1 (6½- or 7-ounce) can tuna, packed in water

2 medium to large tomatoes

2 heaping tablespoons chopped fresh basil or 2 teaspoons dried

2 teaspoons chopped fresh oregano or ⅔ teaspoon dried

4 tablespoons coarsely chopped red onion

5 tablespoons good quality olive oil

4 tablespoons red wine vinegar

Salt and freshly ground black pepper to taste

Bring 2 or 3 quarts hot water to boil in covered pot. Salt, if desired.

Bring hot water to boil in steamer. Remove tough stems from broccoli and cut heads into flowerettes.

Cook shells in rapidly boiling water until tender, about 7 minutes. Steam broccoli about 5 minutes, depending on size of flowerettes. Drain shells and rinse in cold water until cooled. Drain broccoli and rinse under cold water until cool.

Meanwhile, drain tuna and rinse under cold water; drain. Cut tomatoes into large cubes. Chop fresh basil and oregano. Beat together oil and vinegar and beat in basil and oregano. Chop onion. Combine broccoli, tomatoes, onion, shells, and tuna. Mix in dressing gently. Season with salt and pepper. Serve at room temperature.

Cheese, garlic, and parsley bread

3 ROLLS

3 sourdough or French rolls

1 cup coarsely grated Monterey Jack cheese

1 large clove garlic

4 tablespoons minced fresh parsley

Turn oven to broil.

Cut rolls in half. Grate cheese. Put garlic through press or mince finely. Mince parsley. Mix cheese with garlic and parsley. Pile the mixture generously on each roll half and broil until cheese is melted and bubbly.

A SPECIAL SEAFOOD DINNER FOR FOUR

Scallops with garlic and parsley

Sherley's tomatoes

Curried rice

Peaches and blueberries

I tried out this menu on friends, serving Quick Cheese Tomato Fondue (see page 309) before dinner and Raspberry Yogurt sauce with fruit (see page 328) for dessert.

The main part of the meal took 35 minutes to prepare, but I found I had enough food for six people. So you should be able to make this menu for four in the allotted 30 minutes. If not quite, it's worth every extra second!

I can't pull any punches about one ingredient— scallops are expensive, at least where I live. This is probably a meal for special occasions, particularly if you are counting your pennies.

STAPLES

flour	onion
olive oil	rice
salt	curry powder
pepper	chicken or vegetable stock or broth
butter	mayonnaise
garlic	
lemon	

SHOPPING LIST

1½ pounds scallops
  about ½ cup
  parsley

⅓ cup (1½ ounces)
  slivered almonds

½ cup seedless
  grapes

3 tablespoons
  Parmesan cheese

3 tablespoons
  scallion

4 small tomatoes
  (peaches,
  blueberries)

GAME PLAN:

Chop onion.

Sauté onion in butter.
Add rice, curry, and
stock.

Prepare scallops.

Mince garlic for scal-
lops.

Core and halve
tomatoes; season.

Grate Parmesan; chop
scallion and parsley and
mix with mayonnaise;
spoon over tomatoes.

Turn on broiler.

Heat oil and butter for
scallops; add garlic.

Cook scallops.

Chop parsley for scal-
lops.

Toast almonds.

Broil tomatoes.

Add grapes to rice.

Cut lemon.

Add parsley to scallops.

Add almonds to rice.

Scallops with garlic and parsley

4 SERVINGS

1½ pounds bay or sea
  scallops

3 tablespoons flour
  Salt and white pepper
  to taste

2 tablespoons olive oil

2 tablespoons butter

2 medium cloves garlic

⅓ cup chopped fresh
  parsley
  Lemon wedges

Wash scallops and drain thoroughly. If scallops are large, cut in half. Place flour seasoned with salt and pepper in bowl. Add scallops and, using hands or spoon, coat with flour. Over medium heat, heat oil and butter until hot in skillet large enough to hold all the scallops in one layer without crowding. Or use 2 skillets. Mince garlic or put it through garlic press into skillet. Cook 30 seconds. Add scallops and cook, turning once, until they are cooked through. The entire cooking time is about 4 minutes. Chop parsley. Cut lemon into wedges. Stir in chopped parsley. Remove scallops from heat. Serve on platter with lemon wedges as garnish.

Sherley's tomatoes   4 SERVINGS

3 tablespoons coarsely
   grated Parmesan
   cheese, tightly packed

3 tablespoons chopped
   scallion, white and
   green part

2 tablespoons minced
   fresh parsley

3 tablespoons mayonnaise

4 small ripe tomatoes
   Salt and freshly ground
   black pepper to taste

Turn on broiler.

Grate the cheese coarsely and pack tightly when measuring. Chop scallion; mince parsley.

Combine cheese, scallion, parsley, and mayonnaise. Core and cut tomatoes in half horizontally. Place tomatoes, cut sides up, in shallow baking pan. Season with salt and pepper as desired. Spoon on cheese mixture and broil tomatoes about 4 inches from heat about 2 or 3 minutes, until cheese melts and begins to brown. Don't let tops burn. (If you have a toaster oven, you can also broil the tomatoes in it.)

Curried rice

1 small to medium onion
2 tablespoons butter
1 cup brown or enriched white rice*
1 teaspoon or more good quality curry powder

1½ cup chicken or vegetable stock or broth
⅓ cup slivered almonds
½ cup seedless grapes
Salt and freshly ground black pepper to taste

Chop onion. Heat butter in skillet large enough to hold rice. Add onion and sauté about 5 minutes, until onion softens. Stir in rice and curry powder. Add stock. Bring to a boil. Cover and cook at simmer 15 to 20 minutes, until the liquid has evaporated almost completely and rice is cooked. Meanwhile, toast almonds at 400 degrees for 3 minutes (in toaster oven if you have one). Watch or they will burn. When liquid has almost evaporated, stir in grapes. Season with salt and pepper. Just before serving, stir in almonds.

*See page 74 for directions on how to use brown rice in a 30-minute meal.

LOW-CALORIE MENU
FOR TWO

Chinese fish fillets

Boston lettuce with yogurt-grapefrut dressing

Steamed asparagus

Warm crusty rolls

Strawberries

THIS is a dinner for both the serious dieter and the non-dieter. If you hadn't been told it was a diet menu, would you have known? But as you may have noticed, there is very little oil in the fish dish. There is no oil in the salad dressing, which is made with yogurt instead. But there is no reason to think of yogurt just as a diet dressing. It's delicious under any circumstances.

Asparagus speaks for itself. Was there ever a low-calorie food that tasted so good?

For the non-dieter there are nice warm rolls, slathered with butter if desired.

The strawberries? They give the asparagus a run for its money. Skinny people could put vanilla ice cream under the berries . . .

STAPLES

garlic   soy sauce
powdered ginger   Dijon mustard
peanut oil   salt
rice or white vinegar

SHOPPING LIST

¾ to 1 pound fish fillets, such as flounder, blue, pollock, haddock

1 head Boston lettuce

½ cup plain yogurt

2 tablespoons grapefruit juice

16 to 20 thin asparagus

rolls

(strawberries)

GAME PLAN:

Turn on broiler.

Press garlic; mix with ginger, oil, vinegar, and soy sauce.

Brush fish in pan with basting mixture.

Bring hot water to boil in steamer for as-paragus.

Prepare asparagus.

Wash and dry lettuce; break up into pieces.

Make salad dressing.

Steam asparagus.

Broil fish, basting twice.

Drain asparagus.

Dress salad.

Chinese fish fillets

2 SERVINGS

¾ to 1 pound fish fillets, such as flounder, blue, pollock, haddock

1 small clove garlic

1 teaspoon powdered ginger

1½ tablespoons peanut oil

1 tablespoon rice or white vinegar

1½ teaspoons soy sauce

Turn on broiler.

Put the garlic through press; mix with ginger, oil, vinegar, and soy sauce. Place fish fillets on foil in shallow pan. Brush with basting-sauce mixture. Allow to sit while preparing rest of meal.

To serve: Broil fish about 5 minutes, basting twice. Fish is done when it flakes easily with fork and is no longer translucent.

Boston lettuce with yogurt-grapefruit dressing
2 SERVINGS

---

1 head Boston lettuce
(any lettuce will do)
½ cup plain yogurt
2 tablespoons grapefruit
juice

1 heaping teaspoon Dijon
mustard

Wash lettuce. Dry well and break up, dividing between 2 salad plates. Mix yogurt with grapefruit juice and mustard. Spoon over salad.

Steamed asparagus
2 SERVINGS

---

16 to 20 thin asparagus
spears

Salt to taste

Bring hot water to boil in steamer. Break tough ends off asparagus at point where they break easily. Soak in water for a few minutes to remove any grit.

Steam asparagus 8 to 10 minutes, depending on thickness. As soon as they are crisp-tender, remove from heat.

CHINESE MENU FOR TWO

Shrimp foo yong with soy-ginger sauce

Rice with anise

Snow peas and garlic

*Blueberries, strawberries or bananas
   with yogurt and honey*

STRICTLY speaking, egg foo yong, with or without shrimp, with or without anything else, in fact, is not Chinese. It's our version of Chinese, and it certainly has Chinese flavorings.

There are many places where fresh bean sprouts and fresh snow peas are either not available or mean a trip to another store. Hunting defeats the purpose of these menus. As alternatives, canned bean sprouts may be substituted, but they should be drained and refreshed under cold water. Alternatives to fresh snow peas are either fresh spinach or frozen snow peas, though the latter hardly come out as crisp.

Of course the least expensive way to purchase shrimp is uncooked in the shell, but this is one of those instances where economy has to be substituted for convenience. So buy peeled shrimp—fresh, frozen, cooked, or uncooked. There is plenty of time to cook them as long as you don't have to peel them.

STAPLES

eggs	rice vinegar
onion	soy sauce
vegetable oil	garlic
salt	rice
pepper	aniseed or star anise
ginger	(honey)

SHOPPING LIST

½ pound fresh bean sprouts or 2 cups canned

6 to 8 ounces raw or cooked peeled shrimp, or cooked crab meat, or other cooked fish

½ pound fresh snow peas

(blueberries, strawberries, or bananas, yogurt)

GAME PLAN:

Chop onion for shrimp.

Prepare bean sprouts.

Cook shrimp.

Cook rice with water and aniseed.

Trim snow peas.

Press garlic.

Beat eggs; add bean sprouts, onion, shrimp, and salt and pepper.

Cook pancakes.

Mix soy sauce, vinegar, water, and ginger.

When second batch of pancakes goes on to cook, cook snow peas in small skillet.

Shrimp foo yong with soy-ginger sauce

2 SERVINGS

1 medium onion
½ pound fresh bean sprouts or 2 cups canned
6 to 8 ounces raw or cooked shrimp, peeled, or fresh or frozen cooked crab meat, or other cooked fish
5 eggs

Salt and freshly ground black pepper to taste
2 tablespoons vegetable oil
1 tablespoon soy sauce
1 tablespoon rice vinegar
2 tablespoons water
½ teaspoon chopped fresh ginger

Chop the onion medium-fine. Rinse fresh bean sprouts and drain, or rinse and drain canned ones. If raw, cook shrimp. Drain.

Beat eggs in large bowl. Mix in sprouts, onion, shrimp or crab meat, or fish, and salt and pepper.

Heat 1 tablespoon oil in large skillet. Mix batter, being sure to incorporate eggs with fish and vegetables, and spoon 3 pancakes of it into skillet. Don't worry if pancakes run together. When they are browned on the bottom, separate them, turn, and brown on second side. Keep pancakes warm in oven while using up remaining oil and batter.

Chop fresh ginger. Combine soy sauce, vinegar, water, and ginger. Serve sauce over pancakes. (It is good over the rice, too.)

Rice with anise   2 SERVINGS

½ cup enriched white or   Salt and freshly ground
   brown rice*   black pepper to taste
1 cup water
¼ teaspoon aniseed or 1
   clove star anise

Combine rice, water, aniseed or star anise, salt and pepper and bring to boil. When water boils, reduce heat to below simmer, cover, and cook until water has been absorbed, about 17 minutes. Keep rice warm while preparing rest of dinner.

Snow peas and garlic   2 SERVINGS

1 medium clove garlic   Salt and freshly ground
½ pound fresh snow peas   black pepper to taste
1 tablespoon vegetable oil

Put garlic through press. Cut tips off ends of snow peas. Heat oil in medium skillet. Add garlic and sauté 1 minute. Add snow peas, season with salt and pepper, and sauté quickly 3 to 4 minutes until shiny and hot.

*See page 74 for directions on how to use brown rice in a 30-minute meal.

MEATLESS ITALIAN MENU FOR FOUR

Zucchini and rotini

Tomato and mozzarella salad

Italian bread or dark peasant bread

Lemon ice

THIS menu is so simple and so flavorful you will never even miss the sour cream that has been replaced by yogurt, as it has in so many other recipes in this book.

The tomato, mozzarella, and basil salad is classic Italian. If you have no source for fresh basil, make something else, like tomatoes, mozzarella, and anchovies or onions.

And if you can't find rotini for the main dish, just substitute another spiral-shaped macaroni. The shape helps to catch and hold the sauce.

STAPLES

olive oil	salt
onions	pepper
garlic	fresh basil*

---

*Fresh basil is not available in too many markets. In order to make the salad you must have fresh basil; either grow it in your own backyard or patio, or find a market where you can buy it.

SHOPPING LIST

2 pounds zucchini
⅔ cup plain yogurt
1 pound rotini (spiral macaroni)
1 cup (about 5 ounces) freshly grated Parmesan cheese

2 large tomatoes
3 or 4 ounces mozzarella cheese
fresh basil*
Italian bread or dark peasant bread
(lemon ice)

GAME PLAN:

Scrub and cut zucchini; sauté.

Prepare garlic and onions.

Bring hot water to boil in pot for rotini.

Remove zucchini; sauté garlic and onions.

Slice tomatoes and mozzarella and shred basil.

Cook rotini.

Add yogurt to onion mixture.

Grate Parmesan.

Drain rotini; add to yogurt mixture with zucchini and cheese.

Arrange salads; drizzle on oil.

Zucchini and rotini   4 SERVINGS

2 pounds zucchini
5 tablespoons olive oil
2 large onions
1 large clove garlic
⅔ cup plain yogurt

1 cup finely grated fresh Parmesan cheese
Salt and freshly ground black pepper to taste

Scrub and cut zucchini into thin sticks, about 1½ inches long. Heat oil until hot in heavy skillet. Sauté zucchini until golden and it begins to soften. Chop onions; put garlic through press. Remove zucchini from skillet with slotted spoon and set aside. Add onions and garlic and sauté until onions are golden. Stir in yogurt and cook quickly until mixture has thickened a little. Grate cheese. Add drained rotini, zucchini, and ½ cup cheese. Season with salt and pepper. Toss; heat through. Serve with remaining cheese.

Rotini
4 SERVINGS

1 pound rotini (spiral macaroni)   Salt

Bring 6 quarts hot water to boil in covered pot. Salt, if desired. Add rotini and cook about 9 minutes, until tender but firm. Drain and combine with zucchini mixture.

Tomato and mozzarella salad
4 SERVINGS

2 large tomatoes
3 or 4 ounces mozzarella cheese
¼ cup shredded fresh basil

Good quality olive oil
Salt and freshly ground black pepper to taste

Wash, core and slice tomatoes thickly. Slice cheese thinly. Arrange alternating slices of tomatoes and cheese on individual salad plates. When ready to serve, shred basil over salads. Drizzle on olive oil. Pass salt and pepper.

MENU MINUS MEAT
FOR THREE OR FOUR

Bulgur with everything

*Sherley's creamy dressing for red lettuce
(or green)*

Whole grain pitas or whole grain bread

Navel oranges, apples, or papayas

CAN you imagine trying to figure out what to serve Ralph Nader for dinner? Not only Ralph Nader, but his sister, Claire, and Sid Wolfe, the doctor who is now head of Public Citizen and Public Citizen Health Research Group, and his wife, Suzanne? Having once had the pleasure of eating some of Ralph's mother's wonderful Lebanese cooking, I had some idea of what might appeal to the Naders and I lucked out.

I doubled the recipes. Claire brought a loaf of her wonderful whole-grain bread; I added the Mexican Orange Dip (see page 311) and the Chèvre with Hazelnut Oil (see page 310) for cocktails, and the Frozen Fruit Ice (see page 326) to complete the meal. Despite the fact that the main course was made for 6, it was easy to have it ready in 30 minutes. There was even some time to clean up.

Sherley's salad dressing is my good luck recipe. Ever since I started writing cookbooks, Sherley Koteen, whom I have known since I moved to Washington in 1959, has contributed a recipe to every book I've written. A book would be naked without a recipe from her. She's a wonderful cook.

Red lettuce may not be available everywhere. I first had it in Colorado. Beautiful red-tipped leaves make a handsome salad. If you can't find it, any firm lettuce, but iceberg, will do.

STAPLES

onion	mayonnaise
oil	olive oil
oregano	red wine vinegar
salt	basil
pepper	tarragon
Dijon mustard	garlic

SHOPPING LIST

1 cup bulgur (cracked wheat) (appx ½ lb.)

28- or 29-ounce can tomatoes

1 cup dry curd cottage cheese (or skim milk cottage cheese)

12-ounce can whole kernel corn

1 cup (4 ounces) Cheddar cheese

¾ pound red or green lettuce

½ dozen large whole-wheat pitas or loaf whole grain bread

(navel oranges, apples, or papaya)

GAME PLAN:

Sauté onion in oil.

Add bulgur; stir.

Add tomatoes and oregano.

Wash greens.

Prepare salad dressing.

Add cottage cheese and corn to bulgur.

Heat pitas or bread.

Top bulgur with cheese and melt.

Dress salad.

Bulgur with everything   3 or 4 SERVINGS

1 large onion
3 tablespoons oil
1 cup fine bulgur
  (cracked wheat)
  28- or 29-ounce can
  tomatoes
1 teaspoon dried oregano
1 cup dry curd cottage
  cheese

12-ounce can whole
kernel corn
Salt and freshly ground
black pepper to taste
1 cup coarsely shredded,
  tightly packed Cheddar
  cheese

Coarsely chop onion. Heat oil in large skillet; add onion and sauté over medium heat until onion begins to take on color and soften. Add the bulgur and stir to coat well. Add tomatoes and liquid from can, breaking the tomatoes with your fingers as you put them in skillet. Add oregano. Stir; reduce heat, cover, and simmer about 15 minutes, until bulgur is almost tender. Stir in cottage cheese. Drain liquid from corn and stir in. Season with salt and pepper. Sprinkle with cheese. Either cover for a minute or two to melt the cheese, or run under broiler to melt cheese and brown a little. (If you put under broiler, remember to preheat it.)

Sherley's creamy dressing for red lettuce (or green)

3 or 4 SERVINGS

¾ pound red or green lettuce

1½ teaspoons Dijon mustard

1 teaspoon mayonnaise

¼ cup good quality olive oil

2 scant tablespoons red wine vinegar

¼ teaspoon dried basil or 1 teaspoon chopped fresh

½ teaspoon dried tarragon leaves or 1½ teaspoons chopped fresh

Salt and freshly ground black pepper to taste

1 small clove garlic

Wash greens and drain. Pat dry with paper towels. Place in salad bowl or on individual salad plates.

Beat mustard and mayonnaise. Add oil in a very thin stream, beating constantly with wire whisk. Dressing should remain thick. Beat in vinegar in thin stream. Dressing should be thinner but still creamy. If using fresh herbs, chop. Add herbs and salt and pepper. Put garlic through press and beat in.

MEATLESS MENU FOR FOUR

Green and yellow pasta

Oriental cucumbers

Garlic bread

Peaches, pears, or strawberries

THE Italians call the mixture of green and yellow pasta hay and straw but it carries a much different and more complex sauce. Of course, if you should happen to have easy access to fresh pasta, by all means use it.

This pasta dish I would describe as "new" American eating; the garlic bread as old; and the cucumbers somewhere in between . . . or maybe from left field!! No matter, the combination of cuisines is excellent and makes a good vegetarian meal.

STAPLES

garlic

butter

fresh basil*

salt

pepper

rice or white wine vinegar

brown sugar

---

*Fresh basil is not available in too many markets. In order to make the salad you must have fresh basil; either grow it in your own backyard or patio, or find a market where you can buy it.

SHOPPING LIST

½ pound spinach noodles

½ pound wide egg noodles

about ¾ pound zucchini or ½ pound mushrooms

1 pint plain yogurt

3 tablespoons parsley (if you have no basil)*

½ cup (about 2½ ounces) grated Parmesan

2 medium to large cucumbers or 6 to 8 small pickling cucumbers

½ pound Italian or French bread

(peaches, pears, or strawberries)

GAME PLAN:

Turn oven to 400.

Boil water for pasta.

Prepare zucchini and garlic; sauté.

Combine garlic with butter and melt.

Prepare cucumbers and combine with vinegar-brown sugar mixture; chill.

Cook pasta.

Slice bread and brush with garlic butter; brown.

Add yogurt to zucchini.

Chop basil or parsley.

Drain pasta.

Grate Parmesan.

Combine pasta with yogurt mixture, basil, and salt and pepper.

Green and yellow pasta   4 SERVINGS

½ pound spinach noodles
½ pound wide egg noodles
2 or 3 medium zucchini
(about ¾ pound) or ½
pound mushrooms
2 cloves garlic
2 tablespoons butter

2 cups plain yogurt*
3 tablespoons chopped
fresh basil or parsley
Salt and freshly ground
black pepper to taste
½ cup freshly grated
Parmesan cheese

Bring 6 quarts of hot water to boil in covered pot. Salt, if
desired. Cook pasta according to package directions, until
al dente. Meanwhile, scrub and cube zucchini and put
garlic through press. Melt butter and sauté zucchini and
garlic in hot butter over high heat in skillet until zucchini
becomes golden and is tender. Turn off heat and stir in
yogurt while pan is still on stove. This will keep yogurt
warm but it won't curdle.

Chop basil or parsley. Grate cheese. When pasta is
cooked, drain well and stir in yogurt mixture. Stir in basil
or parsley; season with salt and pepper. Keep warm. Serve
with cheese.

Oriental cucumbers   4 SERVINGS

2 medium-large
cucumbers or 6 to 8
small pickling
cucumbers
½ cup rice or white wine
vinegar

2 tablespoons firmly
packed brown sugar

Peel waxed cucumbers; thinly slice cucumbers. Combine
vinegar and brown sugar. Stir cucumbers into mixture and
mix well. Chill until serving time.

---

*In place of yogurt, you can use half yogurt, half sour cream.

Garlic bread   4 SERVINGS

---

4 to 6 tablespoons butter   ½ pound loaf Italian or
1 large clove garlic   French bread

Turn oven or toaster oven to 400 degrees.
  Melt butter. Put garlic through press and add to butter.
Slice bread in half lengthwise. Spread cut sides of bread
with garlic butter and heat 5 to 10 minutes.

VEGGIE MENU FOR TWO

Tofu pasta sauce

Spaghetti squash

Sandy's salad

Apple wedges, or strawberries with yogurt and brown sugar

WHILE this is a meatless spaghetti sauce, it has a replacement for the traditional ground beef—tofu. Tofu, or soybean curd, an integral component of Chinese and Japanese cuisine, is beginning to catch on here. It is very low in calories, has much vegetable protein, and takes on the flavor of the ingredients with which it is mixed. It gives body to a sauce, and you feel as if you are eating something a lot more substantial than tomatoes with seasonings.

To keep the calories down, use spaghetti squash instead of pasta. It has the texture of spaghetti without the calories.

Inspiration for the salad came from Sandy Rovner who sits across from me at my office. She brought in a mushroom and greens salad with feta for lunch one day and I snitched a piece. It tasted delicious and didn't even have any dressing on it yet. The cheese made the difference.

Drizzling just a little olive oil on the salad is much easier than making a dressing, and there is plenty of flavor from the cheese. But be sparing with the oil and be sure it's of very good quality or it will be very noticeable and could ruin the salad.

It's simple not only to double these recipes and stay within the 30 minutes; you could even triple them and still be finished in 30 minutes.

STAPLES

olive oil	oregano
onion	red wine vinegar
garlic	salt
red or white wine	pepper
basil	(brown sugar)

SHOPPING LIST

1 pound tofu (soybean curd)	8 medium mushrooms
29-ounce can tomato purée	4 ounces feta cheese (apples or strawberries, yogurt)
2 pounds spaghetti squash	
¼ pound fresh spinach	

GAME PLAN:

Chop onion and garlic and sauté with tofu in hot oil.

Cook squash.

Prepare spinach and mushrooms.

Add remaining sauce ingredients to skillet.

Arrange salad plates; crumble on feta cheese.

Tofu pasta sauce 　　　　　　　　2 SERVINGS

1 large onion
1 large clove garlic
2 tablespoons olive oil
1 pound tofu (soybean curd)
1 29-ounce can tomato purée
⅓ cup red or white wine

2 tablespoons red wine vinegar
1 teaspoon dried basil
½ teaspoon dried oregano
Salt and freshly ground black pepper to taste

Chop onion; mince or put garlic through press. Heat oil and cook onion and garlic over medium heat until tofu is ready to add. Drain liquid off tofu; break tofu up into ½-inch pieces and add to onion and garlic mixture as it cooks. Cook until liquid is gone and then add tomato purée, wine, vinegar, basil, oregano, and salt and pepper. Cook over low heat, stirring occasionally, until squash is ready.

Serve sauce over spaghetti squash quarters.

Spaghetti squash 　　　　　　　　2 SERVINGS

1 small spaghetti squash (about 2 pounds)

Water

Cut squash into quarters. Remove seeds. Place in pot with enough water to come up to just below cut surface of squash. Cover and boil until squash is tender, about 20 to 25 minutes. Check once in a while to be sure water has not cooked away. Serve topped with tofu pasta sauce.

Sandy's salad

¼ pound fresh spinach
8 medium mushrooms
4 ounces feta cheese

Olive oil of good quality
Salt and freshly ground
black pepper to taste

Wash spinach and remove tough stems. Drain and dry on paper towels. Place spinach on 2 salad plates. Rinse mushrooms and trim off ends of stems. Slice mushrooms directly onto salad plates. Crumble cheese on top. Serve oil separately, allowing each person to dress and season salad to taste.

MEXICAN MENU WITHOUT MEAT FOR THREE

Tortilla stack with chile-tomato sauce

Avocado-onion salad

Pineapple or mango

THIS recipe started out as enchiladas, but in a 30-minute meal there isn't time for such niceties as rolling tortillas. The solution was to make layers of tortillas, filling, and sauce.

If you can't find roasted red pepper, substitute pimiento and add an extra tablespoon of vinegar. Leftover pimientos, by the way, will keep almost indefinitely if you add some vinegar to the jar.

How spicy this menu is is determined by how hot you like your chile powder. It comes in several strengths, from mild, like paprika, to numbing, like cayenne.

STAPLES

onions

mild to hot
chile powder

ground cumin

coriander

salt

pepper

red wine vinegar

white vinegar

marjoram

oil

hot pepper sauce

SHOPPING LIST

1 large green bell
pepper
1-pound package
tofu (soybean curd)
4-ounce can
chopped black
olives
6 corn tortillas
12-ounce can
whole kernel corn
1 cup Cheddar
cheese

1-pound can
tomato purée
1 very large ripe
avocado
1 tablespoon parsley
1 small jar roasted
red peppers or
sliced pimiento
(pineapple or
mango)

GAME PLAN:

Turn on oven.

Prepare onion and
green pepper for tor-
tillas and cook.

Mash tofu; add tofu and
seasonings; add olives.

Steam tortillas.

Drain corn.

Make Chile-Tomato
Sauce.

Grate cheese.

Assemble casserole and
bake.

Prepare salad.

Tortilla stack with chile-tomato sauce

3 SERVINGS

- 1 large onion
- 1 large green bell pepper
- 2 tablespoons oil
- 1-pound package tofu (soybean curd)
- 1½ teaspoons mild to hot chile powder
- ½ teaspoon ground cumin
- ¼ teaspoon coriander
- 4-ounce can chopped black olives
- Salt and freshly ground black pepper to taste
- 6 corn tortillas
- 12-ounce can whole kernel corn
- 1 cup coarsely grated Cheddar cheese
- Chile-Tomato Sauce (see recipe)

Turn oven to 350 degrees.

Coarsely chop onion; seed and chop green pepper. Heat oil in large skillet. Sauté onion and green pepper until onion is soft. Drain liquid from tofu and mash. Add to skillet with chile powder, cumin, and coriander. Drain liquid from olives and add. Stir and cook until tofu has dried. Season with salt and pepper.

Steam tortillas either by wrapping in aluminum foil and heating in oven or by steaming over hot water in a steamer. Drain liquid from corn. Grate cheese.

In small casserole place 2 tortillas. Top with ⅓ of the tofu mixture; top with ⅓ of the corn and tomato sauce. Repeat layering 2 more times, ending with tomato sauce. Sprinkle with cheese. Bake until 30 minutes are up, or for about 15 minutes.

Chile-tomato sauce

1-pound can tomato
purée (2 cups)

2 tablespoons white
vinegar

1½ teaspoons mild to hot
chile powder

½ teaspoon ground cumin

½ teaspoon coriander

Few drops hot pepper
sauce

Combine all ingredients in a saucepan and simmer a few
minutes.

Avocado-onion salad 3 SERVINGS

---

1 very large ripe avocado

1 small onion

2 to 3 tablespoons red
wine vinegar

1 tablespoon chopped
fresh parsley

½ teaspoon dried
marjoram leaves

1 roasted canned red
pepper or 2 tablespoons
sliced pimientos

Cut avocado into small cubes. Chop onion medium-fine.
Mix avocado and onion with vinegar. Chop parsley. Add
with marjoram to avocado. Slice pepper into strips and
add. Mix well.

MEATLESS ITALIAN MENU FOR TWO

Green beans, new potatoes, and pesto

Tomatoes with capers

Warm Italian bread

Fruit and cheese

MOST of us first heard of pesto when it was served on top of linguine. But a closer look at some Italian cookbooks would have revealed other delightful uses for pesto, and as cooks in America become more sure of themselves and more innovative they too are trying pesto with lots of different vegetables.

Not long ago I did a story about Pierre Franey, the fine French chef, cookbook author, and newspaper columnist. Franey was putting together a menu for a magazine story and decided to try pesto with zucchini. It was delightful.

I've used pesto on spaghetti squash and mixed pesto with pasta and chicken in a salad. There are so many ways it can be tried. All you need is a source of fresh basil and for most people that means growing it themselves. Although I did notice an encouraging trend in Washington last summer: one of our largest supermarket chains had begun to carry fresh basil, along with other fresh herbs. A first!

One more thing about this menu: Americans are used to eating foods either piping-hot or refrigerator-cold. Many other cultures eat food at room temperature and for some dishes that is the best way. Room temperature allows the full flavor to come out. So don't chill the pesto dish and don't let the tomatoes be too cold either.

STAPLES

olive oil	salt
garlic	pepper
capers	fresh basil*

SHOPPING LIST

- 6 (10 ounces) new potatoes
- ½ pound green beans
- 2 tablespoons parsley
- ¼ cup pignoli (pine nuts)
- ½ cup (2½ ounces) Parmesan cheese
- 1 large tomato
- Italian bread
- (fruit, cheese)

GAME PLAN:

Cook potatoes.

Bring hot water to boil in steamer for beans.

Cut off tips of green beans and wash.

Steam green beans.

Pick basil leaves.

Prepare pesto and process.

Drain cooked green beans and run under cold water. Cut in half.

Slice tomatoes; drizzle with oil; top with capers.

Arrange green beans on platter.

Heat bread.

Drain and cut up potatoes; arrange on platter.

Place pesto in center of platter.

---

*If you are growing basil in your yard, on your terrace or patio, then it's a staple. Otherwise you will have to put it on the shopping list. Unfortunately there aren't too many stores that carry it, so this may not be a menu for you!

Green beans, new potatoes, and pesto

2 SERVINGS

6 golf-ball-sized (10 ounces) new potatoes
½ pound green beans
2½ cups tightly packed fresh basil leaves
2 tablespoons coarsely chopped fresh parsley
6 tablespoons good quality olive oil

1 large clove garlic, halved
¼ cup pignoli (pine nuts)
½ cup freshly grated Parmesan cheese

Scrub potatoes, but do not peel them. Cook in water to cover in covered pot, about 20 minutes. Drain. Do not peel.

Bring water to boil in steamer for green beans. Trim and wash beans. Steam beans about 7 to 9 minutes, until they are crisp-tender; drain and run under cold water. Cut in half.

Combine basil with parsley, oil, garlic, pine nuts, and Parmesan in food processor with metal blade or in blender. Process until rough paste is formed.

Cut potatoes into quarters and arrange on platter with green beans. Place pesto in center of platter and serve.

Tomatoes with capers

2 SERVINGS

1 large tomato or 2 small
Good quality olive oil
2 teaspoons capers

Salt and freshly ground black pepper to taste

Cut tomato in thick slices. Arrange on individual salad plates. Drizzle with olive oil. Sprinkle with capers. Season with salt and pepper.

EASTERN EUROPEAN MENU FOR THREE

Polenta with cottage cheese and tomato sauce

Red, white, and green vegetables

Orange sections

EVERYONE associates polenta with Italy, but it is served in Eastern Europe, too. If you have any left over, it's wonderful the next day, cut in squares and sautéed in butter.

You can put any kind of spaghetti sauce on top of polenta. If you have someone in the family who is not fond of cornmeal, just tell them to add lots of sauce, cottage cheese, and yogurt. Then you can't taste the polenta!

The combination of tomato sauce with the cottage cheese and yogurt mixes the Italian with the Eastern European style for serving cornmeal, where it is known as *mamaliga*. Actually sour cream is traditional, but the tang of yogurt is even better and, of course, less fattening.

STAPLES

salt
pepper
olive oil
onion

garlic
sesame oil
red wine vinegar

SHOPPING LIST

1 cup yellow cornmeal

12 ounces cottage cheese

½ pint plain yogurt

¼ pound mushrooms
16-ounce can tomato sauce

1 large or 2 small cucumbers

1 large red bell pepper
bunch scallions
(oranges)

GAME PLAN:

Bring water to boil for polenta.

Prepare polenta and add to water; cook.

Chop onion and press garlic for sauce; cook in hot oil.

Slice mushrooms and add to oil.

Peel and slice cucumbers; seed and slice red pepper; chop scallions.

Cook vegetables in sesame oil.

Add tomato sauce to onion and garlic.

Add vinegar to vegetables and season.

Polenta with cottage cheese and tomato sauce   3 SERVINGS

1 cup yellow cornmeal
1 cup cold water
Salt to taste
12 ounces cottage cheese

1 cup plain yogurt
Tomato-Mushroom Sauce (see recipe)

Bring 3 cups hot water to boil in covered pot. Mix cornmeal with cold water. Stir into boiling water until smooth; reduce heat. Cover and cook very slowly over very low heat until mixture is very thick. Stir occasionally. It will take about 15 minutes. Season with salt.

Spoon cornmeal onto plates. Pass cottage cheese, yogurt, and tomato-mushroom sauce separately.

Tomato-mushroom sauce   3 SERVINGS

1 **large onion**
1 **large clove garlic**
2 **tablespoons olive oil**
¼ **pound mushrooms**

16-**ounce can tomato sauce**
Salt to taste

Chop onion coarsely. Put garlic through press. Heat oil in skillet. Sauté onion and garlic until mushrooms are ready to add. Rinse mushrooms and trim off ends of stems. Slice mushrooms into skillet and cook until onion is soft. Add tomato sauce and cook over medium heat until rest of dinner is ready, just a few minutes.

Red, white, and green vegetables   3 SERVINGS

1 **large or 2 small cucumbers**
1 **large red bell pepper**
1 **bunch scallions**
2 **tablespoons sesame oil**

4 **teaspoons red wine vinegar**
Salt and freshly ground black pepper to taste

Peel cucumbers if waxed and slice thinly. Seed pepper and slice into strips. Trim scallions; wash and cut green part into 1-inch pieces. Heat oil in skillet. Add vegetables and cook, stirring occasionally, until cucumbers are wilted. Stir in vinegar and season with salt and pepper.

COASTAL MENU WITHOUT MEAT FOR THREE

Sunburst potatoes, vegetables, and cheese

Sourdough rolls and butter

Sherbet or ice cream

THIS is a variation of a dish I had on the Pacific Coast Highway near Santa Barbara in a counter-culture restaurant: Baked potatoes, lots of butter, and miso were used. Try as I would I couldn't get potatoes, no matter the size, to bake in 30 minutes, even when I cut them in half and put a skewer through them.

I tried serving this with another vegetable dish, but even my 6-foot-2-inch son said he couldn't eat more than the potato dish with some bread.

You can serve other kinds of bread, but the tang of the sourdough, which is available in heat-and-serve form all over my East Coast city, is a perfect foil for the vegetables.

STAPLES

salt   butter

pepper

SHOPPING LIST

12 (1¼ pounds) small
new potatoes
1 medium head
cauliflower
6 carrots
2½ cups (about 8
ounces) coarsely
grated cheese,
such as Cheddar,
Muenster, or
Monterey Jack

1 pint plain yogurt
sourdough rolls or
bread
(ice cream or
sherbet)

GAME PLAN:

Scrub potatoes and
cook.

Break cauliflower into
flowerettes.

Scrape carrots and slice
thinly on diagonal.

Steam cauliflower and
carrots.

Grate cheese.

Measure out yogurt.

Warm rolls.

Serve potatoes with
yogurt, vegetables, and
cheese.

Sunburst potatoes, vegetables, and cheese

3 SERVINGS

12 (1¼ pounds) small new potatoes

1 medium head cauliflower

6 carrots

2½ cups coarsely grated cheese, such as Cheddar, Muenster, or Monterey Jack

1½ cups plain yogurt
Salt and freshly ground black pepper to taste

Scrub potatoes; place in pot with water to cover. Cover and boil, about 20 minutes, until tender but not mushy. Break cauliflower into small flowerettes. Scrape carrots and slice thinly on the diagonal. Bring water to boil in steamer. Steam carrots and cauliflower about 15 minutes. Salt, if desired.

Grate cheese. Measure out yogurt. To serve, cut open the potatoes and place in deep, individual serving dishes. Top the potatoes with some yogurt, then some vegetables, then some cheese. Serve with the remaining cheese and yogurt and salt and pepper.

MEATLESS MENU FOR TWO

Zucchini frittata

Pita

Spinach salad with golden door dressing

Blueberries and strawberries or grapefruit and banana

A frequent complaint from cooks for two is that there are too many loose ends—leftovers—because you can't buy things in small quantities. This meal makes an effort to use one of the ingredients in two different recipes. It may sound repetitious but the way the ingredient, spinach, is used, it tastes completely different each time. Between the ½ pound spinach in the frittata and the cup, more or less, in the salad, all of the 10-ounce bag can be used at one meal.

There will still be loose ends—2 egg yolks. Either freeze them and use for hollandaise some other time or cook them and crumble for garnish on a salad.

The leftover onion can be used to season almost anything you cook the next night or three nights later.

Don't worry about extra cheese. It has a long shelf life.

STAPLES

garlic

salad and olive oil

thyme

rosemary

salt

pepper

apple cider vinegar

basil

Dijon mustard

eggs

SHOPPING LIST

1¼ pounds zucchini

1 large shallot

2 tablespoons grated Parmesan cheese

2 ounces Monterey Jack cheese

10-ounce package fresh spinach or 1 pound fresh loose spinach

2 large pitas

1 small red bell pepper

1 small red onion (optional)

(blueberries and strawberries or grapefruit and banana)

GAME PLAN:

Scrub and grate zucchini.

Prepare garlic, shallot, and spinach.

Sauté garlic and shallot.

Grate Parmesan and Monterey Jack cheeses.

Prepare fresh herbs, if used.

Combine drained zucchini with spinach, thyme, basil, rosemary, salt and pepper; cook.

Combine Parmesan with beaten whole eggs and whites.

Seed and cut red pepper; slice onion, if used.

Add egg mixture to zucchini and cook.

Make salad dressing.

Heat pitas.

Top frittata with Monterey Jack cheese.

Arrange salad plates and dress salads.

Zucchini frittata   2 SERVINGS

1¼ pounds zucchini
1 large clove garlic
1 large shallot
2 teaspoons salad oil
½ pound fresh spinach from bag or 12 ounces loose fresh spinach
1 teaspoon dried basil or 1 tablespoon minced fresh
1 teaspoon dried thyme or 2 teaspoons minced fresh

1 teaspoon dried rosemary or 2 teaspoons minced fresh
Salt and freshly ground black pepper to taste
2 tablespoons grated Parmesan cheese
2 ounces Monterey Jack cheese
3 eggs
2 egg whites

Scrub and grate zucchini coarsely into a bowl. Mince garlic and shallot and sauté in oil until soft. Wash spinach and remove tough stems. Shake to dry. Chop fresh herbs, if used. Drain off excess moisture from zucchini. Add with spinach, thyme, basil, rosemary, and salt and pepper to garlic mixture and cook until softened and liquid is absorbed.

Grate Parmesan and Monterey Jack cheeses. In separate bowl beat whole eggs with egg whites. Add Parmesan. Pour over zucchini mixture and cook until golden on the bottom. Turn frittata with spatula. Sprinkle Monterey Jack cheese over frittata and allow to melt or run under broiler, if desired.

Serve pieces of frittata stuffed into pita, if desired.

Spinach salad with golden door dressing

2 SERVINGS

1 small clove garlic
2 tablespoons apple cider vinegar
2 tablespoons olive oil
1 teaspoon Dijon mustard
Salt and freshly ground black pepper to taste

1 small red bell pepper or ½ of 1 large one
1 small slice red onion (optional)
1 or 2 cups raw spinach

Put garlic through press or mince. Combine with vinegar, oil, mustard, and salt and pepper. Shake well or whisk.

Seed and cut red bell pepper into julienne strips. Slice onion and separate into rings. Wash spinach and remove tough stems. Drain well. Divide spinach between 2 plates. Top with pepper and onion rings. Whisk dressing onto salads.

SAN DIEGO VEGETARIAN MENU FOR TWO

Deborah's huevos rancheros

Boston or bibb lettuce with buttermilk dressing

Crusty dark bread and butter

Fruit and ice cream

THIS is the perfect meal after a weekend of too much indulgence. It's light, and for the serious dieter fine without the bread, or at least without the butter. If you have dessert, not counted in the 30 minutes, though it could be in this meal it's so quick to prepare, the dieter can also do without the ice cream.

Deborah Szekely, owner of the Golden Door in Escondido, California, is busier than most working women. She prefers to entertain with dishes she can prepare in a matter of minutes. This is a favorite of hers for Sunday brunch. I think it works splendidly for Monday night supper, too.

STAPLES

salad oil	pepper
onion	eggs
basil	garlic
oregano	dill
salt	butter

SHOPPING LIST

- 1 small red or green bell pepper
- 16-ounce can peeled tomatoes
- ¼ pound Muenster cheese
- ¼ cup buttermilk
- ¼ cup cottage cheese
- ¼ pound Boston or Bibb
- dark bread
- (fruit, ice cream)

GAME PLAN:

Chop onions, pepper. Heat oil. Sauté onion and pepper in oil.

Cube cheese.

Chop garlic and dill.

Blend buttermilk, cottage cheese, onion, garlic, dill, and salt in blender.

Arrange greens on salad plates.

Add tomatoes, basil, oregano, and salt and pepper to skillet.

Spoon dressing over salads and refrigerate.

Take butter out to soften.

Make wells in tomato mixture and drop eggs into wells.

Top with cheese; cover and cook until done.

Toast bread.

Deborah's huevos rancheros

2 SERVINGS

1 large onion
1 small red or green bell pepper
1 tablespoon salad oil
1 cup canned peeled tomatoes
¼ teaspoon dried basil or 1 scant teaspoon of chopped fresh
¼ teaspoon dried oregano leaves or 1 scant teaspoon of chopped fresh

Salt and freshly ground black pepper to taste
4 eggs
4 1-inch squares Muenster cheese, ¼ inch thick

Coarsely chop onion. Seed and chop pepper. Finely chop 1 teaspoon of the onion and set aside for salad dressing. Heat oil in skillet large enough to hold eggs. Sauté onion and pepper in oil about 5 minutes. Drain and crush tomatoes with fingers before adding to skillet with basil, oregano, and salt and pepper. Cover; cook over low heat 10 minutes. Make 4 wells in tomato mixture and break 1 egg into each. Cut cheese into cubes. Top each egg with some of the cheese. Cover skillet and cook about 10 minutes, or until eggs are done to taste.

Boston or bibb lettuce with buttermilk dressing 2 SERVINGS

1 teaspoon chopped fresh dill or ¼ teaspoon dried
¼ cup buttermilk*
¼ cup regular or low fat cottage cheese
1 teaspoon finely chopped onion (see Deborah's Huevos Rancheros)
⅛ teaspoon minced garlic
Salt to taste
¼ pound Boston or Bibb lettuce

Chop fresh dill.

Combine buttermilk, cottage cheese, onion, garlic, and dill in blender and blend. Season with salt. Arrange lettuce on 2 salad plates and dress. Refrigerate until serving time.

---

*Unless you drink buttermilk, it's not worth it to buy a quart (the only size we have available in Washington) in order to use just ¼ cup. Freeze a quart of buttermilk in small amounts to use as needed. If the quantities frozen are small enough they will defrost quickly, especially when blended.

MEATLESS MENU FOR THREE OR FOUR

Macaroni and cheese "nouvelle"

Cucumbers in orange sauce

Stewed tomatoes

Apples or strawberries with honey

WHAT makes the macaroni and cheese nouvelle? It's less fattening than the traditional cheese sauce that is usually made with flour. It really isn't necessary to get a good consistency to the sauce. The paprika gives it the color you might expect to find in a package of macaroni and cheese, if that's important to you.

The simple flavors of the macaroni dish are well complemented by the spicy seasoning of the tomatoes and the tanginess of the orange-flavored cucumbers.

STAPLES

butter	pepper
onions	paprika
garlic	curry powder
milk	cloves
salt	(honey)

SHOPPING LIST

8-ounce package small elbow macaroni

2 cups (7 to 8 ounces) grated Cheddar or other cheese

2 large cucumbers or 6 to 8 small pickling cucumbers

1 orange

½ cup orange juice

28-ounce can tomatoes

(apples or strawberries)

GAME PLAN:

Bring water to boil in pot for macaroni.

Prepare onion, garlic, and cheese.

Cook macaroni.

Chop onion and combine with tomatoes, curry powder, and cloves; cook.

Prepare cucumbers and cook.

Cook onion and garlic.

Grate orange rind and add with juice and salt and pepper to cucumbers.

Drain macaroni.

Add macaroni, milk, cheese, and salt and pepper to onion and garlic mixture.

Macaroni and cheese "nouvelle"

3 or 4 SERVINGS

1 8-ounce package small elbow macaroni
1 small onion
1 clove garlic
2 tablespoons butter
2 cups grated white Cheddar cheese, or other cheese

1 cup milk
Salt and freshly ground black pepper to taste
Paprika

Bring 3 quarts hot water to boil in covered pot. When water is boiling, add macaroni and stir.

Chop onion and mince garlic or put through press. Grate cheese.

When macaroni is cooked, drain and return pot to stove. Melt butter; stir in onion and garlic and cook until onion is soft. Add macaroni, milk, cheese, and salt and pepper. Cook quickly until mixture begins to boil and cheese melts. Serve sprinkled with paprika.

Cucumbers in orange sauce

3 or 4 SERVINGS

2 large cucumbers or 6 to 8 small pickling cucumbers*
2 tablespoons butter

½ cup orange juice
Grated rind of 1 orange
Salt and freshly ground black pepper to taste

Peel and cut cucumbers in half lengthwise. Slice in about ¼-inch-thick slices. Melt butter in saucepan; add cucum-

---

*If you can get the little pickling cucumbers, they are crisper and usually aren't waxed.

bers and sauté about 3 or 4 minutes. Grate orange rind. Add orange juice, rind, and salt and pepper. Cook briskly so orange juice reduces and thickens slightly. Serve.

Stewed tomatoes 3 or 4 SERVINGS

1 medium onion	¼ teaspoon curry powder
1 28-ounce can tomatoes	⅛ teaspoon cloves

Chop onion. Combine all ingredients in saucepan and cook briskly to reduce liquid. Reduce heat and simmer until serving time.

MENU WITHOUT MEAT FOR THREE

Low-calorie cheese soufflés

Mexican zucchini

Warm pitas

Broiled grapefruit halves with honey

If a 30-minute meal isn't the perfect time to make a soufflé, there is no perfect time. It is definitely a last-minute dish, but if baked in a standard-sized soufflé dish it would take too long. This soufflé is low calorie and is not made in the classic way, but it still puffs up nicely and that's what a soufflé is all about. The secret is baking the soufflé in small baking dishes so that they will be done in 15 minutes.

To round out the meal, Mexican zucchini is filling, and pitas, which make nice containers for the zucchini dish if you like, all add up to more than enough for dinner.

STAPLES

eggs	oil
instant dry milk powder	onion
tarragon	garlic
dill	oregano
salt	(honey)
pepper	

SHOPPING LIST

2¼ cups (about 7½ ounces) sharp cheese, such as Cheddar, Jalapeño spiced

3 tablespoons parsley

1 pound zucchini

12-ounce can corn niblets

16-ounce can tomatoes

6 small whole-wheat pitas

(grapefruits)

GAME PLAN:

Turn oven to 425.

Separate eggs; mix yolks with cheese, dry milk, herbs, and seasonings.

Chop onion and press garlic for zucchini.

Beat whites.

Sauté onion and garlic in oil.

Fold whites into cheese mixture and spoon into soufflé dishes; bake.

Prepare zucchini and add with tomatoes, oregano, and salt and pepper to onions.

Heat pitas.

Just before serving, add corn to zucchini and heat through.

Low-calorie cheese soufflés

6 eggs

2¼ cups coarsely grated sharp cheese, such as Cheddar, Jalapeño spiced

¼ cup instant dry milk powder

1 tablespoon fresh dill or 1½ teaspoons dried dillweed

3 tablespoons chopped fresh parsley

Dash tarragon

Salt and freshly ground black pepper to taste

Turn oven to 425 degrees.

Separate eggs. The best way to do this is to separate the yolk from the white over a small container, removing the white from the small container to the mixing bowl after each egg is cracked. That way if you should be unlucky and some yolk gets into the white it will not spoil all the whites, just the one being separated.

Lightly beat the yolks. Grate the cheese coarsely. Add to the yolks with the powdered milk. Chop the parsley and fresh dill if you are using it. Add parsley, dill, tarragon, and salt and pepper to the yolks.

Have ready two ungreased 2-cup (approximately) soufflé dishes. Beat whites with a pinch of salt until they are stiff. Fold whites into yolk mixture and spoon into soufflé dishes. Bake in preheated 425 degree oven 15 minutes, until tops begin to brown. You will have a French-style soufflé, soft in the middle.

Mexican zucchini   3 SERVINGS

1 small onion
1 medium clove garlic
2 tablespoons oil
1 pound zucchini
1 16-ounce can tomatoes

½ teaspoon oregano
Salt and freshly ground black pepper to taste
1 12-ounce can corn niblets

Chop onion. Put garlic through press. Heat oil in skillet. Sauté onion and garlic until onion is translucent. Meanwhile, scrub and trim zucchini. Slice zucchini thinly and add to onion. Squeeze tomatoes through fingers to break up and add to zucchini. Don't add the juice from the can. Season with oregano and salt and pepper. Cover and simmer until zucchini is crisp-tender, about 10 minutes. Just before zucchini is cooked, add corn and stir. Heat through.

CALIFORNIA MENU
FOR FOUR

California picadillo

Avocado salad

Tortillas

*Cream cheese and guava paste with
    crackers or fruit*

THE original recipe for picadillo calls for long simmering and still longer baking. It has been streamlined with no ill effects as you will see. The recipe really serves more than enough for four people, but it freezes very well and you can save the leftovers for two for some night when you don't want to do any cooking at all.

The trick to this meal is to find two RIPE avocados the same day you want to use them. If you are thinking that you might want to serve this meal one day during the week, then when you are in the store for another meal you could buy the not-so-ripe avocados (which most of them are) and keep them in the kitchen for three or four days.

Serve the picadillo either over tortillas or serve the tortillas with the avocado salad. Typically picadillo is served topped with shredded lettuce.

STAPLES

onions	lemon
vinegar	chile powder
cinnamon	salt
cloves	pepper
ground cumin	

SHOPPING LIST

1 pound ground beef

16-ounce can tomatoes

½ cup raisins

2 4-ounce cans chopped green chiles

12-ounce can whole kernel corn

4-ounce can chopped black olives

2 ounces slivered or sliced almonds

4 ounces grated Cheddar cheese

2 avocados

1 large tomato

4 to 8 corn tortillas

(3 ounces cream cheese, can guava paste, crackers or fruit)

dried or fresh cilantro (Chinese parsley)

GAME PLAN:

Turn oven to 500.

Brown beef; chop onion and add to beef.

Prepare avocados; sprinkle with lemon juice.

Pour fat off beef; add tomatoes, vinegar, cinnamon, cloves, cumin, chile powder, raisins, chiles, corn, and olives.

Warm tortillas.

Grate cheese; add with almonds to beef.

Chop tomato, onion, cilantro; add to avocado with salt and pepper.

California picadillo

4 to 6 SERVINGS

1 pound ground beef
1 large onion
1 16-ounce can tomatoes
2 tablespoons vinegar
1 teaspoon cinnamon
Pinch ground cloves
¼ teaspoon ground cumin
1 teaspoon pure chile powder*
½ cup raisins

1 4-ounce can chopped green chiles, drained
1 12-ounce can whole kernel corn
1 4-ounce can chopped black olives
½ cup slivered or sliced almonds
1 cup grated Cheddar cheese

Brown beef. Coarsely chop onion and add. Sauté until onion begins to soften. Pour off excess fat. Add tomatoes and liquid, breaking up tomatoes with fingers, plus vinegar, cinnamon, cloves, cumin, chile powder, raisins, green chiles, corn, and olives. Heat to boiling; reduce heat and simmer 10 minutes. Grate cheese. Stir in almonds and sprinkle with cheese; cover and cook 10 minutes.

Avocado salad

4 SERVINGS

Juice of 1 lemon
2 large ripe avocados
1 large tomato
1 medium onion
¾ of 4-ounce can chopped green chiles

1 teaspoon dried cilantro or 1 tablespoon chopped fresh cilantro (Chinese parsley)
Salt and freshly ground black pepper to taste

*If pure chile powder is not available, you can use chili powder, the mixture of several spices.

Cut the avocados in half; remove pits and peel. Coarsely mash flesh. Sprinkle lemon juice over mashed avocados. Coarsely chop tomato. Chop onion medium-fine. Chop fresh cilantro. Combine all the ingredients and serve with tortillas.

Tortillas

1 or 2 PER SERVING

4 to 8 corn tortillas

Turn oven or toaster oven to 500 degrees.

Wrap tortillas in aluminum foil and heat in oven or toaster oven about 10 minutes.

A "LITTLE" STEAK
DINNER FOR TWO

Beef teriyaki

Green beans, tomato, and savory

Boiled new potatoes

Peaches or nectarines

FOR some people this dinner may have not enough meat and too many vegetables. You can add more meat and still use the same amount of marinade. You can also reduce the number of potatoes by two and reduce the amount of green beans to a half pound, but keep the rest of the recipe for the beans in the same proportion.

If you don't slice the steak thin, it will be tough. You could use tougher cuts of meat if you planned this dinner the night before and marinated the meat overnight, but then it wouldn't be a true 30-minute from-start-to-finish meal.

STAPLES

ginger	onion
garlic	savory
sugar	salt
soy sauce	pepper
olive oil	

SHOPPING LIST

10- or 12-ounce bone-in sirloin steak or 8 ounces boneless steak

¾ pound green beans

1 large tomato

6 to 8 (10 to 12 ounces) small new potatoes

(peaches or nectarines)

GAME PLAN:

Combine ginger, garlic, sugar, soy, and water. Thinly slice steak and marinate.

Cook potatoes.

Prepare green beans; cook.

Turn on broiler.

Chop onion and press garlic for beans.

Cut tomatoes into chunks.

Broil meat and baste.

Pour water off beans. Add oil and onion, garlic, savory, and tomato to skillet; cook uncovered.

Heat remaining marinade.

Beef teriyaki   2 SERVINGS

---

1 teaspoon chopped ginger

1 small clove garlic

1 teaspoon sugar

3 tablespoons soy sauce

½ cup water

10- to 12-ounce bone-in sirloin steak or 8 ounces boneless sirloin

Chop ginger. Put garlic through press. Combine ginger, garlic, sugar, soy sauce, and water in large bowl. Thinly slice steak across the grain, place pieces in marinade, and turn to coat.

Ten to 15 minutes before serving time, heat broiler. Place steak pieces in shallow broiler pan covered with foil, if desired, to save washing and broil 5 to 7 minutes on each side, turning and basting once. Heat remaining marinade and serve with teriyaki.

Green beans, tomato, and savory

2 SERVINGS

¾ pound green beans
1 medium onion
1 small clove garlic
1 large tomato

1 tablespoon olive oil
½ teaspoon savory
Salt and freshly ground black pepper to taste

Trim and wash beans. Place enough water in large skillet to cover bottom of skillet. Add beans. Cover, bring to simmer, and simmer 5 minutes. Meanwhile, chop onion and put garlic through press. Cut tomato into large chunks. Drain water from skillet; return to heat and dry out before adding oil, onion, garlic, savory, tomato, salt and pepper to taste, and green beans. Cook, uncovered, until all vegetables are tender.

Boiled new potatoes

2 SERVINGS

6 to 8 (about 10 to 12 ounces) small new potatoes

Scrub potatoes, but do not peel them. Cook in water to cover in covered pot until tender, about 15 to 20 minutes. Drain. Serve whole, unpeeled.

Serve with some of the marinade, if desired.

HUNGARIAN MENU
FOR FOUR

Beef paprika "stew"

Broad egg noodles

Hungarian cucumber salad

Grapes with camembert

WELL, of course, the Hungarians don't make stews with ground beef, but you can get the Hungarian flavor with the combination of seasonings even with ground beef, and get it quickly. Don't forget the sweet Hungarian paprika. It's essential for the authentic Hungarian flavor. Marinating cucumbers in vinegar and water with a little sugar is also traditionally Hungarian. Please don't make any snide comments about the sugar. It adds flavor but not many calories since little of it is consumed.

The starch to have with a Hungarian stew is the wonderful galuska—dumplings—but you couldn't even get them done if you did nothing else for the 30 minutes, so that's one pleasure you will have to forgo for this meal. Substitute a broad egg noodle. In my part of the country, there is a Pennsylvania Dutch egg noodle that looks rather like small pieces of lasagna. It does nicely, but any broad egg noodle will work to sop up the sauce.

STAPLES

onions

cooking oil

beef bouillon or stock

sweet Hungarian
paprika

caraway seeds

marjoram

white vinegar

sugar

salt

pepper

SHOPPING LIST

1½ pounds ground
beef

2 small green or red
bell peppers

14- to 16-ounce
can peeled
tomatoes

2 large cucumbers

8 ounces extra broad
egg noodles

(grapes,
Camembert)

GAME PLAN:

Prepare onions and
peppers.

Cook onions and pep-
pers in hot oil.

Brown beef.

Bring water to boil for
noodles.

Add stock, seasonings,
and tomatoes to beef.

Make dressing for
cucumbers.

Boil noodles.

Slice cucumbers and
add to dressing.

Drain noodles.

Beef paprika "stew" 4 SERVINGS

2 medium onions
2 small red or green bell peppers
2 tablespoons cooking oil
1½ pounds ground beef
½ cup beef stock or bouillon
2 teaspoons sweet Hungarian paprika

½ teaspoon caraway seeds
½ teaspoon dried marjoram
4 to 6 small peeled canned tomatoes
Salt and freshly ground black pepper to taste

Chop onions. Seed and slice peppers into ¼-inch strips. Heat oil in large skillet. Add onions and peppers and cook over medium-high heat until onions are soft. Add beef, raise heat, and brown, stirring. Drain off excess fat. When beef has browned, add bouillon, paprika, caraway seeds, and marjoram. Add tomatoes, squeezing them in your hand to break them up. Season with salt and pepper and cook until serving time.

Broad egg noodles 4 SERVINGS

8 ounces (about 4 cups) extra wide egg noodles

Salt

Bring 3 quarts hot water to boil in large covered pot. Add salt and noodles and stir. Cook, uncovered, about 15 minutes, until noodles are al dente. Drain.

Hungarian cucumber salad

4 SERVINGS

½ cup white vinegar
½ cup water
2 to 3 teaspoons sugar

Salt and freshly ground
black pepper to taste
2 large cucumbers

Combine all ingredients but cucumbers. Peel cucumbers if waxed. Slice cucumbers very thin, stir into dressing, and refrigerate, stirring occasionally, until serving time.

TEX-MEX DINNER FOR THREE

Chili

Beans with onion

Chicory with vinaigrette

Apples with camembert

IF I were a member, the Chili Appreciation Society would drum me out for this recipe, but that doesn't stop it from being a pretty good tasting chili even if I took too many shortcuts.

Note that chili, as in what was reputedly first served in Texas jails, has an "i" on the end, while the chile, as in pepper, ends in "e." That's the best way to keep them straight.

An elegant vinaigrette is hardly the traditional accompaniment to chili; it's perfect, though, because it can hold its own.

STAPLES

onions	salt
garlic	pepper
oregano	olive oil
mild and hot chile powder	capers
ground cumin	

SHOPPING LIST

1 pound ground beef	1 teaspoon green or black olives
2 8-ounce cans tomato sauce	1 teaspoon parsley
15-ounce can beans, such as pinto, kidney, Great Northern, navy	1 teaspoon pickles
	½ pound chicory (apples, Camembert)
3 tablespoons apple cider vinegar	

GAME PLAN:

Brown beef.

Prepare onion and garlic; add to beef with seasonings.

Chop onion for beans; cook with beans.

Add tomato sauce to chili.

Prepare salad dressing.

Prepare greens.

Dress salad.

Chili   3 SERVINGS

---

1 pound ground beef	1¾ teaspoons ground cumin
1 large onion	Salt and freshly ground black pepper to taste
1 large clove garlic	
1 teaspoon oregano	2 8-ounce cans tomato sauce
1½ teaspoons mild chile powder*	
¼ teaspoon hot chile powder*	

---

*Mild chile powder resembles paprika; hot chile powder resembles cayenne. If you can't find the authentic Mexican types, substitute paprika and cayenne.

Brown beef in large skillet, stirring to break up pieces. Drain off fat. Chop onion and put garlic through press. Stir onion and garlic into skillet with oregano, mild and hot chile powders, cumin, and pepper. Stir and simmer a minute or two. Add tomato sauce; stir, reduce heat, and simmer gently about 15 minutes. Season with salt, if desired.

Serve with Beans with Onion on the side.

Beans with onion   3 SERVINGS

15-ounce can pinto or kidney beans	1 small onion

Drain most of the liquid from beans. Chop onion medium-fine. Add to beans in pot and simmer until chili is done. Serve with chili.

Many canned beans contain chemicals to aid in the retention of color. Root around on the bean shelf. You should be able to find some kind of beans without the additive EDTA. It may not be pinto or kidney beans, but that's okay. With the onion and the texture, you will get the same effect.

Chicory with vinaigrette   3 SERVINGS

½ pound chicory	1 teaspoon chopped fresh parsley
5 tablespoons olive oil	
3 tablespoons apple cider vinegar	1 teaspoon chopped capers
1 teaspoon chopped green or black olives*	1 teaspoon chopped sour pickle

*Do not use those packed in salt or oil.

Wash the lettuce and drain well. Dry on paper towels.

Beat the oil with the vinegar. Chop the olives, parsley, capers, and pickle into the dressing. Arrange lettuce on individual plates; spoon well-blended dressing over leaves.

ITALIAN MENU FOR FOUR

Spaghetti squash with meat sauce

Chunky tomatoes and cucumbers

Breadsticks

Berries or pears

MEAT sauce is a nostalgia food for me. As a child we had it for dinner once a week and I got the leftovers, complete with cold spaghetti, for breakfast the next morning. I loved it. Still do. When my mother and I used to go on picnics in a park just outside my hometown of Waterbury, Connecticut, there would often be an Italian family simmering a meat sauce over the grill . . . and I had cold sandwiches!!! How I wanted some of that meat sauce!

Contrary to popular American belief, a sauce bolognese, of which this is a facsimile, is not simmered for hours and hours, so don't worry about how quickly this is cooked.

And unlike the old days most of us today are a little more concerned about our calories. Spaghetti squash, therefore, makes a wonderful substitute for pasta. It has the same texture but is low in calories.

STAPLES

onion	pepper
garlic	red or white wine
oregano	vinegar
basil	olive oil
salt	

SHOPPING LIST

1 pound ground beef	2 large tomatoes
28- or 29-ounce can tomato purée	2 large cucumbers
medium green bell pepper	2 tablespoons ~~parsley~~
3-pound spaghetti squash	12 to 16 breadsticks (berries or pears)
1 cup (about 4½ to 5 ounces) Parmesan cheese	

GAME PLAN:

Cook squash.

Brown meat.

Chop onion; press garlic, prepare green pepper; add to beef.

Make salad dressing.

Add tomato purée, oregano, basil, salt, and pepper to beef; cook over low heat.

Prepare cucumbers and tomatoes; mix with salad dressing.

Coarsely grate Parmesan.

Drain squash; cover with sauce.

Spaghetti squash   4 SERVINGS

1 3-pound spaghetti
squash
Salt

Water

Cut squash into quarters. Remove seeds. Place in pot with enough water to come up just below cut surfaces. Cover and cook over medium-high heat until squash is tender, about 20 minutes. Season with salt, if desired. Serve topped with Meat Sauce.

Meat sauce   4 SERVINGS

1 pound ground
beef
1 large onion
1 large clove garlic
1 medium green bell
pepper
1 (28- or 29-ounce) can
tomato purée
1 teaspoon dried oregano

2 tablespoons chopped
fresh basil or 2
teaspoons dried
Salt and freshly ground
black pepper to taste
1 cup coarsely grated
Parmesan cheese

In large skillet brown beef in its own fat. While beef is cooking, chop onion coarsely and add to beef. Put garlic through press and add to skillet. Seed and cut up green pepper into medium chop and add. Cook until onion is soft and beef is brown. Pour off excess fat. Add tomato purée and pour a little water into can to remove residue; add to skillet. Chop fresh basil. Add seasonings; cover and cook over low heat, stirring occasionally, until serving time. Meanwhile grate cheese.

Serve sauce over spaghetti squash quarters and pass cheese separately.

Chunky tomatoes and cucumbers

4 SERVINGS

2 large cucumbers*
2 large tomatoes
2 tablespoons chopped fresh parsley
¼ cup olive oil

¼ cup red or white wine vinegar
1 teaspoon dried oregano
Salt and freshly ground black pepper to taste

Peel cucumbers if waxed. Cut into bite-sized chunks. Core tomatoes and cut into bite-sized chunks.

Chop parsley. Beat oil and vinegar together. Beat in oregano and mix in parsley and salt and pepper. Pour over tomatoes and cucumbers and refrigerate until serving time. Stir before serving.

---

*If you can find pickling cucumbers, they are even better, and much crunchier, and they usually aren't waxed. Use 6 to 8 pickling cucumbers.

CHINESE MENU FOR TWO

Chinese beef and noodles

Leaf lettuce with garlic-caraway dressing

Tangerines, nectarines or grapes

THE tang of the salad dressing in this menu is an excellent foil to play off against the gentle spiciness of the beef.

Originally the beef and noodle recipe was made with strips of steak. The following is not only more reasonable, it cooks more quickly.

STAPLES

soy sauce	lemon
dry sherry	caraway seeds
ginger	dry mustard
garlic	salt
olive oil	pepper

SHOPPING LIST

½ pound ground beef
3 ounces Chinese
vermicelli or 4
ounces Italian
vermicelli
5 to 7 ounces (½
package) frozen
peas
2 scallions
1½ tablespoons
buttermilk or plain
yogurt

2 tablespoons
parsley
¼ pound leaf lettuce
(tangerines,
nectarines, or
grapes)

GAME PLAN:

Prepare ginger and
garlic; combine with soy
and sherry and mix
with meat in skillet.

Bring water to boil in
pot for vermicelli.

Prepare salad dressing.

Cook vermicelli.

Wash and drain greens.

Cook meat; add peas.

Chop scallions.

Drain vermicelli; add to
meat.

Dress greens.

Sprinkle beef and ver-
micelli with scallions.

Chinese beef and noodles   2 SERVINGS

½ teaspoon minced fresh
  ginger
1 large clove garlic
4 teaspoons light soy
  sauce
4 teaspoons dry sherry

½ pound ground beef
½ to ¾ package frozen
  peas
2 large scallions

Mince the ginger; put the garlic through a press.

Combine soy sauce, sherry, ginger, and garlic in skillet large enough to hold meat. Stir in the meat and allow to sit while preparing other parts of the meal.

Sauté the meat mixture until cooked through. About 2 minutes before serving, stir in the peas and cook until heated through. Chop scallions.

Stir drained vermicelli into meat mixture. To serve, sprinkle with scallions.

Vermicelli   2 SERVINGS

---

3 ounces Chinese
  vermicelli or 4 ounces
  Italian vermicelli

If using Chinese vermicelli, bring hot water to boil in kettle. Pour over vermicelli and allow to soak about 15 minutes. Drain.

If using Italian vermicelli, bring 3 quarts hot water to boil in covered pot. Salt, if desired. Add vermicelli and cook about 3 minutes, until al dente. Drain.

Leaf lettuce with garlic-caraway dressing

2 SERVINGS

1 small clove garlic

¾ teaspoon fresh lemon juice

2 tablespoons chopped fresh parsley

2 tablespoons olive oil

1½ tablespoons buttermilk or plain yogurt

½ teaspoon caraway seeds

⅛ teaspoon (or less) dry mustard

Salt and freshly ground black pepper to taste

¼ pound leaf lettuce

Put garlic through press into bowl. Add lemon juice. Chop parsley and add. Combine all ingredients but greens and whisk with wire whisk.

Wash and drain salad greens. Place greens on 2 salad plates and dress.

TUESDAY NIGHT
SPECIAL FOR THREE

Individual meat loaves

Steamed cauliflower

Cheese bread

*Broiled grapefruit sprinkled with brown
sugar*

TUESDAY night special means nothing to anyone
who wasn't always served meat loaf on Tuesday
night as I was. Some of the versions my mother
made were wonderful: some, like the one with the
hard-cooked egg in the center, were awful. I'm not
sure why, but to this day I don't like finding slices
of hard-cooked egg in my meat loaf. Otherwise I
love it hot, at room temperature, or cold. As a kid,
the Tuesday night meat loaf became Wednesday
lunch with white bread and catsup. Even though I
don't eat white bread anymore, there are two ways
I still like it: holding a slab of meat loaf or covered
with tuna salad.

To make meat loaf fit into a 30-minute meal, it
had to be transformed into individual servings that
would bake quickly. You can do that with any kind
of loaf—turkey, chicken, ham.

The cauliflower was also part of the Tuesday
night special, but not the part I liked as a child.

And the cheese bread is a modern innovation,
which adds zest to the simple meal.

STAPLES

onion	salt
oregano	pepper
basil	mayonnaise
~~garlic~~	~~(brown sugar)~~

SHOPPING LIST

1 pound ground beef
8-ounce can tomato sauce
1 medium head cauliflower
1 tablespoon parsley (optional)
12 ounces French bread or baguette

6 tablespoons plain yogurt
½ cup (2 to 2½ ounces) sharp cheese, (such as Cheddar, Parmesan)
(grapefruits)

GAME PLAN:

Turn oven to 450.

Prepare onion and garlic; mix with remaining meat-loaf ingredients; fill muffin cups and bake.

Bring water to boil in steamer for cauliflower.

Prepare cauliflower.

Grate cheese; mix with yogurt and mayonnaise; spread on bread.

Steam cauliflower.

Toast bread.

Individual meat loaves   3 or 4 SERVINGS

---

1 medium to large onion
1 clove garlic
1 pound ground
  beef
¾ teaspoon oregano

1 teaspoon basil
Salt and freshly ground
  black pepper to taste
1 8-ounce can tomato
  sauce

Turn oven to 450 degrees.

Chop onion medium-fine. Put garlic through press. Mix all ingredients together. (It's fastest with your hands.)

Fill approximately 16 medium muffin cups with mixture. Place in oven as soon as the cups are filled and bake about 20 minutes, until fat that has been rendered is bubbling and meat is cooked through. Drain off fat and serve. (Good cold, too, for brown-bag lunch.)

Steamed cauliflower   3 SERVINGS

---

1 medium head
  cauliflower
Salt

1 tablespoon chopped
  fresh parsley (optional)

Bring hot water to boil in steamer.

Wash and trim green leaves from cauliflower and break head into flowerettes, trying to keep them fairly uniform in size. Steam about 10 minutes, depending on size, until crisp-tender. Season with salt. Chop parsley. Serve sprinkled with parsley, if desired.

Cheese bread

3 SERVINGS of 4 ounces of bread per person

12 ounces French bread or baguette

½ cup coarsely grated firmly packed sharp cheese, such as Cheddar or Parmesan

6 tablespoons plain yogurt

6 tablespoons mayonnaise

Preheat oven to 450 degrees.

Slice bread or baguette in half lengthwise. Grate cheese. Mix yogurt, mayonnaise, and cheese together and spread over cut sides of bread. Toast in oven (can be done in the oven with the meat loaf) 10 minutes, until tops begin to brown and bubble.

STIR-FRY MENU FOR TWO

Stir-fried beef and tomatoes

Vermicelli

Oriental broccoli

Honeydew or frozen fruit

AT one time I made this recipe with flank steak, once considered an inexpensive meat. No longer. Skirt steak, if you can find it, and that's often the problem, is cheaper and more tender. One supermarket in which I shop also sells very thinly sliced top round, about ⅛ inch thick. That works well, too.

If it is not tomato season and you want to make this, use cherry tomatoes. They haven't learned how to gas them yet so they can't pick them green.

Vermicelli comes in different thicknesses in Oriental markets. The kind you want is thick enough to hold its shape without turning into a pasty mass when dissolved. You can also boil vermicelli a few minutes instead of soaking it. If you can't easily get Oriental vermicelli, substitute Italian vermicelli. Different but good.

STAPLES

soy sauce

dry sherry or apple juice

garlic

ginger

vegetable oil

egg

rice vinegar

onions

SHOPPING LIST

8 ounces skirt, flank, or very thin top round steak

3 medium tomatoes or ½ pint cherry tomatoes

3 stalks broccoli

3 ounces Chinese vermicelli or 4 ounces Italian vermicelli

(honeydew or frozen fruit)

GAME PLAN:

Slice meat; make marinade and add steak.

If using Chinese vermicelli, cover with boiling water.

Prepare and steam broccoli.

If using Italian vermicelli, bring hot water to boil.

Cut up onions, press garlic, and cook in hot oil.

Make dressing for broccoli.

If using Italian vermicelli, cook.

Cut up tomatoes.

Cook beef.

Dress broccoli.

Remove beef and add tomatoes and marinade; cook.

Return meat to skillet.

Drain vermicelli.

Stir-fried beef and tomatoes
2 SERVINGS

8 ounces skirt, flank, or thinly cut top round steak

1 tablespoon soy sauce

2½ tablespoons dry sherry or apple juice

1 teaspoon finely chopped ginger

2 medium onions

2 cloves garlic

1 tablespoon vegetable oil

3 medium tomatoes or ½ pint cherry tomatoes

Slice beef on the diagonal across the grain into ¼-inch-wide strips. Mix soy sauce and sherry. Chop ginger finely and add to soy/sherry mixture. Add beef and stir to coat well. Chop onions coarsely. Put garlic through press. Heat oil in skillet. Sauté onions and garlic over medium heat. When onions are soft but not brown, stir in meat, without marinade. Chop tomatoes. Cook meat until it loses its redness. Remove meat. (Don't worry if onions go with it.) Add tomatoes and marinade. Cook until tomatoes are soft. Stir in beef and cook until heated through.

Vermicelli
2 SERVINGS

3 ounces Chinese vermicelli or 4 ounces Italian vermicelli

Cover Chinese vermicelli with boiling water and allow to sit 15 minutes. Drain and serve as base for the beef and tomatoes.

If using Italian vermicelli, bring 3 quarts hot water to boil in large covered pot. Salt, if desired. Add vermicelli and cook, uncovered, until al dente, about 3 minutes. Drain.

Oriental broccoli   2 SERVINGS

3 stalks broccoli   1 tablespoon vegetable oil
1 egg yolk   ½ teaspoon soy sauce
1 tablespoon rice vinegar

Bring hot water to boil in steamer.

Trim broccoli of tough stems and cut top part of stems and flowers into individual strips. Steam broccoli until crisp-tender, about 7 minutes. Beat yolk in small bowl. Beat in vinegar. Beat in oil and soy sauce and whisk thoroughly until slightly thick and foamy. When broccoli is cooked, drain and run under cold water. Drain again. Pour dressing over thoroughly drained, cool broccoli.

MOCK CHILI MENU FOR TWO OR THREE

Chili and sausage
Romaine salad with garlic dressing
Spaghetti squash
Frozen yogurt

WELL of course it isn't real chili, what with ground beef instead of chili chop, with the beans right in with the beef, but it tastes very good, even if it hasn't been simmered for 3 hours. Using spaghetti squash instead of spaghetti (as in Cincinnati chili) makes for a somewhat less calorific meal.

Cutting up the squash is the only way to get it cooked in the prescribed 30 minutes. But it still has the consistency of spaghetti when you pull it off the skin with a fork.

STAPLES

onion
garlic
ground cumin
chili powder
paprika
salt

pepper
apple cider vineger
sesame or olive oil
Dijon or German-style mustard
butter (optional)

SHOPPING LIST

½ pound ground beef

½ pound spicy or hot sausage

   16-ouncè can tomatoes

2 16-ounce cans beans (any kind without preservatives)

4 to 6 ounces romaine lettuce

1 small spaghetti squash (2 or 3 pounds)

1 tablespoon parsley cheese (optional) (frozen yogurt)

GAME PLAN:

Prepare and cook squash.

Sauté beef and sausage.

Prepare onion and garlic.

Prepare romaine, garlic, and parsley.

Drain fat from meat; add onion and garlic.

Combine garlic, parsley, vinegar, oil, mustard, salt, and pepper.

Add spices, tomatoes, and beans to meat.

Dress salad.

Drain squash.

Chili and sausage

2 or 3 SERVINGS

½ pound ground beef

½ pound spicy or hot sausage

1 medium onion

1 clove garlic

1 teaspoon ground cumin

1 teaspoon chili powder

½ teaspoon paprika

   Salt and freshly ground black pepper to taste

1 16-ounce can tomatoes

2 16-ounce cans beans,* without preservatives

---

*Some canned beans are free of preservatives. Check the labels.

Sauté beef and sausage until ground meat browns. Coarsely chop onion. Put garlic through press. Drain off all excess fat and add onion and garlic. Cook until onion is soft. Stir in spices. Mix well. Add tomatoes and liquid, breaking tomatoes up with fingers, and beans and cook until mixture is hot and flavors have blended, 10 minutes or more.

Romaine salad with garlic dressing

2 or 3 SERVINGS

4 to 6 ounces romaine
1 small clove garlic
1 tablespoon minced fresh parsley
2 tablespoons apple cider vinegar
2 tablespoons sesame or olive oil

1 teaspoon Dijon or German-style mustard if available†
Salt and freshly ground black pepper to taste

Wash romaine. Drain. Put garlic through press. Mince parsley. Combine with the remaining ingredients and mix or beat thoroughly. To serve, pour over Romaine on individual salad plates.

Spaghetti squash

2 or 3 SERVINGS

1 small spaghetti squash (2 or 3 pounds)

Water

Cut squash into quarters. Remove seeds. Place in pot with enough water to come up to just below cut surfaces of the

†German-style mustard, or New Orleans mustard, has bits of mustard seeds in it. Either of the mustards is delicious.

squash. Cover and cook rapidly until squash is soft and tender, about 20 to 25 minutes.

Drain and serve with chili, some of which may be spooned over the squash.

If you prefer, the squash may be served either with a little butter, salt and pepper, or some grated cheese.

TWO DISH MENU FOR FOUR

Beef and bulgur

Braised fennel

Bananas with yogurt and brown sugar

BULGUR, known under various other spellings, is a very popular grain in the Middle East. It is getting more popular here, but not enough so that it is readily available in the supermarket "straight." In other words without spices in a box. Bulgur is a very reasonable grain, but not when it gets boxed in a fancy package and a few spices are added.

You ought to do your own seasoning of bulgur. You can treat it like rice in many ways or if you are familiar with buckwheat groats (kasha) you can season it the way you season them.

For the cheapest bulgur, which comes in fine and coarse cut, the fine is often called cracked wheat, make a trip to the natural food store when you have a chance and buy it by the pound. It keeps well.

There is more than enough protein in the beef and bulgur dish and plenty of bulk so you don't need much more to complete the meal. A simple vegetable is perfect.

Fennel is much admired in the Mediterranean. Slowly but surely it is making its way into the ordinary American supermarket.

Some people describe it as a large bunch of celery and its texture is similar, but it has a distinctly anise flavor.

While it isn't a matter for this menu, fennel is wonderful blanched, chilled, and served with a hearty oil and vinegar dressing.

STAPLES

onion	pepper
garlic	butter
dry sherry	chicken stock or broth
oregano	(brown sugar)
salt	

SHOPPING LIST

1 pound ground beef
8 medium-large mushrooms
¾ cup bulgur (cracked wheat)
4- or 5-ounce can chopped black olives
16-ounce can tomatoes

1 cup (about 4 ounces) Muenster or Monterey Jack cheese (optional)
2 tablespoons parsley (optional)
1½ pounds fennel
(4 bananas, yogurt)

GAME PLAN:

Cook beef.

Prepare onion, garlic, and mushrooms. Add to meat.

Add bulgur, olives, tomatoes, sherry, oregano, and salt and pepper.

Prepare fennel.

Cook fennel in butter and broth.

Grate cheese; chop parsley.

Cover bulgur with cheese and melt; sprinkle with parsley.

Beef and bulgur

4 SERVINGS

1 pound ground beef
1 large onion
1 large clove garlic
8 mushrooms
¾ cup bulgur (cracked wheat)
1 4- or 5-ounce can chopped black olives
1 16-ounce can tomatoes

½ cup dry sherry
1 teaspoon oregano
Salt and freshly ground black pepper to taste
1 cup grated Muenster or Monterey Jack cheese (optional)
2 tablespoons chopped fresh parsley (optional)

Cook beef in skillet in its own fat, stirring to break up. Meanwhile, chop onion coarsely, put garlic through press. Coarsely chop mushrooms. Drain off most of fat from meat, add onion, garlic, and mushrooms, and cook until onion begins to soften and meat has lost its pinkness. Add bulgur, olives, tomatoes with liquid, sherry, oregano, and salt and pepper. Cover and simmer over medium heat about 15 minutes, or until bulgur is soft. (If there is not enough liquid in canned tomatoes to keep mixture moist, add a little water.) Meanwhile grate cheese if you are using it, and chop the parsley. About 2 minutes before dish is done, add the cheese and sprinkle it on top. Cover and cook until cheese melts. Serve with parsley, if desired.

Braised fennel

4 SERVINGS

1½ pounds fennel
3 tablespoons butter
1 cup chicken broth or stock

Salt and freshly ground black pepper to taste

Wash fennel, remove leafy portions if they have been left on. Remove tough outer portion of stalk. Slice bulb crosswise so that you end up with pieces much like you would have if you had cut a stalk of celery crosswise.

If there is any leafy portion, chop about 1 tablespoon coarsely. Heat butter in skillet. Add broth, sliced fennel, and optional chopped leaves. Season with salt and pepper. Cover and cook over medium heat, about 10 minutes, until fennel is tender-crisp. Drain and serve.

SAN FRANCISCO MENU
FOR TWO OR THREE

Joe's special

Pita breads

Orange and onion salad

Pears and blue cheese

JOE's Special, straight out of San Francisco, has been changed a little over the years. In this version, tofu has been added. In another, one I had on a visit to San Francisco, the beef had disappeared entirely and the dish was completely vegetarian. However it is served, it is delicious.

There is no rule which says Joe's Special has to be served in pitas; you could serve them on the side with butter.

STAPLES

onion

oregano

marjoram

salt

pepper

Worcestershire sauce

eggs

leftover red or white wine (or wine vinegar)

tarragon vinegar

olive oil

garlic

SHOPPING LIST

½ pound ground beef
4 ounces tofu
(soybean curd)
5 ounces fresh
spinach
2 or 3 large pitas
2 or 3 seedless
oranges

1 small or medium
Bermuda onion
2 or 3 large lettuce
leaves
(pears, blue
cheese)

GAME PLAN:

Brown meat.

Cut up onion; add.
Cook until soft.

Add tofu, oregano, marjoram, salt, pepper, and Worcestershire.

Prepare spinach.

Peel and slice oranges and Bermuda onion.

Make salad dressing.

Add spinach to meat mixture.

Heat pitas.

Spoon dressing over salad.

Stir eggs into meat.

Joe's special

2 or 3 SERVINGS

½ pound ground beef
1 medium onion
4 ounces tofu (soybean curd)
¼ teaspoon dried oregano
½ teaspoon dried marjoram
Salt and freshly ground black pepper to taste

1 tablespoon Worcestershire sauce
½ of 10-ounce package fresh spinach
3 eggs
2 or 3 large pitas

Brown meat. While it browns, coarsely chop onion. Add onion. Cut tofu into small cubes. Stir tofu, oregano, marjoram, salt, pepper, and Worcestershire sauce into meat mixture and continue to cook. Meanwhile, wash spinach and remove tough stems. Add to meat mixture and cook until spinach wilts. While spinach is cooking, warm pitas. Beat eggs lightly. Just before serving, stir in eggs until they are firm, a minute or two. Fill pitas with meat mixture and serve.

Orange and onion salad

2 or 3 SERVINGS

2 or 3 medium seedless oranges
1 small to medium Bermuda onion
2 or 3 large leaves lettuce
4½ tablespoons leftover dry red or white wine*
1½ tablespoons olive oil

2¼ teaspoons tarragon vinegar
1½ tablespoons chopped onion
1 small clove garlic
Salt and freshly ground black pepper to taste

---

*If you have no leftover wine, use wine vinegar.

Peel oranges and slice horizontally. Slice Bermuda onion thinly and break into rings. Break up lettuce leaves and arrange on plates. Top with oranges and onion rings. Whisk together wine, oil, and vinegar. Chop onion finely. Put garlic through press; add onion and garlic to salad dressing. Season with salt and pepper; whisk and pour over salads.

This dressing is enough for 3 salads; if you are serving only 2 you can reduce the amounts as follows: 3 tablespoons wine, 1 tablespoon oil, 1½ teaspoons vinegar, and 1 tablespoon onion.

OLD-FASHIONED MENU FOR TWO WITH NEW TWIST

Deviled pork chops

Poppy seed noodles

Orange-olive salad

Yogurt with bananas and nuts

THE pork chops are an old family recipe, originally made with 2-inch-thick pork chops that took an hour to cook. The poppy seed noodle recipe has been hanging around a long time, too, but the orange-olive salad is new, a variation on a North African salad that is usually made with cumin. If you want to try it that way, you will be delighted with the results.

STAPLES

chili sauce	pepper
dry mustard	poppy seeds
Worcestershire sauce	olive oil
curry powder	garlic
paprika	lemon
salt	butter (optional)

SHOPPING LIST

4 very thin pork chops	12 pitted black olives
4 ounces wide egg noodles	1 small red or yellow onion
½ bunch parsley	(yogurt, bananas, nuts)
2 navel oranges	

GAME PLAN:

Brown pork chops.

Boil water for noodles.

Combine chili sauce, lemon juice, mustard, Worcestershire, curry powder, paprika, pepper, and water for chops.

Chop parsley.

Cook noodles.

Add sauce to chops; cover and simmer.

Prepare oranges; arrange on plates with olives and onion.

Make salad dressing.

Drain noodles; combine with poppy seeds, parsley, optional butter; season.

Deviled pork chops   2 SERVINGS

4 very thin pork chops	⅛ teaspoon curry powder
3 tablespoons chili sauce	¼ teaspoon paprika
1½ tablespoons fresh lemon juice	Freshly ground black pepper to taste
¼ teaspoon dry mustard	½ cup water
2 teaspoons Worcestershire sauce	

Trim fat from pork chops. Heat heavy skillet and grease skillet with a strip of removed fat. Brown chops on both sides. Meanwhile, combine remaining ingredients. When chops are brown, reduce heat; add sauce. Cover skillet and cook just at simmer until chops are tender, about 20 minutes. Serve with sauce.

Poppy seed noodles · 2 SERVINGS

4 ounces wide egg noodles	1 tablespoon poppy seeds
¼ cup chopped fresh parsley	1 tablespoon butter (optional)
	Salt to taste

Bring 3 quarts hot water to boil in covered pot. Add noodles and stir to keep from sticking. Cook about 5 minutes, until noodles are soft. Chop parsley. When noodles are done, drain noodles and return to pot; mix with butter, if used, and with poppy seeds and salt. (The butter is unnecessary if the sauce that is served over the pork chops is served with the noodles.) Keep warm, if necessary, until chops are done. Just before serving, mix with parsley.

NOTE: When chopping parsley for noodles, chop an extra tablespoon for the salad dressing.

Orange-olive salad · 2 SERVINGS

2 navel oranges	1 small clove garlic
12 pitted black olives	1 tablespoon chopped fresh parsley
1 or 2 slices sweet red or yellow onion	Salt and freshly ground black pepper to taste
4 tablespoons good quality olive oil	
4 teaspoons fresh lemon juice	

Peel oranges and section. Arrange on individual plates with 6 olives on each plate. Separate onion rings and place on plates. Beat oil with lemon juice and put garlic through press into dressing. Add parsley. Season with salt and pepper. When ready to serve, whisk dressing over salad.

ONE OF JIM BEARD'S FAVORITE SUMMER DISHES FOR TWO

Garlic sausage

Hot potato salad

Curried tomato salad

French bread

Cherries

THE recipe for hot potato salad has been borrowed from Jim Beard. That is, I borrowed the idea but adapted the recipe for a dinner. I'm not so certain everyone can purchase good garlic sausages in their local supermarkets: I can't. So I found a substitution: Italian sausage meat mixed with extra garlic. It will taste different, but good. There are some other changes, but essentially the idea of garlic sausage with hot potato salad made of new potatoes comes from one of Jim's columns. It is so delicious. The curried tomato salad was my addition.

For some, this meal may have too little meat and too many vegetables. If so, you can change the proportions and cut down on the potatoes while increasing the meat. And if calories are a big concern, you don't have to lap up all the oil in which the potatoes are dressed.

STAPLES

olive oil
white wine vinegar
salt
pepper

Dijon or New-Orleans
style mustard
garlic
curry powder

SHOPPING LIST

8 (12 ounces) small
  red or white new
  potatoes
3 tablespoons
  parsley
½ pound garlic
  sausage or hot or
  sweet Italian
  sausage meat

French bread
(optional)
1 very large or 2
  small tomatoes
1 small red onion
¼ cup yogurt and/or
  sour cream
  (cherries)

GAME PLAN:

Cook potatoes.
Cut up tomatoes.
Chop onion; combine
with tomatoes.
Bring hot water to boil
for sausages.
Chop parsley; mix with
yogurt and curry.

Mix oil and vinegar;
chop parsley and add to
dressing.
Boil sausages.
Heat bread, if being
served.
Quarter potatoes and
mix with dressing.
Dress tomatoes.

Garlic sausage   2 SERVINGS

½ pound garlic sausage,   Italian sausage meat
   such as Kielbasa, or ½   plus 1 small clove garlic
   pound sweet or hot

If you are using sausage meat, mince the garlic and mix
with sausage meat. Shape into sausages.

Bring hot water to boil in covered pot. Add sausages and
cook about 20 minutes.

Serve with a really good mustard, like Dijon or New
Orleans-style, much like German-style.

Hot potato salad   2 SERVINGS

---

8 (12 ounces) small red or   Salt and freshly ground
  white new potatoes   black pepper to taste
5 to 6 tablespoons good   2 tablespoons chopped
  quality olive oil   fresh parsley
2 tablespoons white wine
  vinegar

Scrub potatoes, but do not peel them. Cook in water to
cover in covered pot until tender, about 20 minutes.
Drain. Do not peel. Cut into quarters. Beat together oil,
vinegar, and salt and pepper. Chop parsley and mix well to
blend. Pour over warm potatoes and serve.

Curried tomato salad 2 SERVINGS

1 very large or 2 small tomatoes	¼ to ½ teaspoon curry powder
1 small red onion	Salt and freshly ground black pepper to taste
1 tablespoon minced fresh parsley	
¼ cup plain yogurt or 2 tablespoons plain yogurt and 2 tablespoons sour cream	

Cut tomato up; then gently squeeze out seeds if tomato is very juicy. Chop onion. Refrigerate until ready to serve. Mince parsley. Combine parsley with yogurt, curry powder, and salt and pepper. When you are ready to serve, combine yogurt mixture with tomato and onion.

ITALIAN MENU FOR TWO

Spaghetti carbonara

Peppers, onions and mushrooms

Seasoned bread

Strawberries, peaches, or oranges with brown sugar and sour cream or yogurt

SPAGHETTI carbonara, a classic Italian quick dish, with as many ways to make it as there are cooks, ordinarily doesn't call for nitrite-free bacon, but it's the only way I make it. Still, spaghetti carbonara is not exactly the dish for someone on a low-fat diet, but for those of you out there who don't have to watch your calories, cholesterol, fat, or salt intake, is this delicious!

STAPLES

butter	onions
egg	olive oil
salt	brown sugar
pepper	

SHOPPING LIST

8 ounces spaghetti
2 slices nitrite-free bacon
6 tablespoons (about 2 ounces) freshly grated Parmesan cheese
1 large green bell pepper

¼ pound mushrooms
¼ cup parsley
2 crusty rolls
 (strawberries, peaches or oranges, sour cream or yogurt)

GAME PLAN:

Turn oven to 400.

Bring water to boil in pot for spaghetti.

Slice pepper and onion; sauté in oil

Cook spaghetti.

Fry bacon.

Rinse and slice mushrooms; add to pepper and onion.

Chop onion for rolls and sauté in butter.

Chop parsley; add to butter; spread on sliced rolls.

Toast rolls.

Drain bacon and crumble; grate Parmesan; beat egg.

Drain spaghetti; stir in cheese, egg, butter, and salt and pepper.

Sprinkle on bacon.

Spaghetti carbonara   2 SERVINGS

8 ounces spaghetti
2 slices nitrite-free bacon
6 tablespoons freshly
  grated Parmesan
  cheese
1 egg

2 tablespoons butter
Salt and freshly ground
black pepper to taste

Bring 3 quarts hot water to boil in covered pot. Salt, if
desired. Cook spaghetti 10 minutes until al dente. Meanwhile, fry bacon until crisp; drain thoroughly and crumble.
Grate cheese. Beat egg. Drain spaghetti. While still very
hot stir in egg, then cheese, butter, and salt and pepper.
Blend thoroughly. Sprinkle with crumbled bacon.

Peppers, onions and mushrooms   2 SERVINGS

1 large green bell pepper
1 medium onion
1 tablespoon olive oil

¼ pound mushrooms
Salt and freshly ground
black pepper to taste

Seed and slice pepper thinly. Thinly slice onion. Heat oil
in skillet. Sauté pepper and onion. Rinse and slice
mushrooms. After pepper has been coated by oil and has
begun to soften, about 3 minutes, add the mushrooms and
stir. Cook over medium heat until vegetables are crisp-
tender, about 3 minutes more. Season with salt and
pepper.

Seasoned bread

1 **very small onion**
2 **tablespoons butter**
¼ **cup chopped fresh parsley**

2 **crusty rolls**

Turn oven or toaster oven to 400 degrees. Chop onion finely. Place in saucepan with butter and cook the onion a little, about 2 or 3 minutes. Chop parsley. Remove from heat; stir in parsley. Meanwhile, cut rolls in half. Spread cut sides with butter mixture and toast 10 minutes. Serve warm, not hot.

MELTING-POT MENU
FOR TWO

Pork chops with apple, cabbage and
cumin

Yellow squash with provolone sauce

Bulgur with garlic and parsley

Papaya or frozen fruit

It's typically American to borrow a little from all the cultures that have influenced our cooking. That's what makes cooking so much more interesting in this country than it is anywhere else.

The evolution of these recipes may be of interest. The pork chop dish originally called for coriander. I was working with cumin at the time, testing some recipes, so decided to try it. It took much more than I ever imagined to bring out the flavor over the cabbage.

The squash recipe at one time called for Cheddar cheese and zucchini, but I've gotten very tired of Cheddar in so many recipes; hence Provolone, which is delightfully sharp.

And I do also weary of rice all the time, so I substituted my favorite grain, bulgur, or cracked wheat. It has a chewy texture and nutlike flavor. The recipe called for sautéing the garlic separately but that meant too many pots. By adding the raw garlic just toward the end, so it has enough time to cook a little but still retain its flavor, it imparts a lovely, subtle garlicky flavor to the grain.

STAPLES

onion	butter
ground cumin	chicken stock or bouil-
salt	lon
pepper	garlic
Dijon mustard	lemon

SHOPPING LIST

4 thin pork chops

1 tart red or green
apple

½ pound red or
green cabbage

2 medium yellow
summer squash

¼ cup yogurt

¼ cup sour cream

⅓ cup (about 2
ounces) Provolone

1 tablespoon parsley

½ cup bulgur

(papaya or frozen
fruit)

GAME PLAN:

Heat broiler.

Brown chops.

Cut up apple, cabbage,
and onion.

Cook bulgur.

Add vegetables to chops
with remaining season-
ings.

Steam squash.

Mix sauce ingredients
for squash.

Chop garlic and pars-
ley; add to bulgur.

Drain squash and mix
with sauce; run under
broiler.

Pork chops with apple, cabbage and cumin

2 SERVINGS

4 thin pork chops

1 tart green or red apple

½ pound red or green cabbage

1 small onion

2 to 3 teaspoons ground cumin

2 tablespoons fresh lemon juice

Salt and freshly ground black pepper to taste

Brown pork chops in heavy skillet in their own fat over medium-high heat on both sides. Core and slice the apple thinly; slice the cabbage thinly; slice the onion. When chops are browned remove from the skillet. Add the apple, cabbage, onion, cumin, lemon juice, and salt and pepper to taste. Return chops to skillet and cook, covered, until chops are tender and vegetables are soft. Stir occasionally. Total cooking time about 25 minutes.

Yellow squash with provolone sauce

2 SERVINGS

2 medium yellow summer squash

½ cup plain yogurt and sour cream, combined

1 teaspoon Dijon mustard

⅓ cup (about 2 ounces) coarsely shredded Provolone cheese, lightly packed

Heat broiler. Scrub and trim squash; cut into strips. Steam, in a little water in a skillet, covered, until al dente, just a few minutes. Drain. Mix yogurt with sour cream and mustard. Shred cheese and mix into sour cream. Pour sauce over squash and run under broiler to brown.

Bulgur with garlic and parsley

2 SERVINGS

½ cup bulgur (cracked wheat)

1 tablespoon butter

1 cup chicken stock or bouillon or water

⅛ teaspoon minced garlic

1 tablespoon chopped fresh parsley

Sauté bulgur in hot butter in skillet about 2 minutes. Add stock, cover, and cook until bulgur is tender and liquid has evaporated, about 10 minutes. A few minutes before bulgur is done, mince garlic, chop parsley and stir into bulgur. Cover and finish cooking.

CHINESE MENU FOR TWO

Pork chops with mushrooms

Noodles

Pat's bean sprouts and scallions

Murcotts, strawberries or blueberries

PEOPLE are always saying how quick Chinese food is to cook. Cook is the operative word here. Ordinarily you can spend hours chopping, slicing, mincing, and, in general, making preparations for this quick cooking. But some Chinese food is quick to prepare as well as quick to cook. This menu is one example. There is very little chopping or mincing. And dried mushrooms can be sufficiently softened in 15 minutes to trim and cook.

If you do not keep a stock of Chinese or Oriental dried mushrooms in your cupboard and you aren't likely to find them in your supermarket, though even that is possible these days, substitute other dried mushrooms that the supermarket does carry. If all else fails, use fresh mushrooms. The flavor won't be the same, but the dish will work.

Oriental egg noodles aren't readily available in many supermarkets . . . yet. So if you don't have that on your shelf, substitute American fine egg noodles.

STAPLES

ginger	vegetable oil
soy sauce	sesame oil
sugar	beef stock or bouillon
rice vinegar	salt
dry sherry	pepper

SHOPPING LIST

8 dried mushrooms

4 or 5 thin pork chops

4 ounces Chinese, Japanese, or American fine egg noodles

½ pound bean sprouts

2 bunches scallions (murcotts, strawberries, or blueberries)

GAME PLAN:

Soak mushrooms.

Mince ginger; combine with soy sauce, sugar, vinegar, and sherry and marinate chops.

Bring water to boil in pot for noodles.

Cut up scallions; rinse sprouts.

Cook chops in hot oil on both sides.

Drain mushrooms.

Remove stems, slice and add with stock and marinade to chops; reduce heat, cover and cook.

Cook scallions in hot oil.

Cook noodles.

Add sprouts to scallions with sesame oil; stir-fry.

Add marinade.

Pork chops with mushrooms

2 SERVINGS

8 dried mushrooms,
   preferably Oriental
4 or 5 thin pork chops
1 tablespoon minced
   fresh ginger
3 tablespoons soy sauce
2 teaspoons sugar

4 tablespoons rice vinegar
3 tablespoons dry sherry
1 tablespoon vegetable oil
1 cup beef stock or
   bouillon

Place mushrooms in hottest possible water and soak for 15 minutes. Trim fat from chops. Mince ginger and combine with soy sauce, sugar, rice vinegar, and sherry in bowl large enough to hold chops. Place chops in marinade and turn to coat.

Heat oil in skillet. Remove chops from marinade after about 5 minutes; reserve marinade. Brown chops on both sides over high heat. Drain, stem, and slice mushrooms; add with stock and 3 tablespoons of marinade to chops. Reduce heat, cover and cook chops over low heat until 30 minutes of meal preparation are up. Serve chops and noodles with sauce.

Noodles

2 SERVINGS

4 ounces egg noodles—
   Chinese, Japanese, or
   American fine egg
   noodles

Salt

Bring 3 quarts hot water to boil in covered pot. Salt, if desired. Add noodles and cook about 3 minutes, depending on thickness of noodle. Drain; keep warm and serve with sauce for pork chops.

Pat's bean sprouts and scallions

2 SERVINGS

2 bunches scallions
½ pound fresh bean
   sprouts
1 tablespoon vegetable oil

¼ teaspoon sesame oil
   Marinade from chops
   Salt to taste

Wash scallions and cut in 1-inch lengths. Rinse sprouts and drain. Heat vegetable oil in large skillet. Sauté scallions until soft, about 5 minutes. Add sprouts and stir-fry about 3 minutes, until they begin to lose a little of their crunchiness. Add sesame oil and marinade and stir to mix well. Adjust seasoning and serve.

FAR EAST MENU FOR THREE

Pork saté

Mushrooms and sprouts with mustard-vinegar

Asian rice

Pineapple spears or blueberries

THEY probably never saw an alfalfa sprout in Indonesia, but they'd like them if they did. They go quite well with sates. A true sate is grilled, on a skewer, over coals. There's no time for that here, but you certainly could do it when you have more time.

The turmeric gives the rice a wonderful color as well as distinctive flavor.

All in all, a pretty meal to look at.

STAPLES

creamy peanut butter	red wine vinegar
ground coriander	Dijon mustard
cayenne	thyme
ground cumin	basil
onions	oregano
garlic	rice
lemon juice	turmeric
brown sugar	butter
soy sauce	salt
olive or salad oil	pepper

SHOPPING LIST

1 pound boneless pork	3 ounces alfalfa sprouts
15 medium mushrooms	(pineapple or blueberries)

GAME PLAN:

Turn broiler to 475.

Prepare garlic and onion; combine with remaining ingredients except pork.

Stir in pork, coating well.

Chop onion for rice; cook in butter with turmeric.

Add rice, salt and pepper.

Add water; bring to boil, reduce heat, and cook.

Broil pork.

Prepare mushrooms for salad; arrange on sprouts on plates.

Make salad dressing.

Turn pork and continue broiling.

Dress salad.

Pork saté   3 SERVINGS

¾ cup coarsely grated onion	1 teaspoon ground cumin
1 clove garlic	1½ tablespoons fresh lemon juice
½ cup creamy peanut butter*	1 tablespoon brown sugar
¼ cup water	2 tablespoons soy sauce
1½ teaspoons ground coriander	1 pound boneless pork, cut into ¾-inch cubes
⅛ teaspoon cayenne	

*Use natural peanut butter, made only with peanuts or peanuts and salt.

Set broiler to 475 degrees. Grate onion. Put garlic through press or mince. In large bowl combine all ingredients except pork and mix thoroughly. Add pork and stir so that pork pieces are well covered.

Line broiler pan with foil. Place coated pieces of pork on foil, reserving remaining sauce, and broil about 4 inches from heat 5 minutes. Turn pieces of pork and coat with remaining peanut-butter mixture. Continue broiling 5 minutes longer, or until pork is done.

Mushrooms and sprouts with mustard-vinegar

3 SERVINGS

15 medium mushrooms	1 teaspoon Dijon mustard
3 ounces alfalfa sprouts	¼ teaspoon each dried thyme, basil, and oregano
3 tablespoons olive or salad oil	
3 tablespoons red wine vinegar	Salt and freshly ground black pepper to taste

Wash mushrooms and slice off bottoms of stems. Arrange sprouts on 3 salad plates. Slice mushrooms over sprouts. Combine oil, vinegar, mustard, and seasonings. Beat well. Pour over sprouts and mushrooms.

Asian rice

3 SERVINGS

1 medium onion	Salt and freshly ground black pepper to taste
1½ tablespoons butter	
¾ teaspoon turmeric	1½ cups water
¾ cup enriched white or brown rice*	

*See page 74 for directions on how to use brown rice in a 30-minute meal.

Chop onion finely. Heat butter in heavy-bottomed pan. Add the onion and turmeric and stir well. Cook until onion begins to soften. Add rice, salt and pepper, and water; bring to boil over high heat. Reduce heat to simmer and cook, covered, until all liquid is absorbed and rice is tender, about 15 to 17 minutes.

ITALIAN MENU FOR TWO

Italian sausages in pepper-basil sauce

Spaghetti

Spinach, apple, walnut salad

Melon and lemon wedges

THIS is an early fall menu, when there is still fresh basil, when tomatoes are still luscious, and when apples are already in full season.

In order to make this dish you must have a source of fresh basil for full flavor.

So the spinach salad isn't Italian. It goes so nicely, why quibble!

STAPLES

olive oil

onion

garlic

salt

pepper

fresh basil

(lemon)

SHOPPING LIST

½ to ¾ pound sweet Italian sausages

4 ounces (2 cups) spaghetti

3 small red and/or green bell peppers

2 large tomatoes

1 small tart apple

¼ pound spinach

1 small package walnut meats

(melon)

GAME PLAN:

Cook the sausages in large skillet.

Bring water to boil for spaghetti.

Prepare onion, garlic, peppers, and tomatoes for sausages.

Chop basil.

Cook spaghetti.

Remove sausages, cook onion and garlic.

Prepare spinach.

Cook tomatoes, peppers, and basil, with onion adding sausages.

Toast walnuts.

Slice apple.

Arrange salad.

Make salad dressing.

Drain spaghetti.

Dress salad.

Italian sausages in pepper-basil sauce

2 SERVINGS

½ to ¾ pound sweet Italian sausages

1 medium onion

1 large clove garlic

1 tablespoon olive oil

3 small red and/or green bell peppers

2 large tomatoes

½ cup tightly packed fresh basil*

Freshly ground black pepper to taste

Cook sausages in large skillet until well browned on all sides. Remove sausages and set aside. Pour off fat. Coarsely chop onion. Put garlic through press. Add olive oil to skillet. Add onion and garlic and cook until onion is soft. Seed peppers and cut into strips. Coarsely chop tomatoes. Coarsely chop basil. Add peppers to skillet and cook 3 minutes. Add tomatoes, basil, sausages, and pepper. Stir and cook over medium-high heat for a few minutes. Then cover and continue cooking until tomatoes release their juice and sauce begins to thicken a little. Total cooking time about 25 minutes.

---

*To measure fresh basil leaves, press leaves down in measuring cup with your hand to pack them in tightly.

Spaghetti

2 SERVINGS

4 ounces (2 cups)   Salt
   spaghetti

Bring 3 quarts hot water to boil in covered pot. Salt, if desired. Stir in spaghetti and cook until al dente, about 10 minutes. Drain.

Spinach, apple, walnut salad

2 SERVINGS

¼ pound fresh spinach†   2 tablespoons good
¼ cup walnut meats   quality olive oil
1 small tart apple   Salt and freshly ground
2 tablespoons fresh lemon   black pepper to taste
   juice

Wash and remove tough stems from spinach. Drain. Toast walnuts. Arrange spinach on 2 plates. Core, cut apple in half, and slice thinly. Arrange apple slices on spinach. Whisk lemon juice with oil and season with salt and pepper. Pour over salads. Garnish with walnuts.

NOTE: Some people may find the dressing a bit too lemony. If so, reduce the amount of lemon juice by ½ tablespoon.

---

†If you can find arugula, it's a wonderful substitute.

GERMAN MENU FOR TWO

Bratwurst

Cabbage, apples and onions

Hot potato salad

Pumpernickel rolls or bread

Boysenberry sherbet

A summer or fall menu that certainly is appropriate, if you can find the right potatoes, at other times of the year. It clearly represents the German influence on our cooking.

And for those who worry about nitrites, but can't find nitrite-free hot dogs, bratwurst is more than an acceptable substitute. I think bratwurst tastes better than any hot dog I've ever eaten.

STAPLES

white wine vinegar	salt
dry mustard	pepper
onion	salad oil
paprika	caraway seeds
dillseed	

SHOPPING LIST

4 bratwurst

1 large apple

10 ounces (about 6 to 8) new potatoes

¾ pound red or green cabbage

½ cup plain yogurt or yogurt and sour cream

pumpernickel rolls or bread

(boysenberry sherbet)

GAME PLAN:

Cook potatoes.

Bring water to boil in steamer for cabbage.

Slice onion.

Sauté onion in oil.

Cut up apple.

Cut up cabbage and steam.

Add apple to onion and cook, covered.

Make dressing for salad.

Cook bratwurst.

Add caraway seeds and cabbage to onions.

Cut up cooked potatoes. Dress.

Remove bratwurst from water.

Bratwurst   2 SERVINGS

4 bratwurst*

Cook the bratwurst for 15 minutes in the same water in which the potatoes are cooking.

---

*Alternative is nitrite-free hot dogs.

Cabbage, apples and onions

2 SERVINGS

1 large onion
1 large apple
¾ pound red or green cabbage

1 tablespoon salad oil
1 teaspoon caraway seeds
Salt and freshly ground black pepper to taste

Bring hot water to boil in covered steamer. Slice onion, reserving 1 slice to be chopped into 1 tablespoon for potatoes. Core and slice apple.

Cut cabbage into small wedges and steam. Heat oil in large skillet. Separate onion into rings and sauté in oil until rings begin to soften. Add apple; cover and cook over low heat until apple is soft. When cabbage is cooked, about 12 minutes, drain and add to skillet. Stir in caraway seeds. Season with salt and pepper and keep warm until serving time.

Hot potato salad

2 SERVINGS

6 to 8 (10 ounces) new potatoes
1 tablespoon chopped onion (see Cabbage, Apples, and Onions)
2 tablespoons white wine vinegar
½ cup plain yogurt or ¼ cup each yogurt and sour cream

¼ teaspoon dry mustard
¼ teaspoon paprika
¼ teaspoon dillseed
Salt and freshly ground black pepper to taste

Scrub potatoes, but do not peel. Cook in water to cover in covered pot about 20 minutes, until potatoes are firm but tender. Drain. Do not peel. Cut in quarters or thick slices. Chop onion medium-fine. Mix vinegar, yogurt, mustard, onion, paprika, dillseed. Mix with potatoes. Season with salt and pepper and serve warm.

A HYBRID MENU FOR TWO

Polish pork chops

Macaroni

Curly endive with chili-cumin dressing

Grapefruit with or without honey

THIS is another of those strictly American menus—taking something from Europe, something else from Mexico, and making a match. Polish pork chops originally contained sour cream instead of yogurt and they were made with thick chops. That won't work for a 30-minute meal, but you can still get the flavor using thin pork chops, which seem to be readily available. There is only one trouble with them: sometimes they are tender and sometimes they are tough. There's no accounting for how they turn out, so hope for the best because the flavoring is very nice.

If you like the flavor of Mexican food, you will like the dressing, made with the combined spice called chili powder that is hyped with additional cumin.

STAPLES

onion	red wine vinegar
dry sherry	garlic
salt	chili powder
pepper	ground cumin
salad oil	(honey)

SHOPPING LIST

4 thin pork chops
   6-ounce can
   tomato paste
½ pint plain yogurt
1 dill pickle

¼ pound curly
   endive
4 ounces macaroni
   (grapefruit)

GAME PLAN:

Brown chops on one
side; add chopped
onion, brown on second
side.

Bring hot water to boil
for macaroni.

Add tomato paste,
yogurt, and sherry to
chops; cover.

Make salad dressing.

Cook macaroni.

Wash and dry greens.

Season chops with salt,
pepper, and pickle.

Dress salad.

Drain macaroni.

Polish pork chops   2 SERVINGS

4 thin pork chops
1 small onion
1 6-ounce can tomato
   paste, minus 2
   tablespoons*
1 cup plain yogurt

3 tablespoons dry sherry
   Salt and freshly ground
   black pepper to taste
2 tablespoons finely
   chopped dill pickle

Using a piece of the fat from one of the chops, rub it over
the bottom of a large skillet. When skillet is hot, add chops
and cook over medium-high heat. Meanwhile, coarsely
chop onion and add to chops. Brown chops on both sides.
Mix tomato paste with yogurt and sherry and add to skillet.
Reduce heat; cover and simmer for the remainder of the 30
minutes, or until chops are cooked. Chop pickle. Season
with salt and pepper and mix in pickle.

---

*Reserve for another use. Leftover tomato paste freezes well.

Macaroni   2 SERVINGS

---

4 ounces elbow macaroni   Salt

Bring 3 quarts hot water to boil in covered pot. Salt, if desired. Add macaroni and cook until al dente, about 8 minutes. Drain.

Curly endive with chili-cumin dressing   2 SERVINGS

---

3 tablespoons salad oil
1 tablespoon red wine vinegar
½ small clove garlic
½ teaspoon chili powder

⅛ teaspoon ground cumin
Salt and freshly ground black pepper to taste
¼ pound curly endive

Whisk together the oil and vinegar. Put garlic through press and add with remaining seasonings. Whisk.

Wash and dry curly endive with paper towels. Pour dressing over salad.

ITALIAN MENU FOR TWO

"Veal" parmesan

Pasta pizzaiola

Mushrooms and scallion salad

Frozen or fresh strawberries or peaches

WHEN this was written, veal was over $6 a pound in Washington and that's out of most people's price range. Turkey breast cutlets, a fairly new product on the market, are less than half that price, and, while slices have a tendency to fall apart a bit, it doesn't affect the flavor. What with all the sauce, you'd be hard-pressed to tell these turkey cutlets from veal cutlets. Why didn't the turkey people think of them sooner!

If you serve the frozen fruit, be sure to buy the unsweetened kind and let it sit out before you begin dinner to soften a little. Don't let it become mushy, though.

STAPLES

egg	garlic
salt	onion
pepper	oregano
bread crumbs	thyme
olive oil	lemon

SHOPPING LIST

4 or 5 slices turkey breast cutlets

¼ cup (about 1¼ ounces) Parmesan cheese

¼ pound mozzarella cheese

35-ounce can Italian tomatoes

4 ounces elbow macaroni

¼ pound mushrooms

4 to 6 red or Boston lettuce leaves

1 scallion

(frozen or fresh strawberries or peaches)

GAME PLAN:

Combine egg, salt and pepper; combine bread crumbs and grated cheese.

Prepare onion and garlic and cook in hot oil.

Bring water to boil in pot for noodles.

Dip cutlets in egg, then in bread crumbs.

Add tomatoes, salt, pepper, oregano, and thyme to sauce.

Cook noodles.

Sauté cutlets.

Line salad plates with lettuce; trim and slice mushrooms; slice scallion; whisk lemon juice with oil and season.

Cover cutlets with sauce; top with cheese. Continue cooking.

Drain noodles.

Dress salad.

"Veal" parmesan   2 SERVINGS

1 egg
Salt and freshly ground
  black pepper to taste
¼ cup freshly grated
  Parmesan cheese
⅓ cup fine dry bread
  crumbs

4 or 5 slices turkey breast
  cutlets
3 tablespoons olive oil
¼ pound mozzarella
  cheese
½ of Pizzaiola Sauce

Combine egg with a little salt and pepper. Grate cheese.
Mix bread crumbs with Parmesan. Dip each cutlet in egg,
then in bread crumb mixture. Be sure cutlets are well-
coated. Heat oil in large skillet. Sauté cutlets over medium
heat on both sides. Slice mozzarella. Cover cutlets with
pizzaiola sauce. Top with sliced cheese. Cover skillet and
continue cooking until cheese melts, about 5 minutes, or
run under broiler.

Pizzaiola sauce   2 SERVINGS

2 tablespoons olive oil
1 medium onion
1 large clove garlic
  35-ounce can Italian
  tomatoes

Salt and freshly ground
  black pepper to taste
1 teaspoon dried oregano
1 teaspoon dried thyme

Heat oil in skillet. Coarsely chop onion and put garlic
through press. Add to skillet. Cook over medium heat
until onion is soft. Squeeze tomatoes in fingers to break up
and add with liquid and remaining ingredients. Cook just
below boil 15 or 20 minutes.

Use half of sauce with meat; serve other half over
noodles.

Pasta
2 SERVINGS

4 ounces elbow macaroni   Salt to taste

Bring 3 quarts hot water to boil in large covered pot. Stir in macaroni and cook about 8 to 10 minutes, until macaroni is tender. Add salt, if desired.

Mushrooms and scallion salad
2 SERVINGS

¼ pound fresh mushrooms
4 to 6 red or Boston lettuce leaves
1 scallion
2 teaspoons fresh lemon juice

3 tablespoons olive oil
Salt and freshly ground black pepper to taste

Rinse mushrooms and trim off ends of stems. Slice mushrooms directly onto 2 salad plates that have been lined with lettuce leaves. Slice scallion into thin rounds. Whisk lemon juice with olive oil; season with salt and pepper. Pour dressing over mushrooms and sprinkle with scallion.

CELEBRATION MENU FOR FOUR

Veal picatta "sting"

Whole-wheat pasta with yellow squash and tomato sauce

Whole-wheat breadsticks

Raspberry sorbet

First of all the confession.

The veal isn't veal. Hence the "sting." The veal is turkey cutlets from the breast, indistinguishable from veal when cooked and sauced, and half the price.

(If your store doesn't have turkey cutlets use chicken, but make your store carry them! And if you can't buy whole-wheat pasta or whole-wheat breadsticks, use the regular, but make your store get them, too.)

If you'd like to fancy up the meal a little more, you can top the sorbet with sliced strawberries that have been marinated in a little orange-flavored liqueur. Do that just before you start dinner.

Don't forget to add them to your shopping list!

STAPLES

flour	lemons
salt	butter
pepper	onion
olive oil	garlic

SHOPPING LIST

About 8 to 10 slices (1¼ pounds) boneless turkey breast cutlets

3 tablespoons parsley

1½ pounds yellow squash

35-ounce can Italian tomatoes

½ pound whole-wheat or enriched elbow macaroni

12 whole-wheat or enriched white breadsticks

(1 pint raspberry sorbet)

GAME PLAN:

Prepare onion and garlic for sauce; sauté in butter and oil.

Bring water to boil in pot for pasta.

Prepare squash and add with tomatoes and seasonings to onion and garlic.

Cook pasta.

Flour cutlets.

Squeeze lemon juice.

Cook cutlets.

Cut up lemons.

Drain pasta.

Keep cutlets warm and finish sauce.

Veal piccata "sting"   4 SERVINGS

½ cup flour
Salt and freshly ground black pepper to taste

8 to 10 slices (about 1¼ pounds) turkey breast cutlets

2 tablespoons butter

¼ cup olive oil

6 tablespoons fresh lemon juice

1 large lemon, cut into very thin slices
Finely chopped fresh parsley, about 3 tablespoons

Mix the flour with salt and pepper and dust cutlets lightly on both sides. Heat butter and oil in 2 large skillets. Add the cutlets and cook quickly over high heat on both sides until golden, 4 to 5 minutes total cooking time. Transfer to warm platter. Squeeze lemon juice. Heat lemon juice briefly in skillet, stirring to deglaze pan and remove bits from bottom. Pour sauce over cutlets and garnish with lemon slices and parsley.

Whole-wheat pasta

4 SERVINGS

8 ounces whole-wheat or enriched elbow macaroni

Salt

Bring 3 quarts hot water to boil in covered pot. Salt, if desired. Add macaroni; stir and cook until tender but firm. (Whole-wheat pasta takes a few minutes longer to cook than regular pasta, about 10 minutes.) Drain. Serve with squash and tomato sauce.

Yellow squash and tomato sauce

4 SERVINGS

1 large onion
1 large clove garlic
2 tablespoons olive oil
2 tablespoons butter
1½ pounds yellow summer squash

35-ounce can Italian tomatoes
Salt and freshly ground black pepper to taste

Coarsely chop onion and put garlic through press. Heat oil and butter in skillet and sauté onion and garlic in it until onion is soft. Meanwhile, scrub and slice squash. Crush tomatoes in fingers to break up before adding to skillet with liquid and squash. Season with salt and pepper. Cook over medium-high heat, stirring occasionally. Squash should be tender but not lose its shape.

POOR MAN'S VEAL DINNER FOR FOUR

"Veal" with rosemary

Thin egg noodles

Zucchini with apples

Plums or tangelos

You can make the "veal" dish with chicken breasts if you cannot find turkey breast. Like real veal, the turkey and chicken substitutes cook very quickly.

This is one recipe in which it is difficult to substitute yogurt completely for sour cream because the sauce will be too thin.

The apples give the most delightful sweet touch to zucchini, unexpected but delicious.

STAPLES

butter	salt
garlic	pepper
rosemary	onions
Dijon mustard	

SHOPPING LIST

1 pound boneless turkey breast	2 pounds small zucchini
¼ pound mushrooms	2 medium apples
½ cup dry white wine	8 ounces thin egg noodles
½ cup sour cream	(plums or tangelos)
½ cup plain yogurt	

GAME PLAN:

Sauté turkey in butter; set aside.

Cut up zucchini, onions, and apples.

Slice mushrooms and press garlic; cook in turkey skillet.

Cook zucchini, onions, and apples in butter.

Bring water to boil for noodles.

Add wine to mushrooms and reduce wine over high heat.

Boil noodles.

Add rosemary, mustard, sour cream, yogurt, and turkey to wine in skillet. Season.

"Veal" with rosemary   4 SERVINGS

1 pound turkey fillet
2 tablespoons butter
¼ pound mushrooms
1 large clove garlic
½ cup dry white wine
1 tablespoon fresh rosemary or 1 teaspoon dried

2 teaspoons Dijon mustard
½ cup sour cream
½ cup plain yogurt
Salt and freshly ground black pepper to taste

Cut turkey on the diagonal into ¼-inch-wide strips. Sauté in butter until turkey begins to brown, about 7 minutes. Remove from skillet and set aside. Rinse mushrooms, and trim off ends of stems. Slice. Put garlic through press into skillet with mushrooms and cook until mushrooms begin to soften, about 3 minutes. Add wine and cook briskly over high heat until wine is reduced by half, just a few minutes. Add rosemary, mustard, sour cream, and yogurt. Add the turkey; stir and cook gently until mixture is very hot, about 2 minutes longer. Adjust seasonings.

Thin egg noodles 4 SERVINGS

8 ounces thin egg noodles   Salt

Bring 3 quarts salted hot water to boil in large covered pot. Add noodles and cook 5 minutes, until tender. Drain.

Zucchini with apples 4 SERVINGS

2 pounds small zucchini
6 tablespoons butter
2 onions

2 crisp medium apples
Salt and freshly ground black pepper to taste

Scrub, trim, and slice zucchini into rounds about ⅛ inch thick. Heat butter in skillet. Slice onions thinly and separate into rings. Add zucchini and onions to skillet. Cut apples in half, core, and slice thinly; add to skillet. Season with salt and pepper and cook over medium-high heat until onions are limp.

THANKSGIVING MENU
FOR SIX

Turkey-sesame cutlets

Mushroom rice

Tomatoes provençale

Cranberry-orange sherbet (see page 324)

To make this a complete Thanksgiving dinner it needs a little more than the main course. But before we get to that, I have to be completely honest: it took me 37 minutes to make this dinner for six people. I suspect I could have made it in the allotted 30 minutes if it were only for three or four. I know it definitely could have been done for two.

But for someone who wants to have some kind of Thanksgiving, for someone who hasn't been invited anywhere and doesn't want to be, who doesn't want to go through all that Thanksgiving involves, this is a simple solution. No, there are no candied yams, no relish tray, no pumpkin pie, not even any cranberry-orange sauce, but there is a way to remedy that.

To make a more complete Thanksgiving meal, serve oysters on the half shell with lemon wedges to start the meal. (Be sure the fishmonger opens them for you.) And for dessert see page 324 for a cranberry-orange sherbet.

There's nothing to preparing the oysters; the cranberry-orange dessert can be made either the night before or sometime before you begin the dinner preparations, in only ten minutes.

What to serve as an hors d'oeuvre while you cook? See page 310 for the simplest of all hors d'oeuvres, or choose another one from the hors d'oeuvre chapter.

Add the following items to the staples and shopping list if you add an hors d'oeuvre, first course, and dessert. *Added staples:* lemon, sugar, orange-flavored liqueur, rosemary. *Added shopping list:* log of goat cheese (like Bucheron), hazelnut oil, 30 oysters on the half shell, ½ pound fresh cranberries, 1 medium orange.

STAPLES

soy sauce	ginger
flour	bread crumbs
eggs	salad and olive oil
sesame oil	rice
salt	butter
pepper	garlic
sesame seeds	

SHOPPING LIST

3 pounds boneless turkey breast	1½ pints cherry tomatoes
1½ pounds mushrooms	3 tablespoons parsley

GAME PLAN:

Turn oven to 500.
Cook rice.
Prepare turkey.
Wash mushrooms, trim, and grind.
Sauté turkey.

Cook mushrooms.
Prepare and cook tomatoes.
Mix rice and mushrooms and seasonings.

Turkey-sesame cutlets   6 SERVINGS

3 pounds boneless turkey breasts

1½ tablespoons soy sauce

3 eggs

1½ teaspoons water

1½ teaspoons sesame oil

Salt and freshly ground black pepper to taste

1 cup plus 2 tablespoons soft, fine bread crumbs*

6 tablespoons sesame seeds

1¼ teaspoons powdered ginger

2 or 3 tablespoons flour

6 tablespoons salad oil

Wash turkey breasts and flatten a little with rolling pin. Brush with soy sauce on both sides. Combine eggs, water, sesame oil, and salt and pepper and beat to blend. Mix together bread crumbs, sesame seeds, and ginger. Sprinkle flour on both sides of cutlets. Dip cutlets in egg mixture and then in crumb mixture. Heat oil in 2 large skillets. Sauté cutlets over medium heat until golden brown on both sides, about 15 minutes.

NOTE: There are turkey breast slices and turkey cutlets that are much thicker and larger. This recipe calls for the cutlets.

---

*If you would like to use whole-wheat bread crumbs, perhaps you can find them in a natural foods store, or you can make them yourself in a food processor and keep them in a plastic bag in the refrigerator or freezer to use as needed.

Mushroom rice 6 SERVINGS

1½ cups enriched white or brown rice*

3 cups water

1½ pounds mushrooms

4 tablespoons butter

Salt and freshly ground black pepper to taste

Combine rice with water. Bring to boil. Reduce heat to simmer and cook, covered, until all liquid is absorbed, about 20 minutes. If liquid is not absorbed and rice is cooked, raise heat to evaporate water. Wash mushrooms and trim off ends of stems. Grind mushrooms in food processor with steel blade or in blender until mixture is almost a purée. Heat butter in a large skillet and cook mushrooms until color changes. Mix cooked mushrooms with cooked rice and season with salt and pepper.

Tomatoes provençale 6 SERVINGS

1½ pints cherry tomatoes

2 large cloves garlic

3 tablespoons chopped fresh parsley

½ cup soft, fine bread crumbs

3 tablespoons olive oil

Salt and freshly ground black pepper to taste

Turn oven to 500 degrees.

Wash and stem tomatoes.

Put garlic through press. Chop parsley. Mix garlic, parsley, bread crumbs, oil, and salt and pepper. Place tomatoes in shallow roasting pan. Sprinkle with bread crumb mixture and bake in preheated 500 degree oven about 7 minutes, until tomatoes begin to sizzle and look as if they are about to burst.

---

*See page 74 for directions on how to use brown rice in a 30-minute meal.

LAMB CHOP DINNER FOR THREE

Lamb chops oregano

Sweet potatoes and apples

Baked mushrooms

Fruit sherbet

THERE'S only one dinner featuring lamb in this book. Americans don't eat much lamb and my family is typical. But I must say, after not having had lamb for dinner in years, this was a delightful treat. So tender, flavorful, without that "lamby" taste to which many people object. The tartness of the apples is a nice foil. The sherry in the mushrooms is a dividend for the lamb, too.

STAPLES

butter

lemon

salt

pepper

oregano

nutmeg

cinnamon

ginger

dry sherry

SHOPPING LIST

4 or 5 shoulder lamb chops

3 (about 1 pound) small, long narrow sweet potatoes

2 large tart apples

½ cup orange juice

¾ pound mushrooms

¼ cup parsley (fruit sherbet)

GAME PLAN:

Cook sweet potatoes.

Turn on broiler.

Prepare mushrooms, wrap, and place in oven.

Prepare apples; combine with juice and spices; cook.

Prepare sauce for chops.

Brush chops with sauce and broil.

Combine potatoes with apples.

Lamb chops oregano   3 SERVINGS

4 or 5 shoulder lamb chops

2 tablespoons butter

3 tablespoons fresh lemon juice

1 teaspoon oregano

Salt and freshly ground black pepper to taste

Place chops on broiler rack lined with foil. Combine butter, lemon juice, oregano, and salt and pepper in small saucepan and heat until butter is melted. Brush on lamb chops. Broil about 5 minutes, until brown. Turn, brush with lemon sauce, and continue broiling, about 8 to 10 minutes longer, depending on degree of doneness desired.

Sweet potatoes and apples   3 or 4 SERVINGS

3 (about 1 pound) small, long narrow sweet potatoes

2 large tart apples

½ cup orange juice

¼ teaspoon chopped fresh ginger

¼ teaspoon cinnamon

⅛ teaspoon nutmeg

Salt and freshly ground black pepper to taste

Peel potatoes and cut in half crosswise. Cook in water to cover in covered pot about 25 minutes, until potatoes are tender. Meanwhile, wash apples, quarter, and core. Don't peel. Slice and place in skillet with orange juice. Cook over high heat while chopping ginger. Add ginger with cinnamon, nutmeg, and salt and pepper. Cover and cook a few minutes, until apples soften. Uncover, reduce heat, and simmer apples a few minutes longer.

As potato pieces are tender, remove from water and add to apples. Slice potatoes and mix gently.

Baked mushrooms   3 SERVINGS

¾ pound mushrooms	3 tablespoons dry sherry
¼ cup chopped fresh parsley	Salt and freshly ground black pepper to taste

Rinse mushrooms and trim ends of stems. Place mushrooms in large piece of foil that will make a sealed package around the mushrooms. Chop parsley. Add parsley with sherry and salt and pepper to mushrooms. Seal package tightly so juices cannot leak out. Bake in same oven in which chops are broiling about 20 minutes.

PART **3** | # HORS D'OEUVRES AND DESSERTS

HORS D'OEUVRES AND DESSERTS

HOT HORS D'OEUVRES

Angels on horseback
Chile con queso
Dipping potatoes
Fried brie or camembert
Hot sardines and cheese
Port salut with thyme
Quick cheese tomato fondue
Water chestnuts wrapped in bacon

COLD HORS D'OEUVRES

Chèvre with hazelnut oil
Hummus
Mexican orange dip
Peppery pecans
Pismo beach clam dip
Roquefort butter with walnuts
Salmon caper
Sherried cheddar cheese spread
Sour cream chile dip
Spinach spread
Tapenade

DESSERTS

Amaretto apples
Banana and muenster cheese
Hot chocolate bananas
Grape and nectarine compote
Nectarines vermont
Glazed papaya with rum
Frozen peach purée
Hot peaches in brandy
Peach purée
Peaches stuffed with toasted almond cheese
Golden pears and orange
Stuffed pears
Potted plums
Berries with brandy
Cranberry-orange sherbet
Strawberry and peach sundaes
Strawberries with spicy yogurt
Summer fruit with yogurt and apple or pear butter
Frozen fruit ice
Any fruit with any ice cream
Rum and raisins with ice cream
Yogurt or sour cream dip
Raspberry yogurt sauce
Honey yogurt-tofu sauce
Almost all-purpose sauce
Apricot rum dip
Ricotta sweet for spooning or sipping
Zabaglione
More quick desserts

QUICK HORS D'OEUVRES

Hors d'oeuvres quickly turn a middle-of-the-week dinner into something festive. And in the case of the 30-minute meal-maker, they give him or her the opportunity to prepare the main part of the meal while the guests are content nibbling over cocktails.

These hors d'oeuvres can also stand alone. They can be part of a cocktail party or start any kind of meal. Some of them must be prepared at the last minute; others can be prepared ahead of time. Choose what fits your plan and schedule.

There seems to me to be a lot of recipes in this chapter calling for cheese. Without a doubt, it is because most of the speedy recipes are those with a cheese (or a sour cream) base. If you are in a hurry, you simply haven't got the time to make meat balls or bake savory pastries.

Just as with other recipes in this book, the calorie counts for hors d'oeuvre recipes have been reduced by substituting yogurt for sour cream, either entirely or partially, and by reducing the amount of butter or oil. Once again, salt becomes a matter of personal preference—"salt to taste"—it's up to you.

Angels on horseback   MAKES 12

I can make this only when I happen by a natural foods store that sells nitrite-free bacon, or else I must have some in the freezer. Then, of course, oysters have to be in season. When it all comes together, this makes a speedy and delicious hors d'oeuvre.

12 shucked oysters*
 4 to 6 slices nitrite-free
    bacon

Cut the slices of bacon into lengths just long enough to wrap once around each oyster. Secure with wooden toothpick. To serve: Bake in preheated 450 degree oven about 10 minutes on each side, or until bacon is brown and crisp. Watch carefully. Drain and serve hot.

Chile con queso   8 TO 10 SERVINGS

1 small onion, finely chopped	½ pound cream cheese, cubed
2 tablespoons butter	½ to ¾ cup milk
1 cup canned tomatoes drained and broken up	Salt and freshly ground black pepper to taste
1 4-ounce can green chiles, chopped	8 to 10 flour tortillas

Cook onion in butter until it softens. Add tomatoes and chiles; simmer a few minutes. Add cheese and stir occasionally until cheese begins to melt. Stir in milk. Season with salt and pepper. Serve with broiled tortillas.

To broil flour tortillas, cut each tortilla into 8 or 12 triangles. Place on baking sheet and run under broiler until tops begin to blister and brown.

---

*You can also use shucked cherrystone or littleneck clams.

Dipping potatoes

4 TO 6 SERVINGS

At first glance this seemed to be an hors d'oeuvre for the warm weather, particularly for the season of new potatoes—when those tiny little gems are available from spring to fall. But one chilly November day I pawed through the Red Bliss potatoes at the local food coop and found enough small, but not bite-sized potatoes to try the recipe anyway. I scrubbed them, boiled them 20 minutes, then cut them into quarters and proceeded with the recipe. It works and it's delicious.

16 tiny new potatoes or 8 larger ones, like Red Bliss, that can be eaten skin and all

 1 cup plain yogurt

 1 teaspoon chopped fresh dill

 2 teaspoons chopped scallion

 2 teaspoons red caviar (optional)

Scrub potatoes and bring to boil in water to cover. Depending on size, cook 15 to 20 minutes, until tender but not mushy. Drain. Don't run under cold water.

Combine ¼ cup yogurt with dill; combine ½ cup yogurt with scallion; combine remaining ¼ cup yogurt with caviar. (If you choose not to use caviar, just chop another teaspoon of dill or scallion and combine with the remaining yogurt, incorporating into the original mixture.)

Cut large potatoes into quarters (bite-sized pieces). DO NOT PEEL. Either leave the tiny new potatoes whole or cut in half. Dip the potato piece into the yogurt mixtures. (Forget about toothpicks. They just make things more difficult.) The potatoes are best served warm or room temperature.

Fried brie or camembert   ABOUT 4 SERVINGS

Those 3- to 4-ounce Bries and Camemberts you buy in boxes in the supermarket don't taste like much, certainly not like a wedge of Brie or Camembert from a large, top quality wheel. The best thing to do with one of the little ones is heat it to bring out whatever flavor there is. This method does the trick nicely.

3½- to 4-ounce Brie or Camembert wheel	1 egg, beaten
Flour	Bread crumbs
	2 tablespoons butter

Dip cheese in flour on both sides and on edges. Dip all over in beaten egg; then dip in bread crumbs. Heat butter in small skillet. Over very low heat brown cheese on both sides, then roll on edge to brown entirely. Do this slowly so that the cheese has a chance to melt inside. If you have a chance to leave the cheese at room temperature before heating, so much the better.

Be careful not to puncture or the cheese will run. Serve warm, cut into little wedges, with plain crackers.

Hors D'oeuvres and Desserts / 251

Hot sardines and cheese   MAKES ABOUT 12

Those who like sardines will like this hors d'oeuvre; those who don't, won't.

1 can skinless, boneless sardines	Freshly ground black pepper to taste
¼ cup finely grated Cheddar cheese	Melba rounds or pita triangles
2 teaspoons fresh lemon juice	

Drain sardines and mash. Mix with cheese, lemon juice, and pepper. Spread on melba rounds or pita triangles and toast until mixture is hot. (If you have a toaster oven, this is the perfect place to heat them; if not, preheat the oven to 400 degrees and bake about 7 minutes.)

Port salut with thyme

Port Salut cheese   Olive oil
Dried thyme   French bread slices

Toast the French bread. For each slice of bread, top with slice of cheese, sprinkle with a little thyme, and brush with a little olive oil. Toast until cheese melts and bubbles.

Quick cheese tomato fondue

6 TO 8 SERVINGS

3 cups diced mild cheese, such as Cheddar, Muenster, or Monterey Jack

1 tablespoon Worcestershire sauce

2 medium cloves garlic, minced or put through press

¾ cup tomato purée

3 tablespoons dry sherry French bread, about 6 ounces

Combine cheese, Worcestershire sauce, garlic, and tomato purée in heavy pot. Heat slowly over low heat until cheese melts and mixture is smooth; stir occasionally. Stir in sherry and serve. Keep warm either in fondue pot or in heatproof container on hot tray.

Heat bread or bake long enough to produce crispy crust. Cut bread into coarse chunks and serve with fondue.

Water chestnuts wrapped in bacon

16 TO 20 PIECES

1 8½-ounce can water
chestnuts, rinsed and
drained

3 or 4 slices nitrite-free
bacon

Preheat broiler.

Cut each slice of bacon in half lengthwise. Wrap a piece of bacon once around each water chestnut and fasten with a toothpick. Broil 7 to 10 minutes, until bacon is crisp. Drain and serve warm.

Chèvre with hazelnut oil

Proportions are of no importance in this recipe. The ingredients are:

1 piece of chèvre (goat
cheese), such as
Bucheron or
Montrachet

Hazelnut oil*
Fresh rosemary

Serve a piece of chèvre on a plate. Pour a few tablespoons of hazelnut oil into a small dish and mix with several sprigs of rosemary. Be generous. To eat, cut off a piece of chèvre, place on a cracker, then dribble on top a few drops of oil, being sure to get a little rosemary with it.

---

*Hazelnut oil is expensive even though a very little goes a very long way. If you don't want to spend the money, you can substitute a very fruity olive oil.

Hummus MAKES ABOUT 1½ CUPS

This is the only recipe for the well-known Lebanese chick-pea appetizer I've ever seen that doesn't call for tahini, sesame paste. Instead, sesame oil is indicated. It is something you are more likely to have on hand and it makes a tasty appetizer spread.

2 tablespoons fresh lemon juice

5 tablespoons sesame oil

1 large clove garlic

1 16-ounce can chick-peas, drained

Salt and freshly ground black pepper to taste

¼ cup chopped fresh parsley

Combine lemon juice, sesame oil, garlic, chick-peas, and salt and pepper in blender or food processor with steel blade. Blend or process until smooth. Spoon into serving dish and sprinkle with chopped parsley. Serve with pita bread wedges or plain crackers.

Mexican orange dip MAKES ABOUT 1 CUP

½ pint plain yogurt

2 tablespoons fresh orange juice

1½ teaspoons grated orange rind

½ teaspoon chili powder

½ teaspoon ground cumin

1 small clove garlic, crushed

Mix all ingredients and chill, covered, until serving time. Serve as dip with spears of raw zucchini, cucumber, strips of green pepper, or crackers.

Peppery pecans

½ pound pecan halves
1½ to 2 tablespoons butter

Salt and cayenne to taste

Stir pecan halves with butter in heavy skillet. When nuts are almost toasted, season with salt and as much cayenne as you think people would like to taste! Serve warm or at room temperature.

NOTE: You can use other seasonings, if you like—curry powder, Hungarian paprika, or ground cumin.

Pismo beach clam dip MAKES ABOUT 1¾ CUPS

Well, that's what the original recipe was called, but this doesn't bear much resemblance to it. It was something I had wanted to try for quite a while, but it took me several months before I ran into canned clams without monosodium glutamate.

This dip is wonderful on those rounds of pumpernickel cocktail bread.

½ pint sour cream
2 tablespoons finely chopped onion
1 tablespoon Worcestershire sauce
1 tablespoon fresh lemon juice

¼ teaspoon minced garlic
1 10- or 10½-ounce can minced clams, drained
Salt and freshly ground black pepper to taste

Combine all ingredients and mix well. Serve on pumpernickel cocktail bread.

Roquefort butter with walnuts
ABOUT 4 TO 6 SERVINGS

This is rather salty, because Roquefort is salty. But you can cut down on the saltiness by increasing the fat content!!! Add more butter. Salt, fat, whatever—it's delicious. A little can't hurt.

4 tablespoons butter, softened

¼ pound Roquefort cheese

1 tablespoon brandy

½ cup coarsely chopped walnuts

French bread

Mix the butter with the cheese and brandy. Stir in the walnuts. Slice long, thin French bread into ¼-inch slices. Toast lightly, if desired. Spread with Roquefort butter while still warm.

Salmon caper
MAKES ABOUT 1½ CUPS

8 ounces cream cheese

½ teaspoon anchovy paste

1 7- or 8-ounce can salmon, drained and flaked

2 teaspoons chopped capers

1 tablespoon minced onion

Raw vegetables or crackers

Beat together cream cheese, anchovy paste, salmon, capers, and onion. Spread on crackers or use as dip for raw vegetables.

Sherried cheddar cheese spread
MAKES 2 CUPS

With four ingredients you can turn a slab of Cheddar cheese into an interesting spread that looks as if you've put some work into it. You need either a blender or food processor to make the work easy. It can also be done with a fine grater.

½ pound sharp Cheddar cheese

½ cup dry sherry

1 4-ounce jar minced pimientos, drained

4 teaspoons Worcestershire sauce

If using a food processor, put the cheese through the grater. Then, using the steel blade, combine the cheese with the remaining ingredients. Depending on the size of your food processor, you may have to do this in 2 batches. Process until mixture is smooth.

If using a blender, break up the cheese into cubes and add to blender with other ingredients. Blend until smooth.

Place in small serving dish or crock(s), cover, and chill. Serve at room temperature with thinly sliced black bread or crackers. Keeps for weeks.

Sour cream chile dip
MAKES ½ PINT PLUS

This is good as soon as it is made; it ages nicely and has even more flavor if made ahead of time.

½ pint sour cream

1 4-ounce can green chiles, chopped

1 small onion, finely chopped

1 small clove garlic, minced

Combine ingredients and refrigerate until serving time. Serve as dip with crackers or with raw vegetables—green peppers, cherry tomatoes, zucchini spears. Any left over is absolutely delightful in warm pita.

Spinach spread   MAKES 1½ CUPS

You have to like blue cheese to like this. You don't need a food processor; you can chop the spinach and onion and mash in the blue cheese. The food processor method imparts an emerald green color to the mixture, though.

1 pound fresh loose spinach or 10-ounce package fresh spinach

2 ounces blue cheese

1 small onion

2 teaspoons fresh lemon juice

Salt and freshly ground black pepper to taste

Wash spinach and remove tough stems. Steam spinach in covered pot in its own liquid until wilted. Drain well. Combine spinach with remaining ingredients in food processor with steel blade and process. Chill and serve as dip with cucumber spears, cherry tomatoes, or with plain crackers.

Tapenade   MAKES ABOUT 1½ CUPS

An hors d'oeuvre from Provence, or reasonable facsimile thereof.

¾ cup black olives, cured in oil, drained, pitted

2 tablespoons capers

1 teaspoon anchovy paste or minced anchovy

1 6½- or 7-ounce can tuna, drained

1 clove garlic

½ teaspoon dry mustard

1 tablespoon fresh lemon juice

20 leaves fresh basil or enough fresh parsley, minced, to make 2 tablespoons

Freshly ground black pepper to taste

Place all ingredients in a blender or food processor with steel blade. Process to a paste. Place in bowl and cover. Use as a spread with thinly sliced French bread or black bread.

QUICK DESSERTS . . . FROM SCRATCH

You don't have to cook a 30-minute meal to serve these desserts. They go with any menu.

The majority of them are fruit-based. There is a little sugar, in one form or another, in many of them; a little liqueur; a little jelly; a little honey. I don't believe you have to do without sugar entirely. It's a matter of moderation. I'd rather have one good dessert, complete with the amount of sugar necessary to make it taste right, than seven tasteless creations that have only one thing going for them—the absence of sugar.

The only trouble with sugar in this country is that each of us eats 129 pounds of it every year. If we reduced our intake to what our ancestors consumed fifty years ago, no one would be talking about sugar. The amount of sugar or sweetening in these recipes has been reduced considerably. In some recipes, it has been eliminated entirely.

None of the desserts takes more than a few minutes to prepare. Some take longer than others to chill, freeze, or set. Choose the dessert you want to make depending on the amount of time you have until dinner: 10 minutes? 24 hours?

There are recipes to suit each occasion. Some, like Frozen Peach Purée, are for last-minute dinners. So is the Zabaglione. Several, like the Cranberry-Orange Sherbet and Potted Plums, need a little advance warning.

While ice creams and sorbets are suggested occasionally, no recipes are given. They don't quite fit in with the time concept of the book's recipes and besides, you can buy excellent commercially prepared frozen desserts made with completely natural ingredients.

Amaretto apples

4 SERVINGS

¼ cup sugar
¼ cup amaretto
Grated rind and juice
of 1 orange

4 large firm apples

Combine sugar, amaretto, orange rind and juice in heavy saucepan. Heat slowly to bubbling. Meanwhile, peel, core, and thickly slice apples. As they are sliced, add them to pan. Simmer until apples are tender and all of liquid has evaporated.

Chill and serve plain, with crème fraîche (see page 360), or with whipped cream.

Banana and muenster cheese

To Brazilians, cheese and bananas is a very natural combination. Before you say no, try it.

½ large ripe banana per
person or 1 whole small
banana
Muenster cheese in
slices ⅛ to ¼ inch thick

Cinnamon
Sugar

Slice the bananas in half lengthwise and then into quarters. Sprinkle the quarters generously with cinnamon and very, very lightly with sugar. Cover each quarter with a slice of cheese. Place bananas in buttered shallow baking dish and bake in preheated 400 degree oven about 10 minutes, until cheese is completely melted and bubbly.

Hot chocolate bananas

1 tablespoon butter per banana	2 or 3 small pieces of dark chocolate broken from bar of good quality sweet or semisweet chocolate per each half banana
½ large banana per person or 1 whole small banana	
Cinnamon	

Melt butter in skillet. Peel bananas and split in half lengthwise. Place flat sides down in hot butter. Sprinkle with cinnamon. Sauté a minute or two; turn; place 2 or 3 pieces of chocolate on top of each half. Cook, covered, 2 or 3 minutes longer, until chocolate melts. Spread chocolate over bananas and allow to cool a little before serving so that the full flavors come out.

Grape and nectarine compote   4 SERVINGS

2 tablespoons orange-flavored liqueur	2 large nectarines, halved, pitted, and sliced
1 tablespoon honey	
2 cups seedless green grapes	

Combine liqueur and honey in a bowl large enough to hold the fruit. Add the grapes and nectarines; mix gently and refrigerate, stirring occasionally.

Nectarines vermont   4 SERVINGS

---

2 teaspoons maple syrup
1 medium, ripe
nectarine, cut up, per
person

1 tablespoon toasted
chopped walnuts

Mix maple syrup with nectarines and sprinkle with walnuts.

Glazed papaya with rum   4 SERVINGS

The secret to this recipe is finding a completely ripe papaya, which means it has turned yellow all over. Papaya is one fruit that will ripen after it has been harvested. If you plan ahead then, you can buy a green but softening papaya and in a few days end up with a ripe one.

2 large ripe papayas
2 tablespoons butter
2 tablespoons packed
brown sugar

4 tablespoons dark rum

Pare, seed, and cut papaya into bite-sized cubes. Heat butter in skillet. Add papaya with sugar and stir until papaya softens a little and is heated through. Stir in rum and cook until mixture begins to bubble. Serve warm, not hot, so that flavor will come through.

Frozen peach purée
3 SERVINGS

1 20-ounce package
   frozen peaches
2 teaspoons sugar
2 teaspoons fresh lemon
   juice

4 tablespoons port
¼ cup plain yogurt
½ teaspoon ground
   coriander

Before dinner, take package of frozen peaches from freezer and set aside about ¾ of them. At dessert time, combine the peaches with remaining ingredients in a food processor with steel blade and process until mixture is quite smooth except for some chunks of peach here and there.

If using a blender, you will have to blend in smaller amounts. Serve immediately in sauce dishes.

Hot peaches in brandy
2 OR 3 SERVINGS

This recipe is as sweet as the peaches used. For some it may not be sweet enough. The full flavor of the peaches comes out this way, however.

3 medium, very ripe and
   sweet peaches
3 tablespoons butter
½ teaspoon brown sugar

¼ teaspoon powdered
   ginger
3 tablespoons brandy

Slice the peaches. Melt the butter in a skillet. Stir in the sugar and ginger. Add the peaches and cook over medium heat, stirring occasionally to prevent sticking. When peaches are soft, after about 5 minutes, stir in the brandy and cook another minute.

Peach purée   2 SERVINGS

This recipe can easily be doubled. Consider, too, putting it into individual serving dishes in the freezer for about an hour. It will start to form ice crystals and become a peach freeze.

2 large ripe peaches,
coarsely chopped

1 teaspoon fresh lemon or
lime juice

2 teaspoons undiluted
frozen orange juice
concentrate

1 tablespoon orange-
flavored liqueur

In a food processor with steel blade or in a blender process peaches with remaining ingredients until smooth. (In a blender it may be necessary to do this in 2 batches.) Chill.

If you want to make the purée more than an hour in advance, you will need to add another teaspoon of lemon or lime juice to keep the peaches from turning brown. Cover tightly.

Peaches stuffed with
toasted almond cheese   4 TO 6 SERVINGS

3 medium, ripe and juicy
peaches

3 ounces cream cheese,
softened

⅓ cup (2¼ ounces) toasted
slivered almonds

Cut each peach in half and remove pit. Enlarge the cavity by removing a little of the peach pulp. Reserve pulp for another use or eat!

Combine the cream cheese and almonds and place in the cavity of each peach. Chill until serving time, but do not serve chilled. For best flavor, remove peaches from refrigerator ¾ to 1 hour before serving. Decorate with mint leaf.

Golden pears and orange   4 SERVINGS

2 large, very ripe pears	2 teaspoons brown sugar
1 large orange, thinly sliced	2 tablespoons brandy
2 tablespoons butter	

Cut pears in half and core. Slice thinly. Peel and thinly slice orange. Melt butter in medium skillet. Add pears and orange slices and cook, stirring occasionally, until pears soften. Stir in brown sugar and cook briefly, as sugar begins to caramelize. Pour in brandy; stir and serve.

Stuffed pears   6 SERVINGS

¼ pound Roquefort, Gorgonzola, or Danish blue cheese	⅛ teaspoon mace
	2 tablespoons port
¼ pound cream cheese	6 ripe pears
½ stick butter	

Blend the cheeses, butter, mace, and port. Halve and core the pears, making cavities large enough to hold about 1 tablespoon of cheese filling each. Fill.

Cut off a thin slice from bottom of pear half so that it will sit firmly on the plate. Serve immediately. Or cover and chill but take pears out of refrigerator 10 minutes before serving to allow cheese to warm slightly.

Potted plums   4 SERVINGS

This is a good topping for vanilla ice cream or orange sherbet.

12 ripe Italian purple   1 teaspoon grated orange
    plums   rind
⅓ cup port

Combine ingredients in pot and bring to boil; reduce heat;
cover and simmer, turning once, 5 minutes. Allow plums
to cool in syrup and serve at room temperature or cold.

Berries with brandy   4 SERVINGS

1 quart strawberries,   Sour cream, yogurt, or
   blackberries, or   whipped cream
   blueberries
¼ cup honey
¼ cup brandy

Prepare berries by washing gently and drying well. Blend
honey and brandy and pour over berries, stirring gently to
coat them well. Allow to sit at room temperature for 1
hour. (The sauce mixture will draw juice from the fruit.)
Chill if desired, stirring occasionally. Serve with a bowl of
sour cream, yogurt, or whipped cream.

Cranberry-orange sherbet   6 SERVINGS

*This is a very tart and tangy recipe: some may find they want
more sugar.*

   *Even when it freezes overnight, it is easy to spoon out because
the egg whites keep it from solidifying completely.*

8 ounces (2 cups) fresh
  cranberries, rinsed and
  drained
1 medium orange,
  quartered, seeded, but
  not peeled

4 or 5 tablespoons
  orange-flavored liqueur
5 tablespoons sugar
  Pinch salt
4 egg whites

In a food processor with steel blade or in a blender process cranberries and orange to coarse purée with the liqueur. Add the sugar and salt and continue to purée until smooth, but the mixture will always have some bits of the fruit in it. Adjust sugar to taste.

Beat egg whites until stiff. Stir ¼ of them into the fruit; fold in remaining egg whites. Freeze until needed.

If mixture has frozen for only an hour, or even a couple of hours, serve directly from freezer.

If the mixture is frozen overnight, defrost slightly and beat to make of sherbet consistency.

Strawberry and peach sundaes   4 SERVINGS

2 cups each sliced
  strawberries and sliced
  peaches
¼ cup orange-flavored
  liqueur or orange juice

1 pint vanilla ice cream

Combine sliced fruit with liqueur. Refrigerate until serving time. Scoop ice cream into individual dishes, and top with fruit mixture.

Strawberries with spicy yogurt

4 SERVINGS

1 cup plain yogurt
⅛ teaspoon nutmeg
⅛ teaspoon mace
1 tablespoon bitter orange marmalade

2 pints strawberries, cut in half or quarters

Combine all ingredients but berries. Chill until serving time, or serve immediately over strawberries.

Summer fruit with yogurt and apple or pear butter

2 SERVINGS

½ cup plain yogurt
2 tablespoons apple or pear butter
1 cup blueberries

1 medium peach
2 tablespoons toasted slivered almonds

Mix together yogurt and fruit butter. Divide blueberries between 2 dishes. Place half a cut-up peach in each dish; spoon on yogurt mixture and sprinkle with almonds.

Frozen fruit ice

3 OR 4 SERVINGS

The best frozen fruits are the unsweetened strawberries, peaches, or raspberries sold in plastic packages usually weighing 20 ounces.

Take the package or packages out of the freezer before dinner. At dessert time, place some of the frozen fruit in a food processor with steel blade and add a little honey to taste. Process until a thick purée.

Any fruit with any ice cream

One night after a light meal, dessert seemed called for. Scrounging around in the refrigerator, I found 3 purple plums, ½ peach, and some Smokehouse apples that had been pronounced mealy and not very good. I put a large tablespoon of butter in a medium-sized skillet and melted it. Then I cut up the fruit and put it in the hot butter, stirring occasionally, until it softened. I stirred in 1½ tablespoons Marsala and turned off the heat.

There were 3 tablespoons of a mixture of boysenberry and coffee ice cream in the freezer. It went into the bottom of a dish and I topped it with fruit. For me, the perennial dieter, the fruit alone was plenty.

With the exception of melon, there doesn't seem to be any reason that dribs and drabs of almost any fresh fruit wouldn't do just as well for this recipe.

Rum and raisins with ice cream
3 SERVINGS

1 **pint good quality vanilla   ½ cup dark rum
ice cream**
½ **cup raisins**

Before dinner, soften ice cream and put in individual serving dishes. Make a hollow in the center of each serving and place in freezer. Soak raisins in rum.

To serve, spoon some drained raisins into hollows of ice cream. Heat rum slightly; ignite and pour over ice cream. Bring to table flaming. Or, bring hot rum to table; pour into hollows and ignite.

Yogurt or sour cream dip   4 SERVINGS

1 **cup plain yogurt or sour cream**

1 **teaspoon grated orange or lemon rind**

4 **teaspoons honey**

1 **tablespoon kirsch**

1 **quart strawberries or raspberries, or 4 large peaches, sliced**

Mix yogurt, rind, honey, and kirsch together until well blended. Chill. Serve with choice of fruit.

Raspberry yogurt sauce   3 TO 4 SERVINGS

How to make a little fresh raspberry go a longer way. I served this sauce with white peaches, which made one guest exclaim: "I'm not going to put any sauce on these. I've never had such wonderful peaches in my life." And true, they aren't around very long each summer and perhaps in some places not at all. But if you find them, don't be put off by the green color of their skin, which is what makes people think they aren't ripe. Feel them. If they're soft they are ripe. The skin color is reflected in the flesh color, sort of a whitish green, not peach colored at all. They are by far the most perfumed of all peaches.

⅔ **cup fresh or unsweetened frozen raspberries**

⅓ **cup plain yogurt**

2 **tablespoons crème de cassis**

1 **teaspoon sugar**

Blend all ingredients together in a blender or process in food processor with steel blade until smooth. Chill. Serve over strawberries, blueberries, peaches, or nectarines.

Honey yogurt-tofu sauce
MAKES ABOUT 1¼ CUPS

¾ cup plain yogurt
½ cup mashed tofu
(soybean curd)

1 tablespoon honey
¼ teaspoon vanilla

Whirl all ingredients in a blender or food processor with steel blade. Allow to mellow at least 1 hour. Serve with fruit, such as berries, cantaloupe, peaches, bananas, or as a topping for pancakes.

Almost all-purpose sauce
2 SERVINGS

¼ cup plain yogurt
2 teaspoons orange marmalade

Few pinches cinnamon

Combine and serve over sliced peaches, plums, grapes, berries, oranges, bananas, nectarines, pears, etc., etc.

Apricot rum dip
MAKES ABOUT ¾ CUP

½ cup plain yogurt
2 teaspoons apricot preserves
¼ cup finely chopped pecans or walnuts

2 tablespoons dark rum
Generous pinch cinnamon

Combine all ingredients and mix well. Serve with cantaloupe or other melon spears or with peaches or nectarines.

Ricotta sweet for spooning or sipping

4 SERVINGS

Ricotta, mixed as it is in this recipe, usually finds its way into that wonderful Italian pastry called cannoli. Its subtle, delicate flavor takes nicely to most liqueurs. Try it with the Italian anise-flavored one, with an orange-flavored liqueur, even with rum.

½ pound ricotta

¼ cup milk or cream

2 tablespoons anise-flavored liqueur

1½ tablespoons bitter orange marmalade

⅓ cup toasted slivered almonds

Shaved bittersweet chocolate for garnish (optional)

Place all ingredients but almonds and chocolate in a blender or food processor with steel blade. Process until just mixed. Mix in the almonds and chill until serving time. If the dish will not be served for more than an hour, do not stir in almonds until serving time. Spoon into stemmed glasses and garnish with chocolate, if desired.

Zabaglione

6 OR 7 SERVINGS

The proportions for zabaglione, also spelled zabaione, of sugar, egg yolks, and Marsala vary greatly. This is one of the less sweet versions. If you don't have Marsala and don't feel like buying it (it's cheap and keeps indefinitely), you can use sherry.

This is a recipe for warm zabaglione. Instructions for making a chilled, less sweet zabaglione follow. You can decide which to try based upon when you have more time—before dinner or after the main course.

6 egg yolks

5 tablespoons sugar

¾ cup Marsala

Beat eggs with sugar in top of double boiler until thick. Place over hot water and gradually add Marsala, beating constantly until mixture is consistency of lightly beaten heavy cream. Spoon into serving dishes, preferably long-stemmed glasses, and serve immediately.

To serve cold: Remove zabaglione from heat and place in bowl of ice. Continue beating until mixture is cooled. Refrigerate up to 1 day. To serve, beat 1 cup heavy cream until soft peaks form. Fold into zabaglione and serve. This way the recipe serves 12. If you're serving a small crowd, therefore, make half the original recipe (3 yolks, 2½ tablespoons sugar, 6 tablespoons Marsala, and ½ cup heavy cream).

MORE QUICK DESSERTS

Guava and cheese

Serve canned guava shells with cream cheese on unsalted round crackers.

Green grapes, brown sugar, and yogurt

Place seedless green or red grapes in serving dish. Top with layer of plain yogurt evenly spread to cover surface. Sprinkle with brown sugar. Chill until serving time.

Blueberries and ginger

For each serving of blueberries, finely cut 1 or 2 teaspoons crystallized ginger into dish and mix.

Fruit and spirits

Macerate fruits that have been cut into slices or cubes in liqueur, or liquor. Some combinations may need added sugar. Adjust before serving.

Oranges	**Orange liqueurs**
Apples	**Calvados**
Pineapple	**Rum**
Pears	**Pear brandy**
Peaches	**Orange liqueurs**
Raspberries	**Framboise**
Italian plums	**Slivovitz, plum brandy**
Strawberries	**Orange liqueurs, kirsch**

PART 4 | PREPARE-AHEAD MIXES

CONVENIENCE FOODS

BROWNIE MIX
Brownies   *Brownie crust*

BUCKWHEAT PANCAKE MIX
Buckwheat pancakes

BULGUR PILAF MIX
Bulgur pilaf

HOMEMADE CAKE MIX
Chocolate cake   *White or yellow cake*

SPICE CAKE MIX
Spice cake

CHEESE SAUCE MIX
Medium cheese sauce   *Macaroni and cheese*

BASIC COOKIE MIX
Ginger thins   *Peanut butter cookies*
Sugar crisps

CHILI SEASONING MIX
Chili   *Chili mac*
Chili hors d'oeuvres

CHOCOLATE CHIP COOKIE MIX
Chocolate chip cookies

CORN BREAD OR CORN MUFFIN MIX

Muffins

Cheese onion corn bread

Batter bread

Corn bread pizza

FRUITED RICE MIX

White fruited rice

Brown fruited rice

GINGERBREAD MIX

Gingerbread

Gingerbread boys

ITALIAN SEASONING

Tomato sauce

Mayonnaise spread

POT-TO-PLATE STUFFING

Top of the stove stuffing

Bake in the oven stuffing

SHAKE-IT-AND-BAKE-IT CHICKEN COATING MIX

Baked chicken

Sautéed chicken

SHAKE-IT-AND-BAKE-IT PORK CHOP COATING MIX

Baked chops

Sautéed chops

SPICY SHAKE-IT-AND-BAKE-IT FISH COATING MIX

Baked fish

Broiled fish

Sautéed fish

CRÈME FRAÎCHE
COLETTES
ETERNAL CHEESE MIX
FREEZER-TO-OVEN-TO-TABLE POPOVERS
GREEN BEANS AND SLIVERED ALMONDS À LA BIRD
HELP FOR HAMBURGERS CHILI-STYLE
HELP FOR TUNA STROGANOFF-STYLE

HERB BUTTERS
HOT CHOCOLATE SAUCE
INSTANT BREAKFAST
QUICK ON THE SIDE
SPICED TEA
ZESTY BARBECUE SAUCE

CONVENIENCE FOODS

Interest in homemade convenience products doesn't seem to wane. Whether it's how to make your own corn bread mix or chocolate chip cookie mix, or help for hamburgers or shake-it-and-bake-it, recipes like these are the most popular in *The Washington Post*'s food section. There are a variety of reasons.

Some cooks are looking for ways to save money; some are worried about the chemicals put in ready-made convenience foods; some need to cut down on their salt intake; some feel foods made at home have more nutritional value; some believe homemade tastes better. All the reasons people give for wanting to make these foods themselves make sense.

Commercially prepared convenience foods are not necessarily that convenient. And you have to look at the trade-offs: Is the cost of these products worth the amount of time saved; how much nutrition are you giving up for the time-saving and at what price; how many unknown ingredients are you ingesting in the interests of saving time?

Certainly some of the recipes in this chapter require more effort on the part of the cook than buying the packaged mix. But mixes like those for a cake or Italian Seasoning can be done when you are not tired or in a hurry. Then they can be stored as any store-bought mix would be. In experimenting with these products over the years, I have discovered that even without the preservatives most of them have an extremely long shelf life if stored as directed. I have kept cookie, cake, biscuit, and muffin mixes for six months or longer.

Not all the convenience foods in this chapter are the

put-it-away-until-you-need-it variety. Some of them are meant to be used as made, like the Help for Tuna Stroganoff-Style. Such recipes are included to prove that it takes so little extra time to do it yourself. The bought goods taste OK, but I think I cook better, using my own recipes!

On the other hand, the Chocolate Chip Cookie Mix, the three varieties of Shake-It-and-Bake-It, the Brownie Mix, the Hot Chocolate Sauce, the Zesty Barbecue Sauce, I could go on and on, are much better than anything in the store.

Try them, you won't be disappointed.

Brownie mix MAKES ABOUT 8 CUPS, ENOUGH
FOR 3 8-INCH-SQUARE PANS

---

4 cups sugar

2 cups unbleached flour

1⅔ cups unsweetened cocoa

2 teaspoons salt

1¼ cups vegetable shortening

Put sugar, flour, cocoa, and salt in large bowl and mix until ingredients are evenly distributed. Cut in shortening with pastry blender, two knives, or fingertips until mixture resembles cornmeal. Store in airtight container in cool, dry place.

Keeps 4 to 6 months.

To make brownies: Beat 2 eggs with 1 teaspoon vanilla in mixing bowl and blend well. Measure out 2½ generous cups Brownie Mix, but do not pack down. With spoon beat mix into eggs until batter is smooth. Stir in ½ to ¾ cup coarsely chopped pecans or walnuts. Grease and flour 8 × 8 × 2-inch baking pan. Spoon in batter and spread evenly. Bake in preheated 350 degree oven 25 to 30 minutes, until knife inserted in center comes out clean. DO NOT OVERBAKE. Cool in pan and cut into squares.

NOTE: Can also be baked in 9-inch-square pan, but brownies will be thinner. Bake only about 20 minutes.

To make a brownie crust: Combine 2 cups of Brownie Mix with 1 egg beaten with 1 teaspoon vanilla and mix thoroughly. Grease an 8- or 9-inch pie plate well. Spoon mix into pie plate and press against bottom and sides with fingers moistened with water. Bake in preheated 350-degree oven about 20 minutes. The sides should be well baked, the bottom still soft. Remove from oven and push down bottom to flatten. Cool and fill with choice of ice cream, using about 1 quart.

NOTE: Flavor the crust with other extracts besides vanilla. In place of 1 teaspoon vanilla use ½ teaspoon mint, or rum, or orange extract.

Buckwheat pancake mix

MAKES ABOUT 4 TO 4½ DOZEN 3-INCH CAKES

Some nights you just don't want anything fancy at all. Buckwheat cakes and sausage are more than enough. Not that they aren't good for brunch: they are.

1 cup light buckwheat flour

1 cup unbleached white flour or whole-wheat flour

2 teaspoons baking powder

1 teaspoon baking soda

2 teaspoons sugar

½ teaspoon salt

Mix all the ingredients together and store in airtight container in cool, dry place. Keeps 8 months or longer.

To make buckwheat pancakes: 1 heaping cup Buckwheat Pancake Mix, 1 egg, separated, 1 cup sour milk* or buttermilk, and 2 tablespoons melted butter. Combine the mix with the egg yolk, butter, and sour milk. Beat the white until stiff; fold into batter. Cook on hot griddle or lightly greased heavy skillet. (You will also need to grease the griddle lightly every now and then, depending on how well seasoned it is.) Brown pancakes on one side; turn

---

*To sour milk: Place 1 tablespoon lemon juice or white vinegar in bottom of 1 cup (or larger) measure. Fill the cup with milk at room temperature to 1-cup line and stir. Let stand 5 minutes until it clabbers, until a curd forms in the milk.

when edges begin to brown and bubbles form on surface; cook until golden on second side. Serve with butter and maple syrup, sausages, nitrite-free bacon, eggs, and so on. Makes 20 pancakes.

Bulgur pilaf mix   MAKES ABOUT 5 CUPS, 1¼ CUPS MIX MAKES 4 SERVINGS

4 cups bulgur (cracked wheat)	2 teaspoons dried savory
¼ cup dried parsley flakes	Freshly ground black pepper to taste
⅓ cup dried minced onion	
2 teaspoons dried sage	

Mix ingredients together and store in airtight container in cool, dry place. Keeps 8 months to 1 year.

To prepare: Combine a heaping 1¼ cups Bulgur Pilaf Mix with 2 cups of water in saucepan. Season to taste with salt, if desired. Bring to boil; reduce heat to simmer, cover, and cook until water has been absorbed completely, about 20 minutes.

The same seasonings and ratio of seasonings to grain would make a good white or brown rice mix or a buckwheat groats (kasha) mix. Cooking the rice calls for the same proportion of ingredients and the same technique. Cooking the groats calls for mixing the dry mix first with a slightly beaten egg, then cooking the mixture over medium heat until the egg has been absorbed by the groats and the mixture is dry. Then follow the pilaf recipe to finish.

Homemade cake mix MAKES ABOUT 16 CUPS, ENOUGH FOR 4 CAKES

8 cups unbleached flour
5 cups sugar
3 tablespoons baking powder

2 teaspoons salt
2 cups vegetable shortening

Combine all ingredients in very large bowl. Cut in shortening with pastry blender or your fingers (fingers are better) until crumbly. Store in airtight container in cool, dry place.

Keeps 6 months.

To make a chocolate cake:

3½ cups Homemade Cake Mix
⅓ cup unsweetened cocoa
2 eggs

1 cup milk
1 teaspoon vanilla

Mix Homemade Cake Mix with cocoa. Then beat in eggs, milk, and vanilla, beating at low speed for 1 minute and medium speed for 2 minutes.

Spoon into 2 greased and floured 8-inch-round cake pans and bake in preheated 350 degree oven 20 to 25 minutes, until sides pull away from pan and tops spring back when touched lightly.

For square cake: Bake in greased and floured 9 × 9 × 2-inch baking pan in preheated 350 degree oven about 35 minutes, until cake starts to pull away from sides of pan.

To make a yellow or white cake, leave out cocoa entirely and reduce the milk to ¾ cup.

Spice cake mix   6 8-INCH LAYERS

8 cups unbleached flour, sifted	3 tablespoons ground cinnamon
2¼ cups sugar	1 teaspoon ground cloves
2½ teaspoons baking soda	1½ teaspoons salt
2 tablespoons baking powder	2¼ cups shortening
3 tablespoons powdered ginger	

Sift flour, sugar, baking soda and powder, ginger, cinnamon, cloves, and salt together twice. Cut in shortening with pastry blender or two knives until mixture resembles cornmeal. Store in airtight container in cool, dry place.

Keeps 6 months.

To make a single layer, square cake: Measure 2 cups Spice Cake Mix into a bowl. Combine 1 egg, beaten, ½ cup unsulphured molasses, and ½ cup boiling water. Add ½ to dry ingredients and beat until well blended. Add remaining liquid and beat again. Pour into greased and floured 8-inch-square baking pan and bake in preheated 350 degree oven 30 to 35 minutes. Cool on rack before removing from pan.

A cream-cheese frosting is good with this, especially if flavored with orange rind.

Cheese sauce mix   MAKES 10½ CUPS MIX

1 cup unbleached flour	2 teaspoons paprika
3½ cups dried grated Parmesan cheese	1 teaspoon nutmeg
4 cups nonfat dry milk	1 cup butter, cut into pieces
1½ teaspoons salt, or to taste	

Mix flour, cheese, milk, salt, paprika, and nutmeg in large bowl. Cut in butter with fingertips or pastry blender until mixture resembles coarse cornmeal. Store in airtight container in refrigerator, or freeze, if desired. (It won't freeze solid.)

Keeps 6 to 8 months.

To make medium cheese sauce: Blend ½ cup Cheese Sauce Mix and 1 cup milk in small pot and cook, stirring over medium to low heat, until sauce comes to boil. Reduce heat and simmer about 2 minutes. Makes 1 cup.

Water can be substituted for milk in preparing sauce.

Macaroni and cheese   3 SERVINGS

This homemade version of macaroni and cheese gives you 13 grams of protein versus 8 grams for the packaged product and only 14 grams of fat instead of 29. Both have the same number of calories. The price is approximately the same, a penny or two higher or lower depending on where you live.

1 cup Cheese Sauce Mix   1½ cups elbow macaroni

Cook macaroni in boiling water until al dente, about 8 minutes; drain and keep warm. Combine the mix with 1 cup water and cook over low heat until mixture thickens, a couple of minutes. Combine with the macaroni.

Basic cookie mix   MAKES ABOUT 19 CUPS

Without semisweet chocolate morsels or nuts this is the same mix as used in the Chocolate Chip Cookies.

9 cups unbleached flour
4 teaspoons baking soda
2 teaspoons salt
4 cups shortening

3 cups granulated sugar
3 cups firmly packed brown sugar

In large bowl combine dry ingredients thoroughly. With fingers, two forks, or a pastry blender blend in shortening until mixture is crumbly. Store in airtight container in cool, dry place.

Keeps 3 or 4 months.

Ginger thins   MAKES ABOUT 100

2 cups Basic Cookie Mix
¼ cup unsulphured molasses
½ teaspoon vanilla

1 egg, beaten
½ teaspoon each ground ginger, cinnamon, and allspice

If you want to keep ginger thins cookie mix on hand, add the spices to the dry ingredients and store in tightly covered container.

To make cookies, combine all ingredients and mix thoroughly.

Grease baking sheets and place dabs of dough, ¼ teaspoon or smaller, on sheets, 1 inch apart. Bake in preheated 325 degree oven 7 to 9 minutes. Cool slightly on baking sheets, until cookies firm up slightly. Remove with spatula and cool completely on wire racks.

These can be frozen after baking.

Sugar crisps MAKES ABOUT 80

3 cups Basic Cookie Mix 1 egg
1 teaspoon milk Sugar
1½ teaspoons vanilla

Combine Basic Cookie Mix, milk, vanilla, and egg; blend well. Grease baking sheets with oil. Drop batter by teaspoonsful onto sheets. Sprinkle with sugar, if desired. Bake in preheated 375 degree oven 8 to 10 minutes, until edges start to brown. Cool slightly on baking sheets, then remove. These can be frozen after baking.

Peanut butter cookies

MAKES ABOUT 55

3 cups Basic Cookie Mix ½ cup chunky-style
2 eggs natural peanut butter
1 teaspoon vanilla

Combine Basic Cookie Mix with eggs, vanilla, and peanut butter. Blend well. Grease baking sheets. Drop by heaping teaspoons, 2 inches apart, onto sheets and flatten with tines of fork. Bake in preheated 375 degree oven 10 to 12 minutes, or until edges begin to brown. Cool slightly on baking sheets, then remove. These can be frozen after baking.

Chili seasoning mix

MAKES A LITTLE LESS THAN
1 CUP, 15 TABLESPOONS

---

10 tablespoons minced dried onion (½ cup plus 2 tablespoons)

5 teaspoons dried leaf oregano

3¾ teaspoons minced dried garlic

3 tablespoons plus 2 teaspoons ground cumin

Mix ingredients thoroughly and store in an airtight container in cool, dry place.

Keeps 8 to 10 months, after which it begins to lose strength.

To make chili: 2 or 3 tablespoons Chili Seasoning Mix, 1 pound ground beef, 8-ounce can tomato sauce, 15-ounce can pinto beans.

Brown beef. As it begins to lose fat, stir the chili mix and add 2 tablespoons to beef. When beef is browned, stir in tomato sauce; cook over low heat until mixture is well blended and very hot.

Either cook beans separately, after draining off most of liquid, or stir drained beans into meat mixture. Then the dish becomes chili with beans.

To make chili hors d'oeuvres: Combine 1 teaspoon well-stirred Chili Seasoning Mix with 1 tablespoon softened or melted butter for each flour tortilla. Spread mixture on flour tortilla and broil until mixture bubbles and tortilla puffs and begins to brown, a matter of a few minutes. While still hot, cut each tortilla into 6 wedges and serve warm.

To make chili mac: ¾ pound ground beef, 1-pound can tomatoes, 1 cup elbow macaroni, cooked and drained, 2 or 3 tablespoons Chili Seasoning Mix.

Cook beef in skillet until it loses its color. Drain off fat. Add remaining ingredients and simmer, stirring occasionally, until mixture is well blended and thoroughly heated.

Chocolate chip cookie mix
MAKES 30 3" COOKIES, 40 2" COOKIES

When I did a spot on WRC-TV news showing how to make this chocolate chip cookie mix we had somewhere between 1,500 and 2,000 requests for the recipe. It is based on the original Toll House cookie recipe, created in Massachusetts over fifty years ago. For some, it is still the ultimate chocolate chip cookie.

9 cups unbleached flour
4 teaspoons baking soda
2 teaspoons salt
3 cups firmly packed dark brown sugar
3 cups granulated sugar
4 cups vegetable shortening*
4 cups chopped pecans
4 12-ounce packages semisweet real chocolate chips

Combine dry ingredients in large bowl. Mix in shortening, using fingers. Then stir in nuts and chocolate chips. Store in airtight container in cool, dry place.

Keeps 6 months or longer in cool, dry place. Keeps even longer in the refrigerator or freezer.

To make cookies: Combine 7 cups Chocolate Chip Cookie Mix with 1 teaspoon vanilla that has been mixed with 2 eggs, slightly beaten. This batter is heavy. For the larger cookies, drop batter by heaping tablespoonfuls on greased baking sheets. For smaller cookies, drop by

*You can use butter instead of shortening, but then the mix must be kept in the refrigerator or freezer.

heaping teaspoonfuls. Bake in preheated 375 degree oven 10 to 12 minutes for larger cookies; 8 to 10 minutes for smaller cookies. For flatter cookies, pat down with back of spoon. Cool slightly on baking sheets, then remove. Freeze after baking, if you like.

Corn bread or corn muffin mix

MAKES 10½ CUPS

4 cups unbleached flour
4 cups yellow cornmeal
¾ cup sugar
¼ cup baking powder

2 teaspoons salt
1 cup vegetable shortening

Combine dry ingredients; stir well. Cut in shortening with pastry blender, two knives, or fingers. Store in airtight container in cool, dry place.

Keeps 6 months.

Muffins

MAKES 1 DOZEN MEDIUM-SIZED

1 egg
1 cup milk

2⅓ cups Corn Bread or Corn Muffin Mix

Beat egg and milk together. Lightly stir into Corn Bread or Corn Muffin Mix. (Do not beat out the lumps. Mixture should be lumpy.) Grease 12 medium muffin cups. Spoon mixture into cups, filling ⅔ full. Bake in preheated 425 degree oven 15 to 20 minutes.

Cheese onion corn bread MAKES AN 8-INCH-SQUARE BREAD

1 egg	2⅓ cups Corn Bread or
1 cup milk	Corn Muffin Mix
¼ cup chopped onion	
1 cup coarsely shredded sharp cheese, such as Cheddar	

Beat egg and milk together. Lightly stir into Corn Bread or Corn Muffin Mix. Do not beat out lumps. Stir in onion and cheese. Grease an 8-inch-square baking pan. Pour in batter and bake in preheated 425 degree oven 15 minutes. Cut into squares and serve warm.

Bread can also be made plain, without onion and cheese.

Batter bread OR A REASONABLE FACSIMILE THEREOF—VERY SOUTHERN, VERY GOOD.

6 TO 8 SERVINGS

3½ cups milk	4 eggs, separated
2½ cups Corn Bread or Corn Muffin Mix (see page 350)	2 egg whites

Scald 2½ cups milk. Combine Corn Bread or Corn Muffin Mix with 1 cup remaining milk. Gradually add mixture to scalded milk and cook over medium heat, stirring, until mixture is a thick mush. Remove from heat. Stir in yolks, 1 at a time. Beat 6 whites until stiff but not dry; fold into mixture. Grease a shallow 2½-quart casserole and spoon mixture into casserole.

Bake in preheated 350 degree oven about 50 minutes, until crust is golden.

Corn bread pizza   6 TO 8 SERVINGS

Would this be described as southern Italian-American?

1½ pounds ground beef
 1 cup chopped onion
 2 cloves garlic, minced or
   pressed
 ½ cup chopped green bell
   pepper
1½ 8-ounce cans tomato
   sauce
 2 teaspoons pure chile
   powder*

 1 teaspoon oregano
   Salt and freshly ground
   black pepper to taste
2⅓ cups Corn Bread or
   Corn Muffin Mix (see
   page 350)
 ⅔ cup finely grated
   Parmesan cheese

Brown meat; pour off fat. Add onion, garlic, and green pepper and cook until onion is limp. Stir in tomato sauce, chile powder, oregano, and salt and pepper; set aside.

Prepare Corn Bread or Corn Muffin Mix, using proportions in Muffin recipe (see page 350). Spread batter over bottom and sides of greased 12-inch pizza or tarte pan. Spoon beef mixture evenly over batter and sprinkle cheese on top. Bake in preheated 400 degree oven 20 to 25 minutes, or until cheese is bubbly and crust around sides is well browned.

*Pure chile powder is not a combination of spices; it is from the chile only. Use a sweet mild not hot one.

Fruited rice mix   MAKES ABOUT 8 CUPS MIX

This seasoned rice mix has the distinct advantage of being free of monosodium glutamate, salt, and other unpleasantness. If you want salt in yours, add the amount you like.

4 cups enriched white or brown rice

4 tablespoons minced dried onion

5 tablespoons plus 1 teaspoon instant beef or chicken or vegetable bouillon granules

1 cup dried apricots or apples

1½ cups raisins

1 cup unsalted roasted peanuts or blanched slivered almonds

Freshly ground black pepper to taste

Combine all ingredients and store in airtight packages or containers in cool, dry place.

Will keep 6 months.

To prepare fruited white rice: For 4 servings, combine 1 cup stirred white rice mixture with 2¼ to 2½ cups water, depending on how soft and moist you like your rice, plus 2 tablespoons undiluted frozen orange juice concentrate, and salt to taste. Bring to boil; reduce heat to simmer, cover, and cook, stirring occasionally, until liquid evaporates, about 20 minutes.

(In place of water and orange juice concentrate, substitute 2¼ to 2½ cups orange juice.)

To prepare fruited brown rice: Soak the rice mixture in the liquid in which it will be cooked at least 1 hour before cooking, or all day long, if desired. Then cook according to directions.

Makes 4 cups.

Gingerbread mix   MAKES ABOUT 14 CUPS

8 cups unbleached flour	3 tablespoons powdered ginger
2 cups sugar	
¼ cup baking powder	3 tablespoons ground cinnamon
2 teaspoons salt	
1 teaspoon baking soda	2¼ cups solid vegetable shortening
1 teaspoon cloves	

In a large bowl mix all dry ingredients together until well blended. Mix in the shortening using two knives, a pastry blender, or your fingers until mixture resembles cornmeal. Store in airtight container in cool, dry place.

Will keep 6 months.

Gingerbread   MAKES 9 SQUARES

Excellent served warm with vanilla ice cream or whipped cream.

1 egg	2¼ cups Gingerbread Mix
½ cup boiling water	
½ cup unsulphured molasses	

In bowl combine egg with water and molasses, then stir in mix. Pour into greased and floured 9 × 9 × 2-inch pan and bake in preheated 350 degree oven 20 to 30 minutes, or until cake pulls away from sides of pan and tester inserted in center comes out clean. Cool in pan 10 minutes; then turn out and cool on a wire rack.

Gingerbread boys   MAKES 12 6-INCH BOYS

⅓ cup unsulphured
  molasses
1 egg

¼ cup flour
3 cups Gingerbread Mix

Combine molasses, egg, and flour; stir in Gingerbread Mix and blend until soft dough is formed. Roll out on lightly floured surface to thickness between ⅛ and ¼ inch. Use gingerbread-boy cutter and collect dough scraps to reroll and cut out. Place boys on lightly greased baking sheets. Make eyes, nose, and buttons with raisins, if desired. Bake in preheated 350 degree oven about 12 minutes, until edges brown. When cool remove from sheets.
NOTE: Six cups of the mix can be combined with ⅔ cup

Italian seasoning   MAKES ½ CUP PLUS

unsulphured molasses, 2 eggs, and 1 cup flour to make Gingerbread House. Follow any directions for making house to shape, bake, and construct.

3 tablespoons dried
  oregano
2 tablespoons dried basil
1 tablespoon dried
  marjoram

1 tablespoon onion
  powder
2 teaspoons garlic powder

Combine all ingredients and store in airtight container. Mix thoroughly before using.
  Keeps 8 months.

To use with tomato sauce: Combine 1 tablespoon Italian Seasoning with 2 cups tomatoes, or 15-ounce can tomato sauce or purée.

To use with mayonnaise spread: Combine ½ teaspoon Italian Seasoning with ¼ cup mayonnaise. Spread mixture on flour tortillas or thinly sliced bread. Cut tortillas into 6 wedges or bread into squares. Broil until tops begin to bubble and brown. Serve at room temperature.

Pot-to-plate stuffing   MAKES 20 CUPS

5 tablespoons minced dried onion	1 teaspoon turmeric
5 tablespoons dried parsley flakes	¾ teaspoon nutmeg
7 tablespoons dried celery	1 teaspoon minced dried garlic (optional)
5 tablespoons dried basil	Salt to taste
5 teaspoons paprika	20 cups soft bread cubes, from 22 ounces of bread

Put seasonings in blender; blend to powder. Place bread cubes in large bag and add seasonings. Shake bag so that seasonings stick to bread cubes. Put bread cubes in shallow trays in single layer and allow to dry on the counter for a couple of days, until bread feels stale. Store in plastic bags or plastic containers, tightly closed. Shake from bottom before measuring out.

Keeps 6 months.

In heavy-bottomed pan melt 3 tablespoons butter. Stir in 3 cups cubes until coated with butter. Add ¾ cup boiling chicken, vegetable, or beef broth or water until mixture is moistened. Cover and allow to cook over lowest possible heat about 5 minutes, until stuffing is very hot.

Makes 3 cups.

Stuffing can also be baked in the oven after it has been sautéed in butter and liquid is added. Cover and bake in preheated 350 degree oven 15 to 20 minutes.

NOTES: If you use a salty stock, you may prefer to keep the mix unsalted and adjust seasonings after cooking.

The amount of liquid used depends on whether or not you want a moist or medium-dry stuffing. Alter the amount of liquid to suit your taste.

When using to stuff a bird, allow ½ pound stuffing per pound of bird.

Shake-it-and-bake-it chicken coating mix MAKES 3⅓ CUPS, ENOUGH TO COAT 7 TO 9 POUNDS OF CHICKEN

No MSG, no artificial color, no sweetness, and it tastes much better than what they make in the factory.

1½ cups dry fine bread crumbs	1 teaspoon freshly ground black pepper
1 cup unbleached flour	1 tablespoon dried marjoram
4 tablespoons dried parsley flakes	1 tablespoon dried thyme
1 tablespoon paprika	Salt to taste
1 tablespoon onion powder	4 tablespoons vegetable oil
2 teaspoons garlic powder	

Combine all ingredients but oil and stir to mix evenly. Stir in oil and mix with fork or fingertips to blend completely. Store in airtight container in cool, dry place.

Keeps 4 to 6 months.

To use: For about 2 pounds of chicken, pour about ¾ to 1 cup of mix into a plastic bag. Moisten chicken pieces with water or milk and shake off excess liquid. Add a few pieces at a time to the bag and shake to coat evenly. Place chicken pieces on greased baking sheet and bake in preheated 400 degree oven 30 to 45 minutes, depending on size. Turn once, after 20 minutes.

Chicken can also be sautéed. Brown well on both sides in 2 or 3 tablespoons hot oil; cover, reduce heat, and cook until chicken is tender, total cooking time about 20 minutes.

Shake-it-and-bake-it pork coating mix
MAKES ABOUT 2½ CUPS, ENOUGH TO COAT ABOUT 24 PORK CHOPS

No MSG, no artificial color, no sweeteners, and it tastes much better than the stuff in the box.

- 1 cup yellow cornmeal
- 1 cup cornflake crumbs
- ⅓ cup instant minced onion
- 3 tablespoons dried parsley flakes
- 1 teaspoon instant minced garlic
- 1 tablespoon dried oregano
- 1 tablespoon dried basil
- ½ teaspoon freshly ground black pepper
- Salt to taste
- 2 tablespoons oil

Combine all ingredients but oil and stir to mix evenly. Stir in oil and mix with fork until all of the dry ingredients are moistened. Store in airtight container in cool, dry place. Keeps 6 months.

To use: For 8 pork chops, pour about ¾ cup of mix into a plastic bag. Moisten chops with water and shake off excess liquid. Add a few chops to the bag at a time and shake to coat evenly. Pork may be cooked either of two ways: Bake on rack in shallow pan in preheated 425 degree oven, turning once, 30 to 35 minutes for ½-inch-thick chops; 40 to 45 minutes for 1-inch-thick chops.

Or, sauté in a little oil in skillet until golden brown on both sides. Use about ¼ cup oil for 8 chops.

Spicy shake-it-and-bake-it fish coating mix

MAKES ABOUT 3 CUPS, ENOUGH TO COAT ABOUT 5 POUNDS OF FISH

Not only does this taste better than the commercial version, it has no monosodium glutamate, no sugar, no corn syrup solids, no artificial color, and no BHA.

1½ cups dry, fine bread crumbs

1 cup unbleached flour

4 tablespoons dried parsley flakes

1 tablespoon dried lemon peel

1 teaspoon freshly ground black pepper

1 tablespoon celery seed

1 tablespoon dried marjoram

1 tablespoon crushed dried thyme flakes

Salt to taste

4 tablespoons vegetable oil

Combine all ingredients but oil and stir to mix evenly. Stir in oil and mix with fork or fingertips to blend completely. Store in airtight container in cool, dry place.

Keeps 4 to 6 months.

To use: For each pound of fish, pour a generous ½ cup of mix into a plastic bag. Moisten fish fillets with water and shake off excess liquid. Add a few pieces to the bag at a time and shake to coat evenly. Bake the fillets, skin sides down, on a well-greased baking sheet in preheated 400 degree oven about 20 minutes.

To broil: Allow 8 to 10 minutes on each side for thick fillets; 5 to 8 minutes for thin fillets.

To pan-fry: Brown on both sides in hot oil in skillet over medium-low heat.

Crème fraîche MAKES 1½ CUPS

This is absolutely wonderful with fresh fruit. If the fruit isn't ripe enough or sweet enough, sprinkle with a little liqueur and honey or brown sugar and then top with crème fraîche.

There is a recipe in Pure & Simple for crème fraîche made with buttermilk. It produces a very different product from this one, much thicker and not as tangy.

This version is also probably more practical since you don't have to figure out what to do with all the remaining buttermilk if you don't drink it.

1 cup pasteurized heavy   ½ cup sour cream
   cream*

Whisk the cream with the sour cream in a saucepan until well blended. Over the lowest heat possible cook until the mixture reaches 85 to 90 degrees, but don't let it go above 90 degrees.

Pour the mixture into a jar and put cover on, but keep it ajar. Keep mixture in warm place (back of the stove) at about 75 degrees for 8 hours or longer, until it thickens like yogurt. Stir and cover; refrigerate. If a clear liquid rises to the top, drain it off.

Keeps about 2 weeks.

---

*Do not use ultra-pasteurized cream; it won't work.

Colettes

You've seen these chocolate cups advertised in food magazines. It's no trick to make your own. Keep them in the freezer if you like.

12 ounces semisweet   **½ teaspoon vanilla**
   chocolate
¼ cup butter

Melt the chocolate with butter. Remove from heat and stir in vanilla. Let thicken slightly. Coat inside of 2 thicknesses of medium fluted paper cups with chocolate, using a spoon and your finger to fill in the holes. Do not make walls of chocolate too thin or they will crack when paper is peeled off. Place in muffin tins. Chill in freezer a few minutes and then fill in any places that have not been filled in. Freeze until firm. Remove paper from chocolate cups and fill as desired.

Liqueur-flavored whipped cream is one simple filling. Figure about 1 tablespoon liqueur to 1 cup heavy cream. Or, try sweetened strawberries. Suit your own tastes.

The cups can also be filled with something more elaborate, like chocolate mousse.

Eternal cheese mix

There are relatively few proportions and a lot of advice for making this cheese ball from the bits and pieces of cheese that tend to accumulate if you serve it often.

When you have collected about ½ pound of assorted cheeses, any kind but go easy on the really strong ones like blue, Gorgonzola, or Roquefort, grate them coarsely, or cube them, depending on their hardness. Add about 2 ounces cream cheese. Place the mixture in food processor with steel blade and add ½ teaspoon dry mustard for each

½ pound of cheese, ¼ teaspoon Worcestershire sauce, and 5 tablespoons dry sherry or beer or dry red or white wine. Process until mixture is as smooth as possible. Store in airtight container, a cheese crock or glass jar with screwtop cover will do.

Refrigerate. To serve, return to room temperature for 30 minutes. Serve with crackers or bread. (When you near the bottom of the crock, process whatever cheese you have accumulated, and add the sherry, beer, or wine. Check on bite and add more mustard and Worcestershire as needed.)

Freezer-to-oven-to-table popovers
MAKES 15 TO 18 LARGE

When you eat these you have to throw caution to the wind and slather on the butter!

2 cups unbleached flour	2 cups milk
½ teaspoon salt	4 eggs
2 tablespoons melted butter	

Beat the flour, salt, butter, and milk until smooth. Add eggs, 1 at a time, and beat in until blended. Don't overbeat. Oil custard cups, individual soufflé dishes, individual brioche molds, or large muffin pans generously. Fill half full with batter, no more than that or popovers won't rise. Place cups on trays and freeze. When frozen solid, dip cups quickly in warm water so that frozen batter slips out. Place frozen popovers in plastic bag and seal tightly.

Will keep in the freezer up to 9 months.

To bake: Put frozen popovers back into greased containers in which they were frozen. Bake in preheated 450 degree oven 15 minutes; reduce heat and bake at 350 degrees 15 minutes longer, or until golden.

These can also be baked without freezing. Follow baking directions.

Green beans and slivered almonds à la bird
2 SERVINGS

One can hardly call this a recipe, but this is all there is to those expensive packages of seasoned vegetables. In this instance you eliminate the sugar, which green beans do not need, and you eliminate the BHA that is used in the almonds, which is also particularly unnecessary in something that's frozen. And it costs you less than half of what the combination of almonds, beans, and other unnecessary ingredients costs.

9-ounce package frozen green beans or equivalent amount from 1-pound package

Salt and freshly ground black pepper to taste
3¼-ounce package slivered almonds

Cook green beans according to package directions. While they cook, toast the almonds. Drain beans; season with salt and pepper and sprinkle with almonds.

Help for hamburger chili-style
4 SERVINGS

The packaged variety of this "helper" says it makes 5 servings. You can also make 5 servings out of this recipe, but they, like the number of suggested servings on the package, will be quite small.

What you have eliminated from your diet, without any added burden on your time, are the following items: soybean oil, cornstarch, BHA, sodium sulfite, and so much salt that 1 serving is half the daily amount for most normal people. All the salt disguises the fact there isn't much chili powder or tomato in the packaged product. Finally beet color is used to heighten the color of what dried tomato there is in it.

In this case you can get "a helping hand" for less than half the cost of the packaged mix.

1 pound ground beef	½ teaspoon minced dried garlic
1 cup (4 ounces) uncooked elbow macaroni	1½ teaspoons chili powder
3 tablespoons minced dried onion	⅓ cup tomato paste
	Salt to taste

Brown the meat in a skillet; drain off the fat. Add 4 cups water and the remaining ingredients. Stir and bring to boil. Simmer, uncovered, about 15 minutes, or until mixture is as thick as you like.

Help for tuna stroganoff-style   5 SMALL SERVINGS

The number of servings given for this recipe is 5 small. That's because an equivalent amount of the boxed variety says it makes 5 servings. If it is to be a main dish, it really makes 3 or 4 servings for normal-sized people.

When the price of this was compared to the price of the boxed mix it was 17 cents cheaper. Everything is more expensive now, but the cost relationship between the homemade and the packaged has stayed about the same. It's cheaper to make it at home; it tastes better; it has no additives or preservatives, and it's better for you. What more can you ask with so little work?

3½ cups water	2 tablespoons minced dried onion
2 cups egg noodles	3 tablespoons sour cream
6½- or 7-ounce can tuna, rinsed and drained	½ cup grated cheese such as Cheddar
¼ teaspoon minced dried garlic	Salt and freshly ground black pepper to taste

Combine water, noodles, tuna, garlic, and onion in large skillet. Bring to a boil; reduce heat and simmer, uncovered, about 7 minutes, until all water has evaporated. Stir; reduce heat and then stir in sour cream and cheese. Stir and mix well until cheese melts. Season.

Herb butters   4 OUNCES

There is a very simple formula for herb butters. Once you know it, you can use any herb you want. They are a wonderful convenience food, even though the grocery store hasn't started to stock them yet. But some of the haute carry-outs do, at great price. One in Washington is selling 4 ounces of basil butter for $5! You can make herb butter for the cost of the butter, 2 teaspoons of the dried herb, and 2 teaspoons of lemon juice.

The butter can be used on grilled meats, broiled fish, roasted poultry, steamed vegetables, or as a spread on warm bread. It can also be spread on bread to be toasted. It can be used as a medium in which to sauté vegetables such as tomato slices, zucchini, carrots, and so on.

4 ounces butter, softened
2 teaspoons fresh lemon
   juice
2 generous teaspoons
   dried herb, such as
   oregano, tarragon,
   basil, thyme,
   marjoram, dill, mint,
   parsley, or a
   combination

Blend the ingredients thoroughly, mashing with fork. If butter is not soft enough, or you wish to make a large quantity, the ingredients can be processed in a food processor with the steel blade or in an electric mixer.

Herb butter will keep in the refrigerator as long as any stick of butter does; in the freezer, for months if well wrapped. If you do freeze the butter, freeze it in small portions so you don't have to defrost more than you need at one time.

Hot chocolate sauce   MAKES ABOUT 2 CUPS

3 tablespoons butter	¼ cup light corn syrup
4 ounces unsweetened chocolate	1 cup sugar
	Pinch salt
⅔ cup boiling water	2 teaspoons vanilla

Melt the chocolate and butter in heavy pot over very low heat. Stir in the boiling water with whisk until it is smooth. Whisk in syrup, sugar, and salt. Cook and stir until sauce is smooth and glossy. Remove from heat and stir in vanilla.

Serve the sauce hot over just about anything—ice cream, plain cake—or as a dip for orange sections, apple wedges, chunks of banana.

Refrigerate any unused sauce. To serve: reheat over very low heat. You may need to stir in a tablespoon or so of hot water to make the sauce smooth.

Keeps at least 2 months in the refrigerator.

Instant breakfast   1 SERVING

This instant breakfast costs about 10 cents; the best known brand of powdered instant breakfast is twice the price.

1 cup milk	½ banana or 2 to 3 teaspoons honey
2 tablespoons natural smooth peanut butter	

Place milk, peanut butter, and banana or honey in blender and blend a few seconds. Serve.

Quick on the side 2 SERVINGS

This is not much of a recipe, like several others in this chapter. But it will show you how easy it is to make so many of the convenience foods that cost so much. When I made it it cost 30 cents and the packaged noodles and so-called sauce cost 69 cents.

And here's what you don't get in the homemade version: cornstarch, hydrolyzed vegetable protein, and other natural flavors, dextrose, dried cooked beef, beef fat, dried corn syrup, monosodium glutamate, nonfat milk, sugar, wheat starch, caramel color, wheat flour, spice, freshness preserved with BHA, and propyl gallate. Never mind that there is sugar in three different forms—dextrose, corn syrup, and sugar. And who needs the MSG or the caramel color or beef fat . . .

2 teaspoons beef stock granules

1 tablespoon flour

½ teaspoon minced dried garlic

1 teaspoon minced dried onion

Salt to taste

2 cups (3 ounces) medium egg noodles

Combine the beef stock granules with flour, garlic, onion, and salt, if desired, in medium pot. Add 2¼ cups water and the noodles; stir and cook until noodles are tender, about 7 minutes.

Spiced tea 　　　　　　　MAKES 3 CUPS PLUS

When a half pound of a commercial spiced tea cost $8.50, making it at home cost $3.73.

8 ounces orange pekoe
tea

3 tablespoons dried
orange peel, either
ground or in very small
pieces

6 tablespoons whole
cloves, slightly crushed

2 cinnamon sticks,
crushed (optional)

Combine ingredients and mix well. Store in airtight container in cool, dry place and allow flavors to meld for a few days before using.

Use 1 teaspoon of tea to make a cup of tea.

Keeps at least 1 year.

Zesty barbecue sauce MAKES 2 CUPS

The best-known commercial brand of barbecue sauce lists as its first ingredient corn syrup, followed by distilled vinegar, tomato purée, and salt. It is thinned with water. It also contains artificial color and flavor. It gets its body from the powdered cellulose it contains. You may remember powdered cellulose from a certain high-fiber bread. If you want to make your homemade barbecue sauce last longer, do what the manufacturers do: thin it with water.

1 cup finely chopped onion

3 tablespoons salad oil

2 cups tomato sauce

¼ cup cider vinegar

¼ cup fresh lemon juice

3 tablespoons Worcestershire sauce

2 tablespoons firmly packed brown sugar

2 tablespoons prepared mustard

¼ to ½ teaspoon hot pepper sauce

1 clove garlic, crushed

½ bay leaf, crushed

¾ teaspoon chili powder

Sauté onion in hot oil until tender. Do not brown. Stir in remaining ingredients; bring to boil. Reduce heat and simmer, uncovered, 20 to 25 minutes, until mixture begins to thicken. Cool and pour into a jar with a tight-fitting lid. Store in refrigerator.

Keeps at least 3 months.

Use as you would any barbecue sauce: to grill poultry, beef, pork; to mix with ground beef to make barbecued beef. Or just as a sauce spooned over roasted or broiled meats.

INDEX

Beef *(cont.)*
  paprika "stew," 213–15
  preparation of, 65–66
  steak, stir-fried with toma-
    toes, 233–35
  teriyaki, 210–11
Berries with brandy, 324
Bibb lettuce with buttermilk
    dressing, 194–97
Blueberries
  and ginger, 331
  with yogurt and apple or
    pear butter, 326
Boston or Bibb lettuce with
    buttermilk dressing,
    194–97
Boston lettuce with yogurt-
    grapefruit dressing,
    155–57
Brandy
  berries with, 324
  hot peaches in, 321
  shrimps with apple and,
    126–27
Bratwurst, 276–78
Bread
  batter, 351
  cheese, 229–32
    garlic and parsley, 148–50
  corn
    with cheese and onion,
      351
    mix for, 350
    pizza, 352
  crumbs, whole-wheat, 70,
    295n
  garlic, 169–72
  gingerbread, 354
  herbed pitas, 126–28
  popovers, 362
  seasoned, 257–60
  stuffing, pot-to-plate, 356

Breakfast, instant, 366
Brie, fried, 308
Broccoli
  Oriental-style, 233–36
  steamed, 98–100
  stir-fried, with lemon,
    129–31
  tuna and shells with,
    148–49
Brown rice, 74
  fruited, 353
Brown sugar, green grapes
    with yogurt and, 331
Brownie crust, 340–41
Brownies, 340
  mix for, 340
Brussels sprouts
  glazed, 135–37
  with tomato sauce, 91–93
Buckwheat groats, 98–100
  kasha pilaf, 115–17
Buckwheat pancakes, mix
    for, 342–43
Bulgur
  beef and, 241–43
  with everything, 165–67
  with garlic and parsley,
    261–64
  pilaf, mix for, 342
Butter
  cumin, corn on the cob
    with, 138–41
  herb, 365–66
  lemon, fish fillets with,
    142–43
  Roquefort, with walnuts,
    313
Buttermilk salad dressing,
    194–97

Cabbage
  apples and onions, 276–78

386 / INDEX

Turkey *(cont.)*
veal piccata "sting,"
287–89
"veal" rosemary, 290–91
-sesame cutlets, 295

"Veal" (turkey), 58–59
Parmesan, 283–85
piccata "sting," 287–89
with rosemary, 290–91
Vegetables
potatoes with cheese and,
187–89
red, white and green,
184–86
See also names of vegetables
Vermicelli, 119–21, 225–27,
233–35
Vermouth
salmon fillet poached in,
145–46
zucchini and, 122–24
Vinaigrette dressing, chicory
salad with, 217–20
Vinegar-mustard dressing,
269–71

Walnuts
Roquefort butter with, 313
spinach salad with apples
and, 273–75
Water chestnuts wrapped in
bacon, 310
Watercress and mushrooms
in mustard dressing,
115–18
White cake, 343
White rice, fruited, 353

Whole-wheat bread crumbs,
70, 295n
Whole-wheat pasta, 287–89
with caraway seeds,
108–10

Yellow cake, 343
Yellow squash
with Provolone sauce,
261–63
and tomato sauce, 287–89
Yogurt
chicken with, 108–09
cucumbers with mint in,
145–47
-dill dressing, cucumbers
in, 126–28
-grapefruit dressing,
155–57
green grapes with brown
sugar and, 331
honey-tofu sauce, 329
Mexican orange dip, 311
raspberry sauce, 328
or sour cream dip, 328
spicy, strawberries with,
326
summer fruit with apple or
pear butter and, 326

Zabaglione, 330–31
Zesty barbecue, 369
Zucchini
with apples, 290–92
frittata, 190–92
Mexican, 202–05
rotini and, 162–64
vermouth and, 122–24

A Note About the Author

Marian Burros is the award-winning food critic of *The New York Times*. She also has been an Emmy recipient for her consumer reporting on NBC-TV in Washington, D.C., and is the author of a number of well-known cookbooks, including *Elegant but Easy* and the best seller *Pure & Simple*. Marian, who describes herself as a "cottage industry," is a frequent contributor to many magazines. She has been writing about food—from its politics to its romance—for more than twenty years.

Home delivery from Pocket Books

Here's your opportunity to have fabulous bestsellers delivered right to you. Our free catalog is filled to the brim with the newest titles plus the finest in mysteries, science fiction, westerns, cookbooks, romances, biographies, health, psychology, humor—every subject under the sun. Order this today and a world of pleasure will arrive at your door.

POCKET BOOKS, Department ORD
1230 Avenue of the Americas, New York, N.Y. 10020

Please send me a free Pocket Books catalog for home delivery

NAME _____

ADDRESS _____

CITY _____ STATE/ZIP _____

If you have friends who would like to order books at home, we'll send them a catalog too—

NAME _____

ADDRESS _____

CITY _____ STATE/ZIP _____

NAME _____

ADDRESS _____

CITY _____ STATE/ZIP _____